ETCHING, ENGRAVING
AND OTHER INTAGLIO
PRINTMAKING TECHNIQUES

ETCHING, ENGRAVING
AND OTHER INTAGLIO
PRINTMAKING TECHNIQUES

RUTH LEAF

DOVER PUBLICATIONS, INC.
New York

Published in Canada by General Publishing Company, Ltd., 30 Les-
mill Road, Don Mills, Toronto, Ontario.
Published in the United Kingdom by Constable and Company, Ltd.,
10 Orange Street, London WC2H 7EG.

This Dover edition, first published in 1984, is a republication of the
work originally published by Watson-Guptill Publications, New York, in
1976 under the title *Intaglio Printmaking Techniques*. In the present edition the 16 original color illustrations are reproduced in black and white
in the text (five being reproduced in color on the covers), and the section
"Supplies and Suppliers" has been updated.

Manufactured in the United States of America
Dover Publications, Inc., 31 East 2nd Street, Mineola, N.Y. 11501

Library of Congress Cataloging in Publication Data

Leaf, Ruth.
    Etching, engraving and other intaglio printmaking techniques.

    Reprint. Originally published: Intaglio printmaking techniques. New
York : Watson-Guptill, 1976.
    Bibliography: p.
    Includes index.
    1. Intaglio printing—Technique. I. Title.
NE1625.L4   1984   765   84-4158
ISBN 0-486-24721-X

To Karen, Anita, and Hersh

Acknowledgments

I wish to thank the following people for making this book possible:

David Engler for insisting the book be written and published.

Vera Freeman of Andrews Nelson Whitehead for help with printing papers.

Joseph Martin of Martech for technical information.

Diane Casella Hines, Rene Sax, and Ellen Zeifer for excellent editorial assistance.

Anita Lerner for translating handwritten manuscript into readable type.

Robert Schiavo and Daniel Quat for photographs.

Joyce Hurwitz and Sharen Hedges for illustrations.

And the artists who work in my studio, for their moral support and for some of the fine prints reproduced in the book.

Contents

Introduction

In my book I have tried to present a thorough analysis of intaglio printmaking and related techniques. You can use this book in one of two ways—first as a handbook to augment your knowledge of printmaking, and second as a learning experience to experiment with printmaking. Even if you have never printed before, if you have some background in art and—more important—a strong desire to learn, this book will help you approach printmaking as a new means of expression. This work is not easy technically, intellectually, emotionally, or physically—more than one person has gone home defeated from an arduous afternoon at the workshop! But if you persevere, I'm sure that you'll find printmaking satisfying in all ways.

In the classes at my workshop, I teach printmaking by beginning with the easier methods and working up to the harder ones. If I had arranged my chapters as I teach, the order would be as follows (not including the first six chapters): hard ground, acids, basic printing, soft ground, aquatint, sugar lift, white ground, engraving, drypoint, color printing and embossing, double intaglio, tuilegraphs, viscosity method, viscosity and aquatint, collagraphs, and the Blake transfer method. If you're going to use the book as a handbook, then there's no need to follow the chapters in this order. But if you're either planning to teach printmaking or to learn it on your own—or partially on your own—then it would be a good idea. I think you'll find that once you've conquered the easier techniques, the others will become progressively simpler if only because there won't be so much new material. There are always blockbusters like the viscosity method, but in general, once you become familiar with the ways in which grounds and acids work, you'll find later chapters simple compared with the earlier one.

I also suggest that when you have mastered the simple techniques, you do a plate that combines several grounds so you can see how they work with one another. This is comparable to the point when, in studying a language, you take all you've learned and try to order dinner in a restaurant. Hopefully, you'll get what you want.

Whichever way you approach my book, read the chapters carefully all the way through. Then assemble the materials you'll need before you begin so that you won't find yourself searching for a tinfoil dish or a palette knife when you should be attending to your grounds. Also, approach the techniques slowly—*one step at a time*.

When you've gone through a technique, try to judge the results of your prints and plates impartially. If they seem faulty to you, don't give up—this is the toughness I was talking about. Read the chapter again, looking for the one little thing which you may have overlooked and which could have thrown the whole process off—*and try again!*

Intaglio printmaking is extremely difficult to learn on your own. For one thing, you probably won't want to rush out and buy a $4,000 press to see if you like making prints! The best way to learn is to either take a class and/or join a workshop or studio where other artists are working. (Some workshops insist that you take a course there or elsewhere just so you don't damage the equipment.) Being an artist—and therefore, a highly visual person—you'll find it infinitely easier to learn by seeing others work than by only reading this book. Even if you've been printing for years, a studio will give you a kind of circular benefit in which you'll learn from the other artists as they learn from you. Plus, if you get increasingly involved with your workshop, there will be a common desire to have the studio gain a reputation for producing good work.

At the studio you'll discover that the methods which you learned and which you read about in books are by no means the only way—or even the *right* way—to accomplish certain procedures, but simply *one* of the right ways. If another artist's technique of applying a ground looks as though it might be more comfortable for you, then go ahead and try it. You may like it better than your own way or my way. Printmaking is, after all, a living, developing art form in an expanding field. It's a young, growing medium that has changed in the last 30 years from a technique for producing small hand-held prints to one that can make prints the size of paintings.   Take my book as a starting point or as extra, helpful information. After that, you're on your own!

PART ONE
General Information

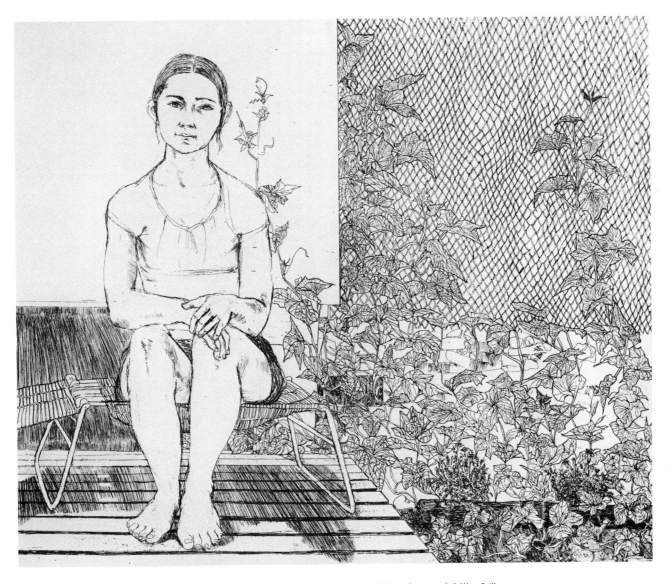

Barbara and the Cucumbers *by Ruth Leaf. Hard ground, 20″ x 24″.*

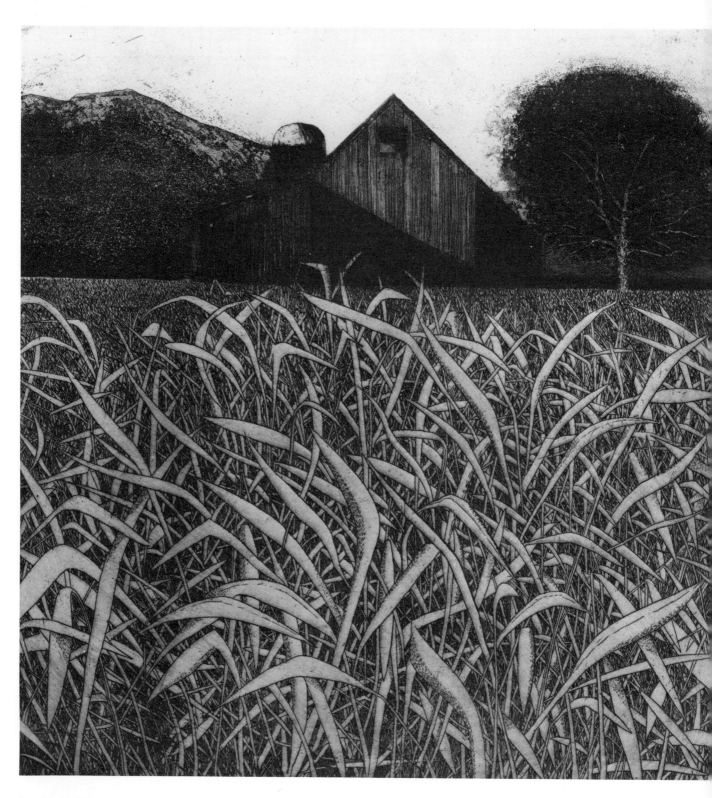

Summer Field *by Bob Kuzyn. Intaglio and engraving, 20" x 20".*

ONE

Materials and Equipment

One of the most exciting aspects of printmaking is the great number of materials and pieces of equipment that you can use. There are, of course, certain things such as metal plates and acids that are indispensable—I describe them here so that you'll be able to work with them in later chapters. (See *Supplies and Suppliers* for information on where to buy these materials.)

However, you're not limited to the materials and equipment which I list. As you print, you may often discover new ways to use old objects—a scrap of lace may give you the texture you want, or spray paint may give you the fine aquatint you need.

PLATES

You can use many different kinds of plates when you print—plates can be made of metal, plastic, Masonite, vinyl, asbestos, and other materials. With the different materials you can achieve different effects.

Zinc. Zinc is the metal most commonly used for etching plates since zinc is easier to work with than steel and less expensive than copper. You'll usually use nitric acid to etch zinc plates, the backs of which are coated with an acid-resistant material so the acid cannot react with the back surface of the plate.

When you etch a zinc plate, you can use any of the grounds described in this book. You can also use this kind of plate for engraving, although the burin will tend to slip: a sheet of zinc is not uniformly hard. Also, zinc is softer and coarser in structure than copper, the best metal to use for engraving.

You can buy zinc plates of .062 to 16 or 18 gauge. The 16 or 18 gauge is a standard commercial size and is therefore more easily obtained, although there are many other gauges—thicknesses—to choose from.

Finally, remember that zinc affects certain colors—yellow ink will turn greenish, and all other light colors such as white will turn slightly gray.

Steel. Polished or commercial grade mild steel—cold roll—.062 to 16 gauge is the best kind of steel to use for etching. You can pull many more prints on an etched or engraved steel plate than on a copper or zinc plate because steel is so much harder—lines and aquatints will wear down and hold less and less ink faster on copper and zinc than on steel. However, steel is very difficult to polish or scrape. Unless you purchase an already polished plate, your print will invariably have a darker tone than a print from a zinc plate bitten in the same manner. And if you want to remove scratches from the plate's surface, you'll have a very difficult time scraping them out.

The backs of steel plates are not usually acid-proof when purchased. Before placing a steel plate in acid—nitric acid—coat the back with a stopout solution, spray paint, or contact paper (see Chapter 12). Use any ground on a steel plate that you would use on a zinc plate, and also try using steel for engravings or drypoints.

Copper. The copper you use for etching and engraving should be cold-rolled, 16 or 18 gauge, and hard rather than soft. Soft copper, used for enameling, is less expensive.

The harder the copper, the better. Remember that rolled copper crystalizes in the direction in which it was rolled and will be harder in that direction. A hammered copper plate would be hard in all directions, but unfortunately, these plates are no longer available. Old copper plates, if you can find them, are as hard as hammered copper because copper crystalizes with time. Also, photoengravers work on copper plates—if you can find some of their used plates, polish the backs and use them.

Copper is very good for engraving and drypoint, as well as for etching. When you etch with copper use Dutch mordant, a solution that is made with hydrochloric acid. You can get very fine lines on a copper plate with hard ground. Soft ground, lift ground, and aquatint may also be used. Don't, however, use white ground on copper.

Copper plates can be purchased with an acid-resistant coating on the back surface. If the plate is not coated, apply a stopout solution to the back of the plate before you put it into the acid.

When you print with color on copper, note that the copper will interact chemically with vermilion. You can use any other color, in general, without trouble.

Brass. Brass plates are more expensive than zinc, are etched with Dutch mordant, and don't come with a acid-resistant coating on the back surface. They can be used in the same manner as copper plates.

Plastic. You can use plates made of Plexiglas, Lucite, or acetate for engravings and drypoints, but not for etching. Plastic plates are less expensive than metal, and they have the advantage of being transparent—you can place your plate directly over a drawing and engrave by tracing the design.

You can sand the surface of the plastic to give your prints some tone. For a variety of lines, try using a power tool to carve into the plate. Finally, remember that plastic scratches easily, so handle it carefully.

Masonite. Masonite can be carved with woodcutting tools and printed just like a metal plate. Or, you can use it as a base for a collagraph (see Chapter 20).

Vinyl Asbestos Tiles. These are the plates used in making tuilegraphs (see Chapter 21). The tiles are manufactured in three sizes: 9″ x 18″, 9″ x 9″, and 12″ x 12″. They come in many colors and textures, some of which can be used for printing reliefs or intaglios. You'll find that the light-colored, non-textured tile is the easiest to work with and draw on.

GROUNDS

Grounds are substances used to coat all or part of the plate's surface. Some—such as hard ground, soft ground, and white ground—act as a stopout solution, an acid-resist. Other grounds—such as lift ground and aquatint—are used with stopouts to create the image on the plate. See Chapters 6, 7, 8, 9, 10, and 11 for further information.

Keep all of your grounds in containers with tight covers to keep dirt and metal particles out and to prevent the solvent in the grounds from evaporating. If the solvent evaporates, the remaining ground becomes hard.

Hard and soft grounds are both used with brushes kept in separate coffee cans ⅓ full of varnolene (see Figure 1). Thus you can use the brush at any time. *Don't put the soft ground brush into the hard ground or vice versa.* If, by mistake, you put the hard ground brush into the soft ground, clean the brush with varnolene and then wash it very thoroughly with mild soap and cold water. If you put the soft ground brush into the hard ground, skim off the surface of the hard ground to make sure that no soft ground remains. Clean the brush with varnolene, but don't use soap and water.

ACIDS AND CHEMICALS

You'll use acids to bite metal plates, and you'll need various chemicals to make biting solutions (see Figure 2). Different acids react with different plates. *Never* put two plates of different metals in the same acid bath either at the same time or at different times. If you do, the acid will act as a conductor, depositing, for instance, zinc on steel and steel on zinc, and you'll have to throw out both plates and the solution.

Nitric Acid. Combine ACS commercial grade nitric acid with water to bite zinc and steel plates. You can also use this acid to bite copper if you want a *very* rough bite.

Hydrochloric Acid and Potassium Chlorate Crystals. Combine these two materials to make Dutch mordant, a solution that is used to bite copper or brass slowly.

Bicarbonate of Soda. Also known as baking soda, this can be used as a safety device to stop the action of any acid if it overheats while you're biting a plate. You'll know acid is overheating when it turns muddy yellow in color and starts to boil and smoke. If you don't have bicarbonate of soda handy when this happens, throw *lots* of cold water into the acid bath. Remove the plate from the bath with gloves on—the metal will be *very* hot.

You can also add bicarbonate of soda or baking soda to acid to stop its biting action completely before you throw it down the sink—this will help your metal plumbing last longer.

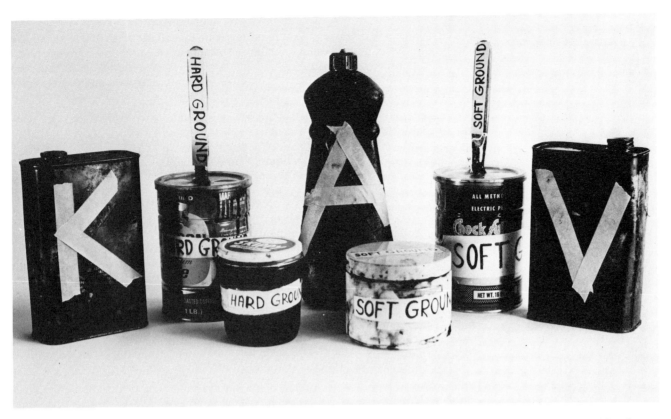

Figure 1. Cans of hard ground and soft ground in front of tins that hold their respective brushes. The three cans of solvents also in the picture are kerosene on the left, alcohol in the middle, and varnolene on the right.

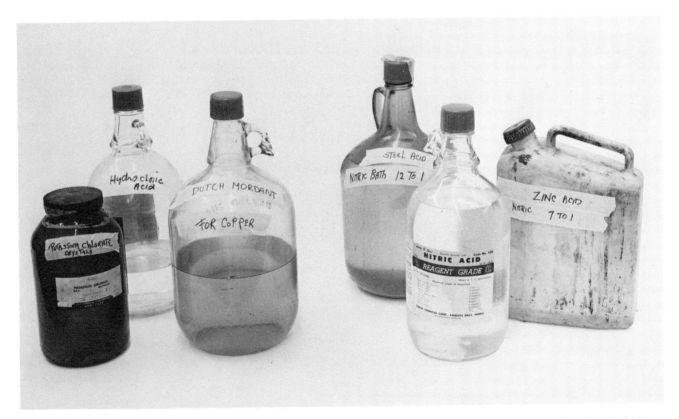

Figure 2. Acids and chemicals, from left to right: potassium chlorate crystals and hydrochloric acid which combine to make Dutch Mordant; a weak solution of nitric acid, 12 to 1, for biting steel plates; pure nitric acid; a medium-strength nitric acid solution, 7 to 1, for biting zinc plates.

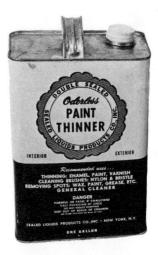

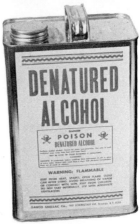

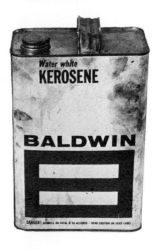

Figure 3. Solvents, from top to bottom: paint thinner, denatured alcohol, kerosene.

SOLVENTS

Solvents dilute and dissolve various materials which you'll use when you make a plate and print it. Among other things, you'll use solvents to clean grounds off your plate, dissolve aquatints made with rosin, dilute asphaltum, and liquify hard and soft grounds. Store all solvents in metal containers with tight, screw-on metal covers (see Figures 1 and 3).

Varnolene. This is an inexpensive thinner which is used instead of turpentine for cleaning plates during printing if you switch colors, for cleaning the bed of the press after printing, and for thinning and removing grounds. When added to hard ground and asphaltum, varnolene keeps them liquid. You'll also use this solvent to clean glass and marble slabs, palette knives, and brushes.

Benzine. You can use benzine in place of varnolene for the same purposes.

Kerosene. You need kerosene to clean rollers—leave a residue of this solvent on plastic or gelatin rollers to help preserve them. *Never use benzine on a roller*—it will dry out the surface. You can also use kerosene to clean a plate before you put it away for the day: a film of kerosene left on the plate will keep the moisture in the air from corroding its surface (see Chapter 23).

Denatured Alcohol. When combined with rosin, this solvent forms a rosin stopout solution (see Chapter 6). Denatured alcohol is also used for removing aquatint and rosin stopout from plates and brushes.

Spirits of Turpentine. This solvent is not used often in printmaking because it tends to be more expensive and oilier than paint thinners like varnolene.

Xylene. This solvent can be used to make hard ground—it acts to combine the powdered ingredients quickly. You don't have to use xylene for this purpose if you just cook the ground longer. Please note that xylene is a highly inflammable solvent.

Acetone. This solvent is used on vinyl asbestos tiles to roughen the tile and cause a tone to appear when the tile is printed. Acetone is also a solvent for spray paint, which can be sprayed on a plate to obtain a very fine aquatint.

INKS

There are basically two kinds of inks you'll use—intaglio inks and surface inks. Intaglio inks are the inks you'll push into the crevices of your plate. After your whole plate is covered, you'll then wipe off the top surfaces with paper, tarlatan, or your hand. Surface inks are the inks you'll roll on the cleaned top surfaces of the plate, over the intaglio, with a roller.

Keep all intaglio inks that don't come in their own cans or tubes in jars with screw tops, such as mayonnaise jars, baby food jars, or cold cream jars (see Figure 4). The tops of these jars and cans often become very difficult to open after you use the ink once or twice. Use a small screwdriver to pry the lid gently to break the seal of dry ink that glues the lid to the jar.

When you're finished printing, put a layer of water in the jar or can to prevent a skin of dried ink from forming on the surface. The water won't affect the ink in any way— just remember to pour it off before you use the ink again.

Offset inks, used by commercial printers, are suitable for surface printing. You can add magnesium carbonate to these surface inks to make them thicker for use as an intaglio ink if you don't mix your own intaglio ink from powders and oil. In general, intaglio inks should be thicker than surface inks. To make the commercial inks dry slower, add a touch of vegetable shortening to the ink and mix it in thoroughly. To keep surface inks for use another day, wrap them in tinfoil or wax paper and put them into a freezer.

If you try the viscosity method of printing (see Chapters 16 and 17), it would be a good idea to get surface inks made by the Lorilleux Company in France (see *Supplies and Suppliers*).

OILS

There are several types of oils that you may want to use in conjunction with your inks and when you work on the plate.

Raw Linseed Oil. You'll need raw linseed oil to combine it with both surface and intaglio inks to thin them and to make the ink less viscous, or oilier. Keep your raw linseed oil in a container such as a vinegar cruet that will allow you to control the flow of the liquid, drop-by-drop.

Heavy Plate Oil. This is linseed oil that has been boiled and reduced to 1/5 of its original volume (don't confuse plate oil with boiled linseed oil). Heavy plate oil is extremely viscous, or thick, and is used for making intaglio inks.

3-in-1 Oil. You can use this machine oil on an India oil stone when you sharpen tools, although a thin film of kerosene would be better. Also coat your plate with it when you scrape and burnish the surface.

ROLLERS

Rollers come in various sizes (see Figure 5)—the length and diameter of the roller needed depends on the size of the plate you are printing. A roller will cover a plate three times the size of the diameter of a roller and one time its length. For example, the largest plate a roller 3″ in diameter and 10″ long will cover is 9″ x 10″. Or, the largest plate a roller 4″ in diameter and 10″ long will cover is 12″ x 10″.

Rollers can be made of plastic, gelatin, or rubber. Gelatin rollers, and some plastic rollers are very soft—they'll sink into deeply bitten areas of your plate as well as cover the surface. Other plastic rollers and some rubber rollers are medium rollers—they won't sink into your plate as much as a soft roller will. The hard rollers are usually made of a synthetic rubber. When you roll them over your plate, they'll touch only the top surfaces.

When you purchase rollers, the word "durometer" will be used to designate the hardness or softness of the roller: the durometer of a soft roller would be about 10 to 20; that of a medium roller would be about 25 to 30; and the durometer of a hard rubber roller would be from 50 to 60.

Rollers are expensive, and the larger ones are custom-made. It usually takes from six weeks to three months, depending on the kind of roller purchased, from the date of your order to the delivery.

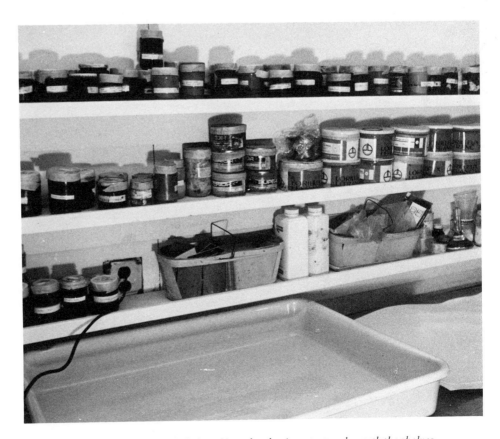

Figure 4. Jars and cans of ink on shelves. Note the plastic water tray beneath the shelves.

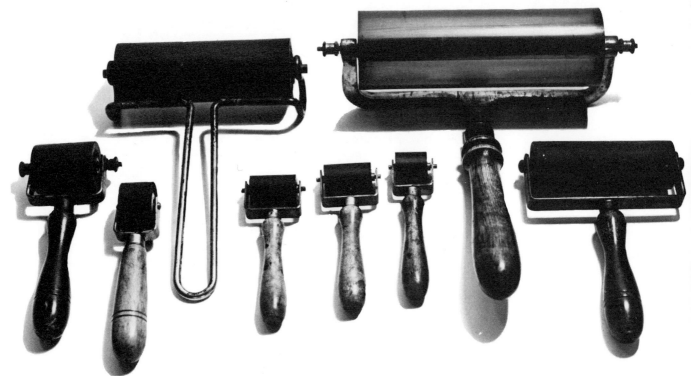

Figure 5. Small rollers. A gelatin (soft) roller is on the upper left, and a plastic (hard) one is on the upper right—note the projections attached to the handles that prevent the soft rollers from touching any surface on which they might be resting. The smaller rollers underneath are hard and are made of rubber. They all have wooden handles—you could easily screw in hooks to hang them.

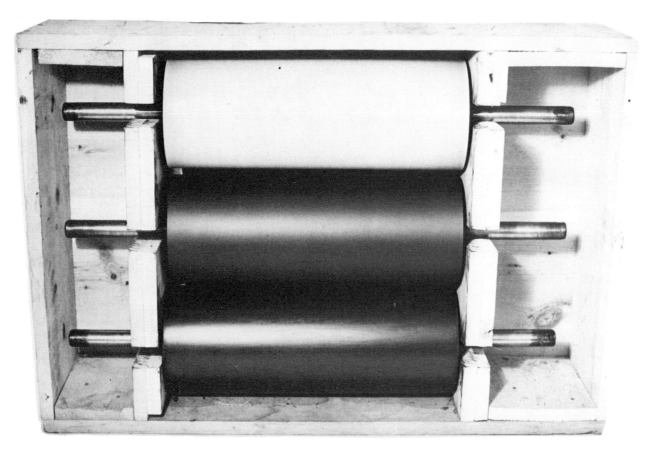

Figure 7. Rollers not in use stacked in a box. The surfaces of the rollers are not touching each other.

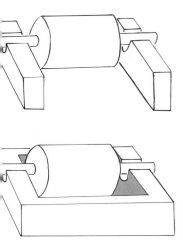

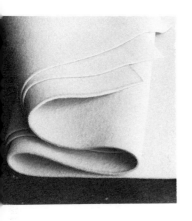

Figure 6. The large roller in the top of this illustration is resting on separate blocks with grooves for the roller's handles. This setup prevents the surface of the roller from touching the slab or table top on which it might sit. The roller underneath rests in a box.

Figure 8. Three wool felt blankets, two 1/16" thick and one ⅛" thick.

Always clean a roller after you use it. Apply kerosene liberally and wipe the roller until no more ink comes off on a clean wiping cloth. Always leave a film of kerosene on a plastic or gelatin roller when you put it away to keep it soft and pliable. Wipe rubber rollers dry. You can wash rubber with soap and water after you wipe them with kerosene if you want to. If you do wash them with soap and water, dry them thoroughly. New materials are always being used to make rollers. Therefore, when buying a custom-made roller, ask the manufacturer what solvent he recommends.

Large rollers, with handles on both sides, should have a box or blocks on which to rest the handles while you're printing (see Figure 6). When you're finished printing, hang them in a dust-free place, if possible (see Figure 7). *At no time should anything touch the surface of the roller besides a wiping cloth, kerosene, or the plate.* Plastic and gelatin rollers will take on the shape of anything that touches them. If you rest one, for instance, against a pegboard wall even for a short time, the roller will have a perfect impression of the pegboard embossed on its surface.

Small plastic and gelatin rollers come with projections attached for the roller to rest on while they aren't being used. Small rollers should have a screw eye or a hole to screwing hook at the end of their handles so that they can be hung up when you're finished printing.

BLANKETS

Blankets, or printing felts, are placed over your damp paper and plate before you print. The blankets act as a cushion as the pressure of the press pushes the paper into the lines and crevices of the plate to pick up the ink.

Blankets should either be finely woven or made of pressed wool felt. You'll need three blankets, two of 1/16" thickness and one of ⅛" thickness (see Figure 8). When you print, you'll place the two thinner blankets directly over the damp paper and plate—the thicker blanket goes on top, under the roller. It's a good idea to rotate the two thinner blankets when the one closest to the paper becomes very damp or absorbs the sizing of the paper.

When the blankets become stiff with sizing, you must wash them. This is an arduous job which cannot, unfortunately, be done by a machine. Wash the printing blankets in a mild soap and ammonia solution in cold water. Use a nail brush to scrub them, and than *press* out the soap and water—never twist or wring a printing blanket. When you finish, place the blankets on newsprint or on a blotter on a flat surface to dry. *Never* hang a blanket over a clothesline, or the line will become embossed into the blanket and will affect your prints. If possible, have two sets of blankets—when one set is being washed, you can use the other.

To determine the size of the blankets you need, measure the length and the width of the bed of the press you're using and subtract 6" from the length to allow for the roller. For a 30" x 50" press bed, for example, you would need two blankets 30" x 44" x 1/16" and one blanket 30" x 44" x ⅛", all of woven or pressed wool felt.

PAPER PRODUCTS

The many kinds of paper products which you'll need for printmaking are described here with the exception of printing paper which is discussed in Chapter 3.

Blotters. Blotters are thick, pulpy paper used for blotting wet paper before printing and for drying prints after printing. Blotters are usually quite large, about 24" x 38".

Proof Paper. Use proof paper—Basingwerk or Radar Vellum—to proof your plates before you use good printing paper.

Newsprint. Many printmakers place a sheet of newsprint on top of their damp proof paper, under the blankets, before they pull a print. This helps prevent the blankets from absorbing the proof paper's sizing. Newsprint may also be placed on top of your print after it's printed, underneath the blotter while the paper is drying. Don't use newsprint (or tissue paper) between dry prints in storage. Both are acid pulp papers which will "burn" your prints. (See *Things Every Printmaker Should Know and Doesn't Know Whom to Ask* at the end of the book.)

Glassene. This is a shiny, smooth paper that you'll need if your intaglio is very deep, since the ink on your print may then be very thick and sticky. You should place a sheet of glassene on top of your print, under the blotter, rather than a piece of newsprint. Newsprint would stick to the ink; glassene won't.

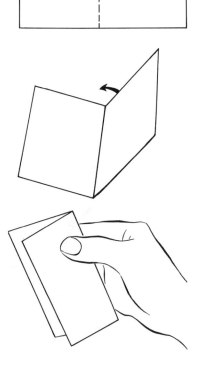

Figure 9. Here you see a 3″ x 5″ cardboard square, top, which you can use to apply ink to your plate. Center, the 3″ x 5″ square is bent in the middle and is used, bottom, to pick up clean printing paper.

Silk Paper. Use silk paper between dry prints in storage to prevent the print on top from absorbing the ink on the print underneath.

Tissue Paper. Tissue paper may be used instead of newsprint between a drying print and the blotter.

Tableau Paper. This is a paper that is used after the tarlatan wipe to wipe more ink off the surface of the plate. This is necessary for inks that are particularly sticky and hard to wipe, such as color intaglio inks. When you print a black or a dark intaglio ink, try using the pages from an old telephone book in place of the tableau paper to get a very clean wipe.

Newspapers. You'll need newspapers in the studio to spread over table tops to absorb solvents, grounds, and inks.

Paper Towels or Lint-Free Cloths. Both of these are indispensable in the studio. You'll use paper towels to dry plates after they've been scrubbed in preparation for putting on a ground, to remove grounds and inks from plates after scrubbing with solvents and a brush, and to dry your hands. You'll need lint-free cloths to clean the bed of the press, to remove grounds and inks from the plate, and to clean rollers.

Wax Paper. You'll need wax paper to cover materials laid on top of a soft ground to create texture before you roll the plate through the press.

Tracing Paper. To transfer a drawing to a plate on which a hard ground has been applied you need tracing paper. You can also draw on tracing paper directly when you lay it over a plate with a soft ground.

Cardboard. Pieces of cut cardboard can be used instead of daubers to apply ink to a plate—there is less danger of the cardboard scratching the plate. The pieces of cardboard should be rectangular and any size that is comfortable for your hand to hold. Discard the cardboard after you use it. Cardboard also makes good clips for handling paper after printing to keep the paper clean (see Figure 9).

Contact Paper. Contact paper is used to protect the surface of the plate when the plate is bitten into free-form shapes in a strong nitric acid bath. You'll also need contact paper to cover the backs of plates, such as brass and steel plates, that don't already have an acid-resistant coating on their back. In addition, contact paper is used to strengthen the backs of tiles and to protect the backs of collagraphs from solvents.

CLEANSERS

Different cleansers are needed for cleaning plates, fabrics, and your hands.

Degreaser. Use Janitor in a Drum on steel plates to remove the protective coating of oil applied by the manufacturer.

Powdered Cleansers. The same kinds of cleansers used for cleaning sinks are used to clean plates before you apply a ground. These cleansers, such as Comet and Ajax, work as well as the whiting and ammonia.

Powdered Soap, or Detergent. This type of cleanser is necessary to clean fabrics that have been pressed into soft ground so you can use them again for texture. Also, Ivory Snow is an ingredient in white ground, and Tide is used in the lift ground formula (see Chapter 6).

Waterless Hand Cleaner. This is good for removing ink and ground from your hands without removing your skin, as coarse abrasive soaps seem to do. The waterless hand cleaner can also be used for cleaning brushes which have been used with stopout—the lanolin in the cleaner preserves the hairs of the brush.

EXPENDABLE INGREDIENTS

The following supplies are used on plates and in making grounds, stopout, and ink:

Asphaltum Powder. Used in making hard ground and stopout, this material is soluble in varnolene or turpentine. You can purchase ready-made asphaltum in liquid form. Always keep liquid asphaltum covered to keep the solvent from evaporating—if the solvent does evaporate, liquid asphaltum becomes unusable. You can try adding benzine to make it more liquid.

Beeswax. This product can be purchased in ½ pound to 1 pound cakes. The pure white beeswax is used as an ingredient in soft and hard ground.

Rosin. Rosin comes in powder and chunk form and is soluble in alcohol. Chunk rosin is used for making aquatints, stopout, and hard ground; powdered rosin is too fine for aquatints, but it can be used in hard ground. However, commercial powdered rosin has impurities which don't dissolve completely in alcohol. Therefore, chunk rosin is better to use when you make stopout, an alcohol-based solution.

Enamel Spray Paint. You can use enamel spray paint on a plate as a substitute for rosin aquatint. The spray will give you a very fine aquatint, but it will break down more quickly in the acid than the rosin will. Also, you can't pull as many prints with a spray paint aquatint as you can with a rosin aquatint since it wears down faster.

Gum Arabic. In powdered form, this is an ingredient in lift ground.

Malachite Green. This pigment is soluble in alcohol and is added to stopout made of alcohol saturated with rosin to make the transparent stopout visible. *Caution*: This is a very concentrated pigment that must be handled carefully. A tiny grain will explode into a virulent green spot on contact with water or alcohol.

Vaseline. An ingredient in soft ground, this material is thinned with varnolene or turpentine. You'll need vaseline to smear over plates you're putting away for a long period of time to protect them.

Magnesium Carbonate. Added to surface inks, magnesium carbonate thickens the ink as an intaglio ink.

Titanium White. This pigment is used in making white ground.

India Ink and Karo Syrup. Both of these ingredients are used in making lift ground.

Shortening, or Solidified Vegetable Oil. Either of these will retard the drying of surface inks. Use only a very small amount.

Gesso (Acrylic Polymer Base), and Elmer's Glue. These two substances are used in making collagraphs (see Chapter 20).

GENERAL EQUIPMENT AND MISCELLANEOUS

The following items are necessary to have for printmaking. Many of them are common objects used in a new way.

Trays. You'll need trays to hold acid and water. The plastic ones used by photographers (see Figure 4), purchased in stores that sell photographic equipment, are quite adequate. The largest standard size of a plastic photographic tray is 24″ x 28″. You can also make wooden trays and coat them with an acid-resistant material such as asphaltum or fiberglass. Or, you can order trays of any size in stainless steel. For small plates, use glass or plastic trays, sturdy Pyrex pans, or plastic kitchen dishes.

Plate Glass or Marble Slabs. A ¼″ thick slab of plate glass or marble is necessary for mixing inks and for rolling surface colors. The size of the slab you need depends on the size of the rollers you use. If you have a roller which is 20″ long and 6″ in diameter, you'll need a rolling surface slightly larger than 20″ x 18″. Since you'll mix your ink on the same surface, it's a good idea to add quite a few inches to each dimension. In the case of the 20″ roller 6″ in diameter, a slab 24″ x 22″ would be the smallest size you should buy. Please note that you must have a separate slab for each color rolled during one printing session. In other words, if you use three surface colors to print one plate, you need three slabs.

Brushes. You need many kinds of brushes in printmaking (see Figure 10). For hard and soft grounds, use 2½″ to 3″ wide bristle brushes—the size of the brush will depend on the size of the opening of the jar containing the ground (see Figure 1). For lift ground or for detailed stopping-out, get good sable brushes which come to a point.

For all other purposes in printmaking, use inexpensive brushes—stopout solutions

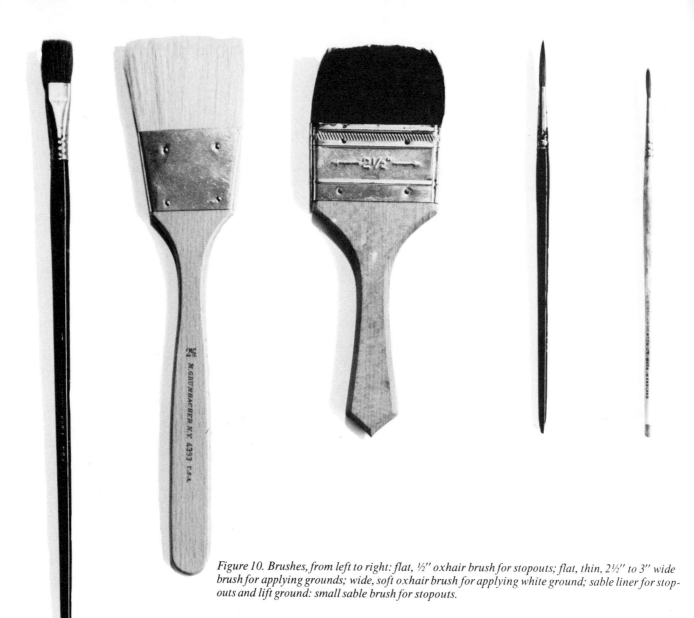

Figure 10. Brushes, from left to right: flat, ½″ oxhair brush for stopouts; flat, thin, 2½″ to 3″ wide brush for applying grounds; wide, soft oxhair brush for applying white ground; sable liner for stopouts and lift ground: small sable brush for stopouts.

Figure 11. Large hot plate used for warming plates, for inking and printing, and sometimes for heating aquatints.

and other liquids such as asphaltum are difficult to remove and brushes deteriorate rapidly. To stop out large areas of the plate, use an inexpensive camel's hair or oxhair brush, ½″ x 1″ wide. You'll need a natural-bristle scrub brush or a toothbrush to remove ink from your plate after you print and to remove grounds after the plate has been bitten. (Don't use plastic brushes as they disintegrate on contact with solvents.) If you clean the brushes thoroughly after each use, they'll last longer.

Palette Knives and Spatulas. These tools are used to grind powdered pigment into heavy plate oil to get color intaglio inks and to mix oil into surface inks.

Gloves. Use vinyl or garden gloves to protect your hands when you are printing.

Plastic Funnels. Large funnels are used for pouring acid into containers of water to make acid solutions of varying strengths, and for pouring acid solutions from trays into bottles for storage. Funnels can also be used to fill solvent containers.

Hot Plates. These are used for heating rosin on plates to melt the rosin and make aquatints. You'll also need hot plates to heat grounds and to warm plates for inking and printing. Some hot plates have thermostats and are made especially for printmakers (see Figure 11).

Rolling Pins. You should roll a rolling pin gently over a blotter covering wet paper so that the blotter will absorb the water from the paper before it's printed.

Tarlatan. This is the starched cheesecloth or cotton crinoline used for wiping intaglio inks on plates.

Sponges. You'll need sponges often in a studio. You should have a clean sponge to brush damp printing paper after blotting to remove any excess material on the paper's surface and to brush up the nap of the paper to make the surface more receptive to ink. Sponges are used with powdered cleanser to remove grease from the plate before you apply a ground. Sponges are also used to create textures in a white ground and to wipe out the water tray to remove all sizing from paper that collects on the tray's surface. Synthetic sponges are much less expensive than real ones and work just as well.

Daubers. Made of strips of old printing blankets or felt, daubers are used to push intaglio ink into the crevices of the plate. After you use a dauber, place it in an airtight, plastic bag so the dauber will stay pliable and dirt-free. Pieces of dirt or dried ink imbedded in the dauber will scratch the plate.

Mylar Tape. This kind of tape is impervious to solvents and is therefore used to protect labels. Labels on ink jars become unreadable when they're covered with spilled ink—if the label is covered with clear Mylar tape, you can easily wipe the label clean with varnolene.

Masking Tape, or Pressure-Sensitive Tape. This tape is used to register the plate when you print a double intaglio; it's used with calipers, and you can place it around the covers of ink jars to keep them air-tight.

Razor Blades. Single-edged razor blades have endless uses—no studio should be without them.

Textures. You should keep a good supply of material with texture around to use with soft grounds. Start collecting textures from hardware stores, fabric shops (remnants of lace and silk, for example), and even automobile graveyards—you can use the textures of gaskets and other flat shapes left behind when motors are taken apart. Many packaging materials, such as corrugated board and plastic with bubbles in it, make interesting textures. Any material that is pliable, such as tinfoil, plastic wrap, or waxed paper, can be used.

Powder, or Talc. Sprinkled on the bed of the press and then wiped off, powder will absorb any excess varnolene that is left on the bed after it's wiped clean. You'll also need powder or talc when you hand-wipe your plate.

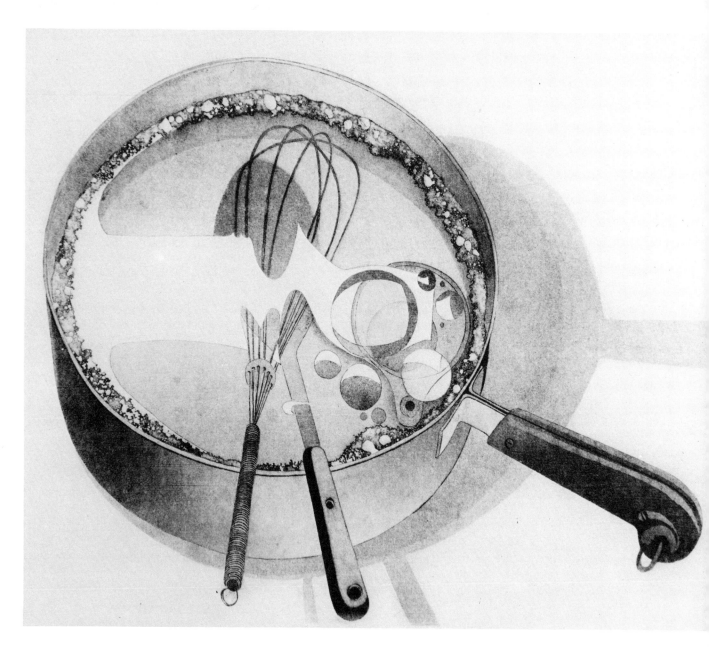

Still Life *by Mary Westring. Intaglio, 16" x 20". Hard and soft grounds.*

TWO

Tools

The tools you can use to make plates and print are as varied and unlimited as your imagination. In this chapter I suggest a basic list of tools you'll need and describe their functions. You can then improvise and discover other tools which will help you achieve the effects you want.

POLISHING STONE

You'll need a polishing stone (see Figure 1) to sharpen burins and scrapers and to polish etching needles. It's a disc-shaped India oil stone, about 3½″ in diameter. The rough, darker side of the stone is used *only* for changing the shape of a tool; the other, smoother, lighter side is used for fine polishing and sharpening. Use light machine oil or 3-in-1 oil or kerosene when you rub any tool on the stone, and *always* wipe the stone clean with kerosene.

ETCHING NEEDLES

An etching needle is usually a long, thin, pointed tool made of metal—Figure 2 contains two good examples. You can use any pointed tool to draw through a ground, but note that a sharp point might scratch the plate underneath. It's a good idea, therefore, to dull the point of an etching needle by holding the tool at the end opposite the point, resting the point on a polishing stone, and dragging the point around the stone in a circular motion (see Figure 3). Always hold the needle at roughly a 90° angle to the stone to round the tool evenly. The point must be smooth or you'll find it difficult to move the needle over the ground without catching the needle in the metal plate.

One type of etching needle that's commonly used is called a scriber. This is a pointed tool held in a chuck, a knoblike holder. The needle is detachable, and you can use the chuck to hold points other than the one it came with, such as phonograph and darning needles.

An ordinary fine sewing needle is good if you want an extremely fine point for drawing very delicate lines on a hard ground. To use this kind of needle, first break it in half. Then force the broken end into the eraser of a pencil. Get a grip on the needle with needle-nose pliers. The rubber will hold the needle firmly, and you'll find the pencil both familiar and comfortable to work with.

DRYPOINT NEEDLE

A drypoint needle is an etching needle with a *very* sharp point that you'll use to scratch into your metal plate. The point must be extremely sharp in order to raise the typical burr—the rough edges on both sides of the scratched line—that will make the print a drypoint. The burr is actually the displaced metal from the scratched line.

Your drypoint needle can have either a diamond point or a carbide steel point. A diamond point is perfect and you'll never need to sharpen it. The steel point must be sharpened periodically with a polishing stone. To do this, put a drop of machine oil on the fine side of the stone. Hold the needle loosely with its top in your left hand so you form an acute angle with the stone (see Figure 4). With your right thumb and third finger, grasp the tool near its base. Move your left hand from side to side while you rotate the needle with your right hand. These two simultaneous movements will cause the tool to be sharpened to an even, sharp point.

BURIN

The burin is a diamond-shaped steel tool—usually referred to in catalogs as a "lozenge-shaped graver"—that is bent at an angle to allow your fingers to clear the plate as you work (see Figure 2). Burins, which you'll use to engrave a plate, come in

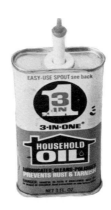

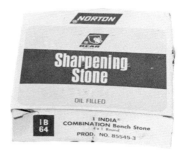

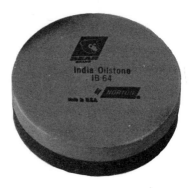

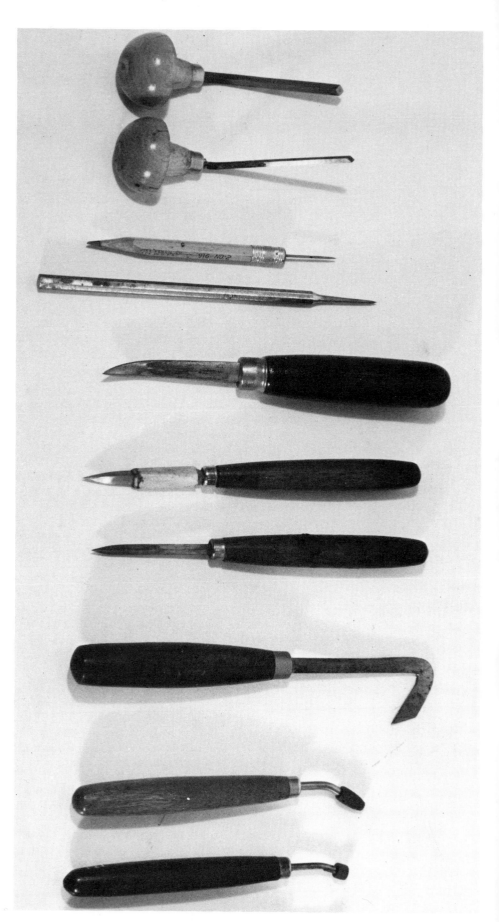

Figure 1. From top to bottom: can of machine oil used with the polishing stone; box polishing stone comes in; polishing stone. The top, lighter half of the stone is the fine side, and the bottom, darker half is the rough side.

Figure 2. A variety of tools mentioned in this chapter, from bottom to top: roulette with lines; irregular roulette; draw tool; small scraper before taping and large, taped scraper; burnisher; dental tool sharpened to a point; sewing needle imbedded in pencil eraser; and Nos. 5 and 10 burins.

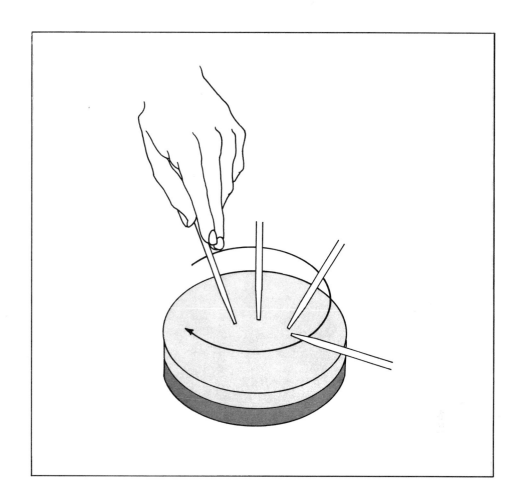

Figure 3. The proper method for rounding the point of an etching needle.

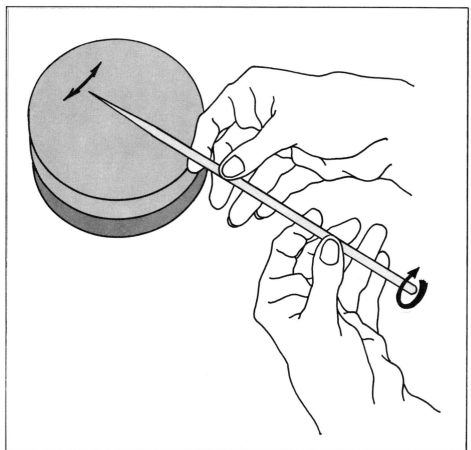

Figure 4. In this illustration, you can see how to sharpen a drypoint needle with a polishing stone coated with machine oil. Rotate the needle with one hand while moving it across the stone with the other.

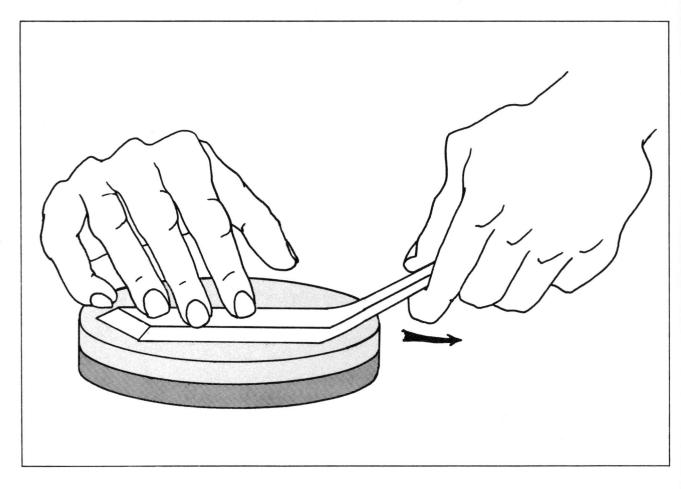

Figure 5 (above). When you remove a burr from the edge of the burin, your hands should be in the position shown. Pull the burin in the direction of the arrow.

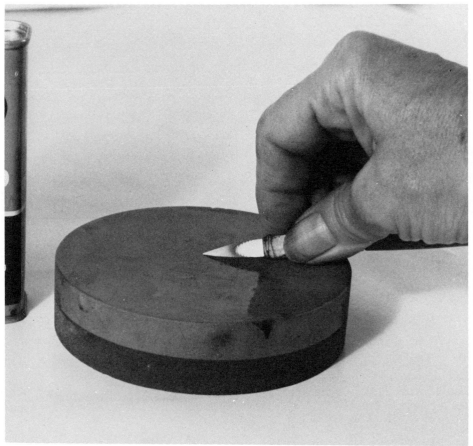

Figure 6 (right). One side of a scraper being sharpened on the fine side of a polishing stone.

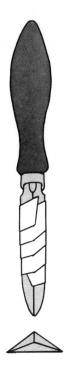

Figure 7. A scraper wrapped in tape. The tape protects your hand from the three sharp cutting edges of this tool.

different sizes, from No. 2 to No. 12. In general, the larger the number of the burin, the larger the burin itself and the wider and deeper the cut the burin will make in the metal. The shanks of sizes Nos. 2 to 5 are quite fragile and break easily from pressure; burins No. 6 and No. 10 are the most serviceable. When you first start to use a burin, you should buy or have access to two sizes—either Nos. 6 and 10, or Nos. 7 and 12. After you get used to two, you can experiment with other sizes.

Burins are used mainly on copper plates, and should be very sharp, since a blunt burin is hard to control. To test the sharpness of a burin, drop the point *gently* on your thumbnail. If it catches in the nail, it's sharp enough; if the point doesn't catch, then the burin should be sharpened.

To sharpen a burin, hold it in your right hand with your fingers on the shank close to the point. Place the flat diamond shape down on the smoother surface of the polishing stone. Then move your hand in a circular motion *without* rocking the tool. Stop every few strokes to look at the flat face of the burin to see if there are any facets, or extra sides, on the diamond shape. A facet indicates that the position of the tool on the stone is incorrect or that you're grinding the tool with a rocking motion. If you see an irregularity in the diamond shape, then you must sharpen the burin on the rougher surface of the stone first—until the facets are gone and the face of the tool is smooth—and then again on the smooth side. If you have trouble sharpening burins, please note that there's a tool called a Graver Sharpener that holds the burin in place while you sharpen it and makes sharpening easier.

When you've finished sharpening the burin and it has passed the thumbnail test, run your fingers along the sides of the tool. You'll notice that the sides near the point have a burr, or raised edges. To remove the burr, place the tool side down on the stone. Place your right forefinger and middle finger gently on top of the burin, holding the tool steady on the stone. Then pull the burin toward you with your left hand, always keeping the burin steady with your right (see Figure 5). Do this once on each side. Be very careful not to rock the tool, or it will destroy the burin's "belly"—the bottom V of the diamond shape—and you'll have to begin to sharpen the burin all over again. See Chapter 19 for information on engraving and on using the burin.

SCRAPER

The scraper is a three-sided, pointed steel tool with three sharp cutting edges attached to a handle (see Figure 2). You'll use this tool to scrape out a texture of a line that isn't wanted, to blunt hard edges on a deeply bitten plate, and to create interesting soft effects.

You must prepare the tool before you use it by sharpening the three cutting edges on a polishing stone. To sharpen the scraper, place one of the three sides flat on the smooth side of the stone and move the tool in a circular motion (see Figure 6). Don't rock the scraper from side to side or you'll destroy the sharp edge. Repeat this procedure with each side of the scraper until all three cutting edges are sharp to the touch. Then wind masking tape around the scraper, leaving ¾" of steel bare below the handle (see Figure 7). The tape will protect your fingers from the cutting edges. Finally, always keep the scraper free from rust by occasionally spreading machine oil on the steel with a cloth.

BURNISHER

The burnisher is a highly polished curved steel tool (see Figures 2 and 8) that is used to polish, or burnish, areas on the plate that have been scraped or lightly scratched. You can also use this tool to remove unwanted texture from an aquatint or a drypoint. The hard surface of the steel burnisher rubbed against the softer metal plate—copper or zinc, for example—polishes the plate so the rubbed area won't hold ink. For best results, put a drop of oil on the plate where you are burnishing.

Like the scraper, the burnisher must be protected against rust by wiping it with oil after you're finished using it.

ROULETTES

Roulettes are steel wheels—with fine raised lines or dots on them—that are attached to handles (see Figure 2). You use this tool by rolling the wheel across the plate while pushing down on the handle. You can also use the roulette on areas where the acid has not bitten the plate evenly—if a tonal area is not uniformly dark, you can darken the

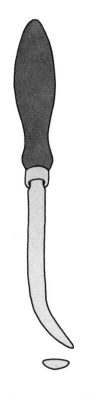

Figure 8. A burnisher. The bottom side is smooth tempered steel and is used for polishing zinc and copper plates.

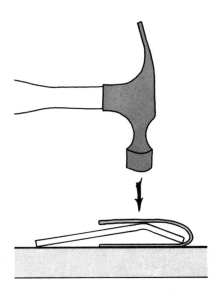

lighter areas by rolling the wheel over them. Remember, though, that the indentation in the plate as well as the raised burr around the edges of the indentation made by the roulette aren't very long-lasting. The pressure exerted by the press when the plate is printed quickly wears the burr down, flattening the indentation so that it holds less and less ink.

HAMMER

A flat-faced hammer is a good tool for straightening the bent corner of a plate. To do this, wrap a piece of blotting paper around the edge of the plate so there's blotting paper both over and under the plate (see Figure 9). Lay the plate on a flat surface and hammer the bent edge until the plate becomes flat.

OUTSIDE CALIPERS

If you have a plate with a depressed area on its surface, you can use outside calipers to correct the depression. The size of the calipers you need depends on the size of your plate: the calipers should be half the size of the longest edge of the plate. For example, a 6″ calipers would be good for a plate 12″ x 12″ and a 9″ calipers would be good for a plate 10″ x 18″.

To correct the depression, put the plate between the two arms of the calipers (see Figure 10). Rest the plate on the table and tighten the set screw—the screw that controls the movement of the two arms of the calipers—until the arms are touching both sides of the plate. Outline the depressed area on the front of the plate by scratching the plate's surface with one arm of the calipers—the arm resting on the back of the plate will simultaneously scratch the outline of the depressed area on the reverse side of the plate.

Now remove the calipers and fill in the space inside the scratched outline on the back of the plate with a pressure-sensitive tape like masking tape. Run the plate through the press with the tape touching the press bed and the surface of the plate up. The thickness of the tape on the back surface will raise the level of the plate on the printing surface.

FLEXIBLE SHAFT

The flexible shaft is a power tool used by hand that looks like a dentist's drill (see Figure 11). You can scrape, polish, and draw on a plate with it. Before you buy a flexible shaft, try to use a few different types so you can decide what kind would be best for you. And, before you begin experimenting, always remember that when you use a flexible shaft or any grinding machinery, *protect your eyes with safety glasses.*

You may find a flexible shaft with a *foot rheostat*—this is a mechanism that controls the speed of the tool—easier to use than a flexible shaft with a hand switch. The foot rheostat leaves your hands free to cope with the plate and with the attachments on the hand piece. To use this machine, turn the motor on, and pick up the hand piece. Then apply pressure to the rheostat with your foot, and the motor will turn the attachment on the hand piece. The more you push down, the faster the tool will turn; with less pressure, the tool will slow down. When you remove your foot, the attachment will stop turning completely although the motor will still be on. Actually, this kind of flexible shaft works rather like an old-fashioned sewing machine.

The hand piece of your flexible shaft should be comfortable to hold and may come with *collets* with capacities of from 1/32″ to ⅛″. By changing the collet you'll be able to use attachments such as *carbide burrs,* which come on different sized shanks of 1/32″ to ⅛″ in diameter. For example, a carbide burr on a shank 1/32″ in diameter will fit into a collet with a capacity of 1/32″. To use a *mandrel* with a shank ⅛″ in diameter, you must change the collet to one with a capacity of ⅛″. Some flexible shaft hand pieces have *chucks* instead of collets to hold attachments. Unlike the collet, the chuck is adjustable to different sizes of shanks. The adjustment is made by turning the chuck with a key made for this purpose.

You can get many different attachments for flexible shafts to use on your plate. Carbide burrs can be used to scrape the levels on a deeply bitten plate very roughly—the plate has to be polished when you're finished scraping. You can also draw directly on the plate with this attachment by using pressure to remove the metal from the plate. Or you can use less pressure and draw through a hard ground with the burr. Always remember that different burrs make different lines on the plate.

Figure 9. Flattening a bent plate with a hammer. The bent plate is wrapped in blotting paper and lies on a firm, flat surface.

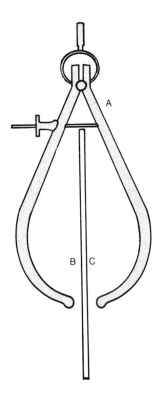

Figure 10. Set your calipers up in this manner to transfer the outline of a surface depression from the front of the plate to the back in order to fill a depression. In this diagram you can see (A) the outside calipers; (B) the front of the plate; and (C) the back of the plate.

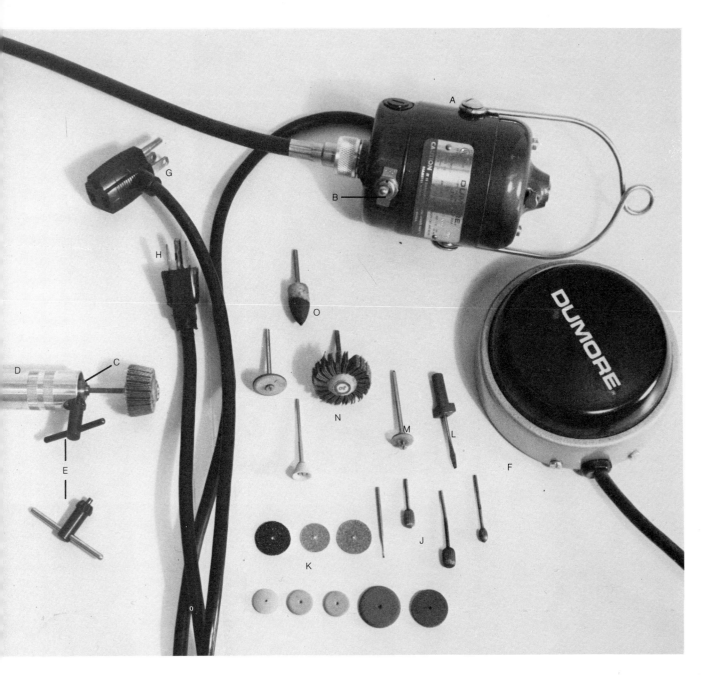

Figure 11. A flexible shaft, and many of its attachments: (A) motor; (B) motor's off-on switch; (C) chuck with ¼" to ⅛" capacity; (D) hand piece; (E) key to the chuck; (F) foot rheostat; (G) plug to foot rheostat; (H) plug to electric outlet; (I) rubber wheels of varying degrees of hardness; (J) carbide drills; (K) sandpaper discs; (L) screwdriver to tighten mandrels onto shanks; (M) mandrels; (N) fan grinders; and (O) buffer.

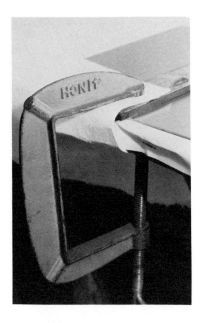

Figure 12 (above). A straight-edge, blotter, and plate clamped to the table, an arrangement which you should duplicate before you use the draw tool.

Figure 13 (right). A draw tool in use. Notice that its cutting edge is on the underside of the hook.

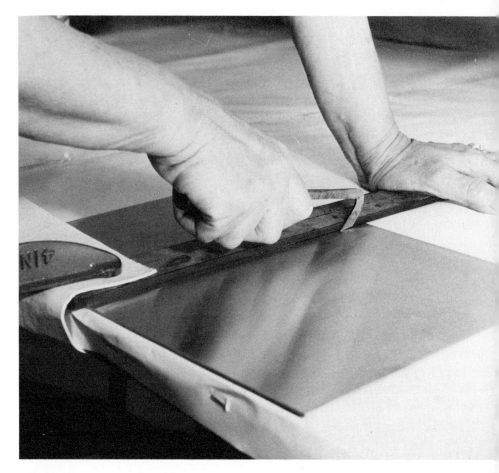

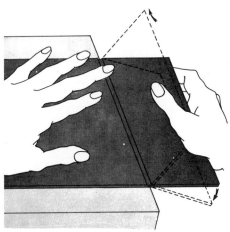
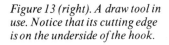

Figure 14 (above). To separate a plate into two pieces after scoring it with a draw tool, bend the piece to be severed first down, then up, and finally back to table level. Repeat if necessary.

Figure 15 (right). A small jigsaw being used to cut a plate.

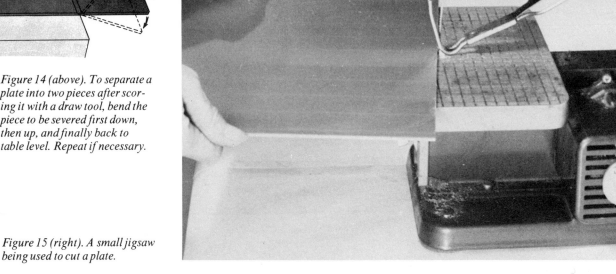

Fan grinders, attachments made from abrasive cloth mounted on shanks, are used to polish the plate. The grades of abrasiveness of the cloth available range from very coarse to very fine.

Mandrels, another attachment, can be used with polishing discs that screw onto the shanks. You can also buy felt wheels, or buffers, to screw onto the same shank—when you use buffers with jeweler's polish, you can get a fine finish on your plate. Finally, you can also polish with rubber wheels.

DRAW TOOL

A draw tool (see Figure 2) is a hook-shaped tool with a cutting edge on the underside of the hook. You can use it to cut plates into different sizes—to do this you also need two C-clamps, a blotter, and a steel straightedge. First lay the plate surface up on a table, place a blotter on top of the plate, and fold the paper underneath the table. Then put the straightedge on top of the blotter. Clamp the straightedge, blotter, and plate to the table so they can't move (see Figure 12). The blotter prevents the clamp from scratching the surface of the plate. Now pull the draw tool lightly along the straightedge (see Figure 13). When you have made a visible indentation, apply heavier pressure.

After the draw tool has cut halfway through the plate, take off the clamp and lift off the straightedge and blotter. Move the plate so that the cut line is even with the table edge. Pull sharply—first down and then up—and separate the plate into two pieces (see Figure 14). The plates will have roughly cut edges that will have to be filed.

Plates can also be cut in rectangular pieces with a guillotine or with metal-cutting shears. You can cut them into puzzlelike pieces with a jigsaw (see Figure 15). If you want your plate cut into many odd shapes, and you don't have access to a jigsaw, you can have it cut professionally at a machine shop or at a sheet-metal shop.

FILES

You'll need files (see Figure 16) to bevel, or smooth into an angle, the edges of the plate. An unbeveled plate may damage your printing blankets and will cut the papers. When you do this, use a rough, flat bastard-cut file first that shears the metal quickly. Then use a fine, flat file to smooth the rough edges left by the first file. It's a good idea to file your plate before you bite it in acid and then to file it again before you print.

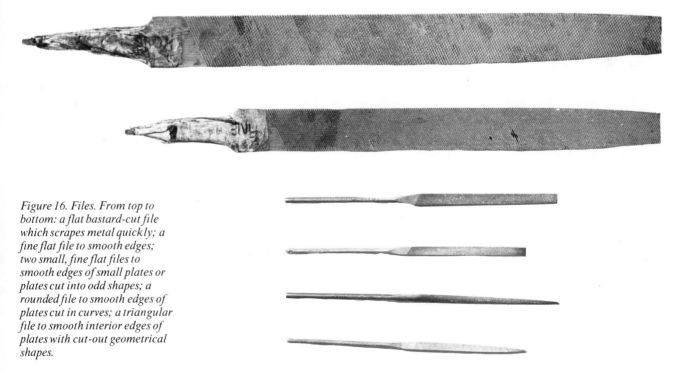

Figure 16. Files. From top to bottom: a flat bastard-cut file which scrapes metal quickly; a fine flat file to smooth edges; two small, fine flat files to smooth edges of small plates or plates cut into odd shapes; a rounded file to smooth edges of plates cut in curves; a triangular file to smooth interior edges of plates with cut-out geometrical shapes.

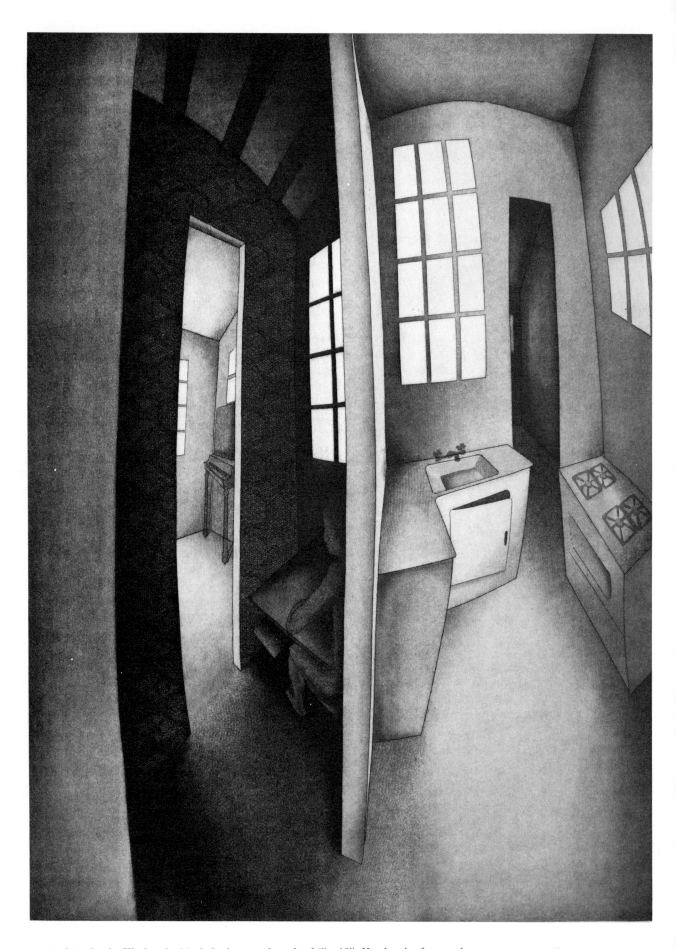

. . . And Again, the Kitchen *by Merle Perlmutter. Intaglio, 24" x 18". Hard and soft grounds.*

THREE

Printing Papers

Your choice of paper, as well as your choice of inks and grounds, will affect the quality of your finished print. There's a wide variety of papers available, all producing different effects and requiring different treatment.

All paper is made from cellulose fiber, a substance found in plants. Before the industrial revolution, papers were handmade from cotton or vegetable fibers, and many of these papers still exist. Today, however, although you can still purchase handmade or mold-made 100% rag paper, most paper is made from wood and rag fibers treated by mechanical or chemical processes. When these recent methods of making paper were first developed, some of the paper disintegrated rapidly. Now, however, there are many companies that manufacture high-quality paper which can be used by artists for printmaking and which will last a long time.

PERMANENCE

How long a paper will last is determined by many factors, one of which is the care with which the chemicals used in the manufacturing process are first neutralized and then eliminated. Another factor in a paper's permanence is the viscosity, or oiliness, of the ink used to make the print. If the ink, which is made of plate oil and powdered pigment, is too oily, the oil will eventually separate from the pigment, leaving a yellow, translucent stain surrounding the inked surfaces and crevices. Finally, the print will not last long in its original state unless it's stored properly. (See *Things Every Print-maker Should Know and Doesn't Know Whom To Ask.*)

SIZING

Different types of paper contain varying amounts of sizing, a glue that serves to strengthen and harden the paper and to make it less absorbent. Sizing for handmade or mold-made paper is usually made from the hides, hooves, or bones of animals. Douglas Howell, who teaches the old techniques for making paper, uses gelatin and plaster of Paris for sizing his handmade papers. Sizing used for commercial paper is a mixture of soda, ash, rosin, and alum.

This sizing must be softened or removed by soaking the paper in water before it can be properly printed. The amount and kind of sizing, as well as the weight of the paper, determine how long a paper should be soaked. The less sizing a paper contains, the less soaking it needs. (See the chart at the end of this chapter.)

RAG CONTENT

Paper may be made of rag and vegetable fibers or 100% rag. If a paper has a 33% rag content, then the other 67% is vegetable fiber. In general, the higher the rag content, the tougher and more durable the paper.

WEIGHT OF PAPER

The weight of a paper tells you how thick or thin the paper is. In the chart at the end of this chapter, the weights of the papers are given in pounds per ream, a standard measure which equals roughly 500 sheets of paper. A paper that weighs 120 pounds per ream will be much thinner than a paper that is the same size and weighs 300 pounds per ream. In general, thicker paper gives a better embossment than thin paper for deeply etched plates.

HANDMADE, MOLD-MADE, AND MACHINE-MADE PAPER

All paper is made of torn rags or of a mixture of torn rags and vegetable fibers that are combined with water and macerated into a pulp. Mold-made and handmade papers are usually equally good quality. In fact, when a machine shakes the mold, rather than a person, the paper will probably be of a more even consistency. Commercial machine-made paper (paper made without a mold) is generally of an inferior quality.

DAMPENING PAPER FOR PRINTING

You must always dampen you paper before printing so it will be soft enough to be pushed into the crevices and lines etched into your plate. You can do this in one of two ways—soak and blot the paper right before you use it, or soak the paper in advance and store it in plastic.

Materials and Equipment
printing paper
water tray
plastic bag or sheet of plastic larger than your paper
¼" thick glass or marble slab larger than your paper

Process. First, fill half the water tray with cold water. Drop one sheet of paper in at a time. Turn each sheet over—*be sure that each one is wet on both sides.* If you put the paper into the water carelessly, air may be trapped between two pieces and one side of each sheet will remain dry. Let the paper soak for about 20 minutes—1 hour for sized paper—(see chart).

If you're printing now, when your plate is ready take out the paper, place it between blotters, and blot it (see Chapter 13, page 141). If, on the other hand, you're preparing your paper a day (or more) before it's to be used, remove the paper one sheet at a time, blot it, and stack it. If you don't want to blot all the paper, wet only half the number of sheets you're planning to use. That is, if you're going to print ten sheets of paper, immerse five sheets in the water. Place one wet sheet of paper on a clean surface. Then set a dry sheet of paper on top of the wet one, and so on—one wet sheet, one dry sheet—until all the papers are stacked.

Place all the stacked sheets into the plastic bag, or wrap them well in the plastic sheet. Smooth the plastic over the paper to remove the excess air until the plastic clings to the paper. Then fold the edge of the bag under or seal the plastic sheet with tape so that no air can get in (see Figure 1).

Now, put the glass or marble slab over the plastic bag and wet paper. The slab will cause the moisture in the bag to distribute itself evenly so all the paper will be perfect for printing in 24 hours. Don't leave the damp paper enclosed in a plastic bag for more than a week in cold weather or two days in hot weather; if you do, the paper will become moldy. To avoid this you could add two or three drops of carbolic acid, also known as phenol, into the water tray before soaking your paper. *Please note that carbolic acid is very caustic.* Use it with the same caution you would use when handling undiluted nitric or hydrochloric acid.

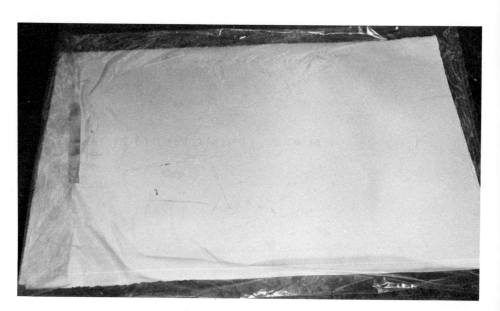

Figure 1. Dampened paper wrapped in plastic.

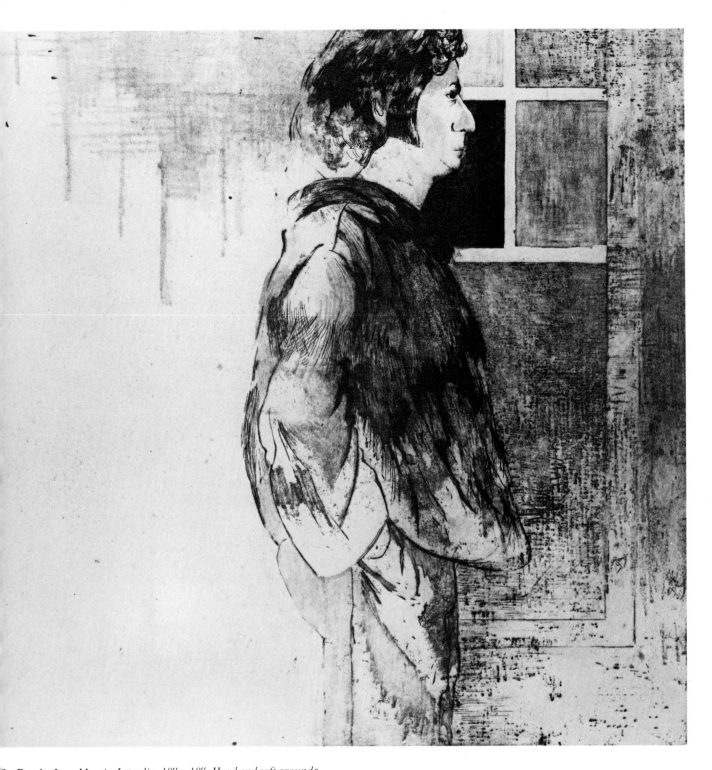

The Boy *by Jean Morris. Intaglio, 18" x 18". Hard and soft grounds.*

PAPER CHART

Name of Paper	Color	Size in Inches	Amount of Sizing	Rag Content
Arches Cover	Buff	22″ x 30″	Half	100%
Arches Cover	White	22″ x 30″ 29″ x 40″	Half	100%
Basinwerk Medium	Off White	26″ x 40″	Full	None
Fabriano Classico Medium	White	22″ x 30″	Full	100%
Classico Medium	White	22″ x 30″	Full	100%
Copperplate	Off White	30″ x 42½″ 22″ x 30″	Some	33%
Waterleaf Crisbrook Etching	White	22″ x 31″	None	100%
Domestic Etching	Off White	26″ x 40″	Half	50%
Dutch Etching	White	22″ x 30″	Half	50%
German Etching	Yellow White	31¼″ x 42½″	None	80%
Watercolor J. Green	Off White	27½″ x 40½″	Full	100%
Rives BFK	White	22″ x 30″ 29″ x 41″	Half	100%
Waterleaf Rives Heavyweight	Off White	29″ x 41″	Little	100%
Murillo	Yellow White	27½″ x 39½″	Full	33%
Italia	White	28″ x 40″	Little	66%
Radar Vellum	White	26″ x 40″	Hard	None

Note: The quality of paper is changing—each package you buy may have slightly different properties.

Weight	Wetting Time	Hand, Machine or Mold-Made	Comments
120 lbs	One hour	Mold-made	Edition paper for all intaglio. Not good for color or deep embossing.
120 lbs 230 lbs	One hour	Mold-made	Edition paper for intaglio and surface color. Not good for deep embossing.
88 lbs	Wets immediately	Machine-made	Proof paper for black intaglio.
140 lbs	One hour or more	Mold-made	Edition paper for intaglio, surface color, and embossing.
300 lbs	One to two hours	Mold-made	Edition paper for color inks, collagraphs, and deep embossing.
240 lbs 125 lbs	Wets immediately	Mold-made	Edition paper for single intaglio. Very fragile when wet.
140 lbs	Wets immediately	Handmade	Edition paper for all intaglio and viscosity printing. Not good for double intaglio.
120 lbs	One hour	Machine-made	Edition or proof paper for all intaglio.
120 lbs	One hour	Mold-made	Edition paper for color inks, all intaglio and double intaglio.
260 lbs	Wets immediately	Mold-made	Edition paper for all intaglio. Not good for printing in color or for double intaglio.
133 lbs	Wets immediately	Mold-made	Edition paper for all intaglio and viscosity printing. Excellent for engraving. Not good for double intaglio.
115 lbs 230 lbs	One hour	Mold-made	Edition paper for intaglio and surface color. Has a tendency to buckle when dry.
240 lbs	Wets immediately	Mold-made	Edition paper for all intaglio. Not good for surface color or double intaglio.
230 lbs	One hour or more	Mold-made	Edition paper for intaglio. Tends to crack under deep embossing.
220 lbs	15 minutes	Mold-made	Edition paper for all intaglio and surface color.
162 lbs	15 minutes	Machine-made	Proof paper for surface color.

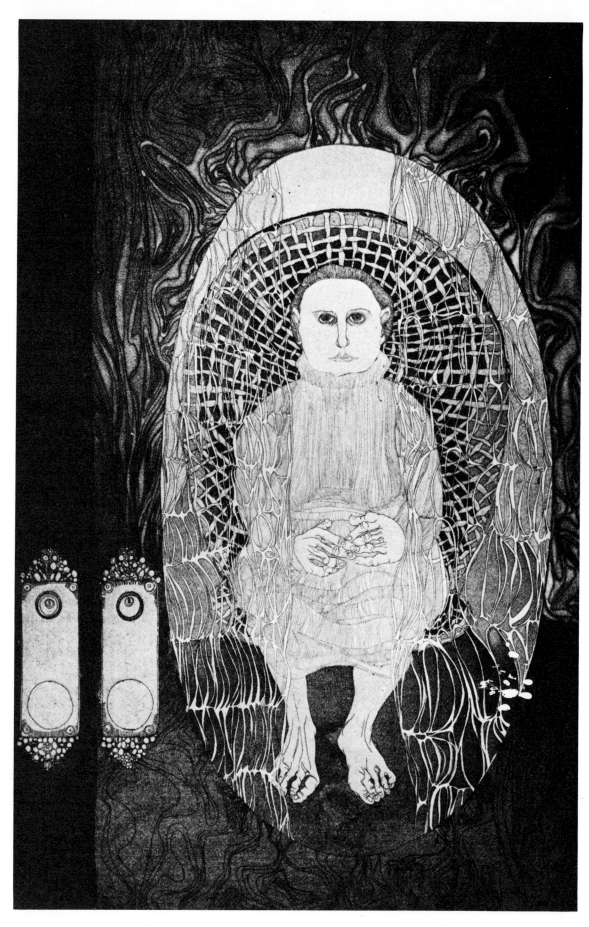

Looking Through a Door Window *by Naomi Hilton. Intaglio, 18″ x 12″. Hard and soft grounds.*

FOUR

Presses

The press is the most expensive single piece of equipment that you'll need to print an etching, drypoint, or collagraph. Because presses are so expensive—they can cost anywhere from $200 for a very small, simple one to $4,500 for a large, complex one—it's a good idea to use someone else's. Or, if possible, join a workshop with presses you can use until you're sure you want to buy one. Try many different kinds of presses, and before you buy the one you think you want, print a large, deeply embossed plate on it. Use high-quality blankets, ink, and paper; and be sure you like the results. If you don't like the prints you pull on the press, don't buy it.

In this chapter, I discuss the different features to look for and be aware of when you use or buy a press. (See *Supplies and Suppliers* at the back of this book for the names and addresses of press manufacturers.)

SIZE OF PRESSES

The press size refers to the size of the press bed—the entire press is actually larger. Bed sizes of etching presses range from 12″ x 24″ to 30″ x 50″, and you can get a larger bed made to order. When you decide to buy a press, first determine the size of your largest plates. The bed of your press should be at least 4″ wider than that. For example, if your largest plate will be 24″ x 36″, then your press should be no smaller than 28″ x 48″. You can, of course, also print that size plate on a much larger press. But don't print miniatures or small plates on a large press unless you lay two 2″ to 3″ wide strips of metal on either side of the plate (see Figure 1). Leave ample room for the printing paper to lie flat between the strips. And be sure that the metal strips are the same gauge, or thickness, as the plate being printed. They'll keep the press roller from warping or even breaking, which can happen if you use enough pressure and enough small plates over a period of time.

PRESS WEIGHT

The weight of the press should be mostly in the rollers and the bed. Always remember that the overall weight of a press is *not* an indication of its quality—a very heavy press may actually have a great deal of its weight distributed in the wrong places, such as in the frame.

If you intend to buy a press, consider its weight with respect to the floor on which you'll place it. A press can be as heavy as a grand piano, about 2,000 pounds. Although you can distribute the weight more evenly by placing a ¾″ piece of plywood under the base of the press, make sure you know how many pounds your floor will hold so it won't collapse.

PRESS ROLLERS

The top roller of the press rides over the blankets, paper, and plate with enough pressure to press the dampened paper down into the lines and grooves of the plate to make an embossment and/or to pick up the ink. The top roller should be large enough to ride up onto the surface of the plate under pressure; if the roller is too small, it will push the plate forward instead. If your roller is very large, though, you'll need a lot of pressure to get a good print. Most top rollers available on standard presses are 6″ or 7″ in diameter, and this size roller works very well.

The bottom roller of the press supports the bed of the press and counteracts the pressure applied by the top roller. Both rollers must be rigid enough so that the pressure exerted by the press is uniformly even.

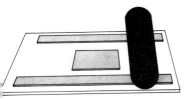

Figure 1. Two long metal strips laid next to the small square plate on the press. Room is allowed for the paper margin between the strips and plate. The cylindrical press roller on the right will roll over the strips when the small plate is printed. This setup will prevent the press roller from warping.

Figure 2. A mint press with a star wheel handle.

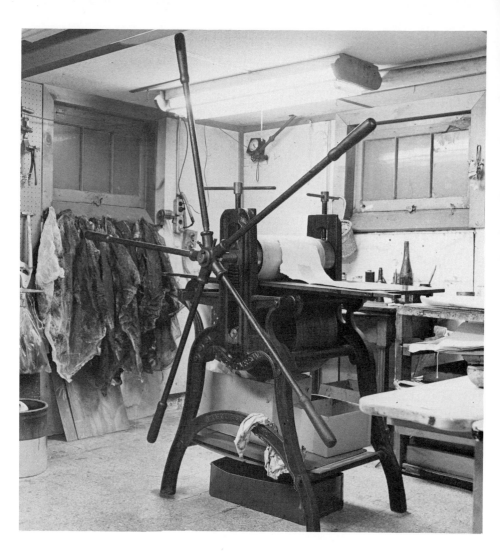

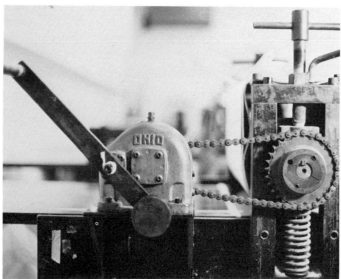

Figure 3. A press with a gearbox mounted to one side.

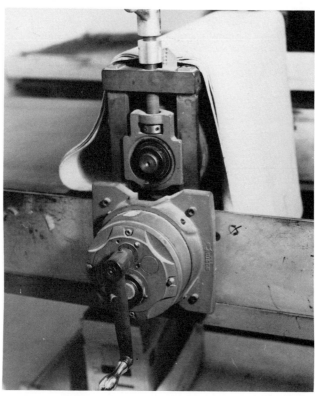

Figure 4. A press with the drive shaft of the gearbox mounted directly through the roller.

PRESS BEDS

The bed of the press is usually made of steel, although the Dickerson press bed is made of pressed Masonite that the manufacturer will replace for a fee when it warps.

The thickness of the bed depends on many things: length, width, and the number of bottom (support) rollers and how they're positioned under the bed. Most presses have four support rollers, and most beds are about ⅝″ thick. The Martech press, an exception, has a ½″ steel bed with eight small rollers supporting the bed. I know of one Martech press that has been used in a studio for six years, and the bed is as straight as it was when it was purchased.

The bed and the handle of the press should be a comfortable distance from the floor for you to work with. The ideal height of the press bed will vary according to your size and work habits, but it will probably be somewhere between your hip and waist, like a kitchen counter. Most manufacturers will supply your press with a metal stand made to order to the height you desire. If you're sharing the press with many people in a studio, the height of the bed will have to be a compromise to suit everyone.

DIRECT DRIVE AND GEAR-DRIVEN PRESSES

The old mint presses that printmakers used to purchase were direct-drive presses—the roller turns 360° when the handle turns 360°. To make this possible, the direct-drive presses have a star wheel handle of five spokes, each three feet in length, leading from the hub of the roller out to the tip (see Figure 2). To pull a print, you put your hands on one spoke, and one foot on another. Then you press down on your foot with your body weight, change spokes, and keep repeating the process until your plate moves through the press.

Presses manufactured today have gears to make them easier to operate. With the average press, you must turn the handle 10 to 24 times to turn the roller 360°, or one complete turn. Ratios of from 10 (turns) to 1 (revolution) to 24 to 1 will satisfy most printmakers. The larger the ratio, the less effort required to turn the handle, but the greater the number of turns required to roll the plate through the press.

The way the manufacturer mounts the gearbox on the press is of the utmost importance. Any gearbox that's off to one side (see Figure 3) will cause side loading in the roller. This results in a skewing action which may or may not be detrimental to the print—it is, however, definitely detrimental to the press. The best type of gearbox, then, is one that goes directly through the center of the roller shaft (see Figure 4).

TYPES OF DRIVES

There are different kinds of drives for presses, one of which is the top roller, or friction drive, the most common type manufactured in the United States. When you turn the handle of this type of press, the top roller supplies the force that drives the bed through the press and creates the pressure necessary for printing. However, even though you turn the handle the bed won't move unless the blankets are engaged—

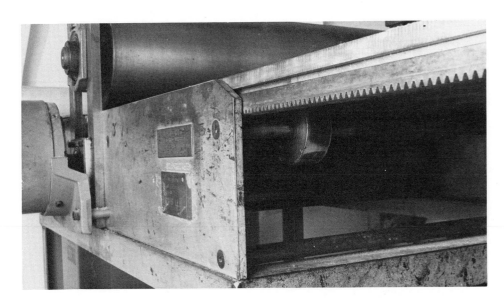

Figure 5. A rack-driven press— the rack itself has a serrated edge.

caught under the roller—or unless the roller lies flat against the bed. One of these two conditions is necessary to supply the contact which causes the friction needed to slide the bed under the roller.

Another type of friction drive is the bottom-roller drive, which is found in most European presses. Here the lower roller forces the bed through the press while the top roller supplies the pressure as it rolls over the plate. Both the top and bottom-roller, friction-driven presses are used to print etchings, drypoints, and collagraphs.

A press with a third kind of drive is the rack-driven press (see Figure 5). This press doesn't have a friction drive—the bed is driven through the press by a gear with a rack arrangement placed on either side of the gear. Both rollers are free to rotate and supply pressure to the plate. The rack-driven press prints intaglio, relief, and lithographic plates.

MOTORIZED PRESS

A motorized press—in which conventional handle of the manual press has been removed and replaced with a geared motor—is the easiest kind of press to use. The motor has a switch with three positions—forward, reverse, and off. When you turn the motor on, the roller rotates and drives the bed through the press until the bed can go no further or until you turn off the motor.

In adjusting the pressure of a motorized press, you're at a disadvantage since it's difficult to tell when you have too much pressure. On a hand press you know you have too much pressure when you have difficulty turning the crank. On the motorized press, you must sense the pressure. And always remember that too high a pressure setting might prove harmful to the plate and the press.

There is, however, a type of motorized press made by Martech that allows you to have both manual control and motorized comfort. On this press, you adjust pressure with a crank handle; then you can either switch on the motor to run the bed through the press or work the press by hand. The drive the motor gives is somewhat like power steering on an automobile: the motor supplies 95% of the power needed, and the printmaker/driver supplies the balance.

The motorized press costs a few hundred dollars more than a manual press of comparable quality. If you're thinking of buying one, try out many different kinds and check the safety features offered by the various manufacturers—they must meet the state and federal safety standards for motorized equipment.

MICROMETER DIALS OR SCREWS

You can control the height of the top roller above the press bed with either two large screws or two micrometer dials on either side of the top roller. You use the screws—which are cheaper than micrometer dials—to determine how much pressure the top roller will exert on the plate. The tighter you turn the screws down, the closer the top roller will be to the press bed, and hence the more pressure the roller will create. You can also turn the screws up—if you want to print a high block of wood, for example—so that the roller is an inch or more above the bed.

The screws can be turned separately, and you *must* adjust them to equal heights so the roller is parallel to the press bed. If you don't do this, the pressure on one side of the roller will be much greater than on the other. Your print may be darker on one side, your plate may move and blur the print, and your blankets may wrinkle.

Micrometer dials are not essential, but they make the adjustment of the roller's height above the press bed much easier. The dials are usually set so when the top roller is resting evenly on the bed, the dials read zero. Thus, if both dials read at the same level, you know that the roller is parallel to the plate. Micrometer dials are very useful in a studio where many people must use the same press and the height of the roller has to be changed often.

FEATURES TO LOOK FOR IN A PRESS

1. All chains or gearboxes should be enclosed.

2. The top roller should have self-aligning ball bearings.

3. Make sure that the press has end-stops—they keep the bed from riding out too far—and hold-downs, which keep the bed level at all times. On some presses the hold-downs and end-stops are on the underside of the bed, one on each side, in order to leave the entire top of the bed free as a working surface.

4. The bed should fit well in its frame so that it moves in a straight line. It should also be level or it will be thrown out of alignment. You can buy leveling pads to put under the legs of the press for balance.

CARE OF THE PRESS

Always oil the parts of your press that require lubrication. Ask the manufacturer where these parts are and how often they should be oiled. Gearboxes are usually filled with oil and need little maintenance, but check to see that the oil is at the level specified by the manufacturer, and add more if necessary.

Don't use excess pressure when you print. The correct amount of pressure for each plate is determined by the print—if the deepest area of the plate is printing well, then the pressure is correct. Excess pressure causes the plate to wear down quickly, makes turning the handle of the press very difficult, and may damage the press. Never print an object or plate that is so uneven in height that it might cause the bed to bounce as the roller passes over it. You may break the roller or dent the press.

Place the press in a studio as far from the acid baths as possible—the acid may cause the metal on the press to corrode. You should wax the rollers of the press with a very hard paste wax to help keep them from corroding. Whenever the wax wears off, apply another coat. (You cannot wax the bed of the press because the wax will wear off when you clean it with solvent while you print.) Also, you should wipe the bed with kerosene every night to prevent it from rusting.

Don't leave your printing blankets engaged, or caught in the press, overnight. The damp printing paper causes the blankets to become wet, and the moisture will cause both the roller and the bed to rust.

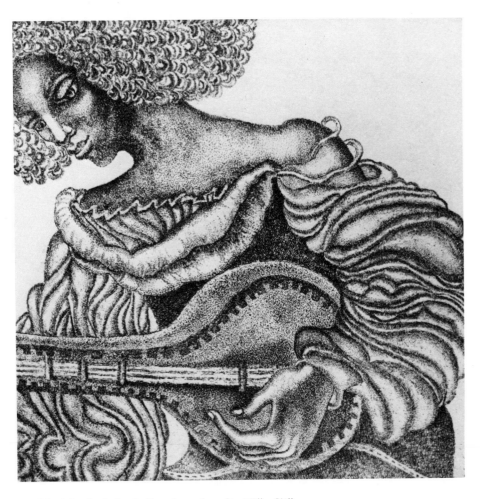

The Musician *by Rolande Grataloup, Intaglio, 5½″ x 5½″.*

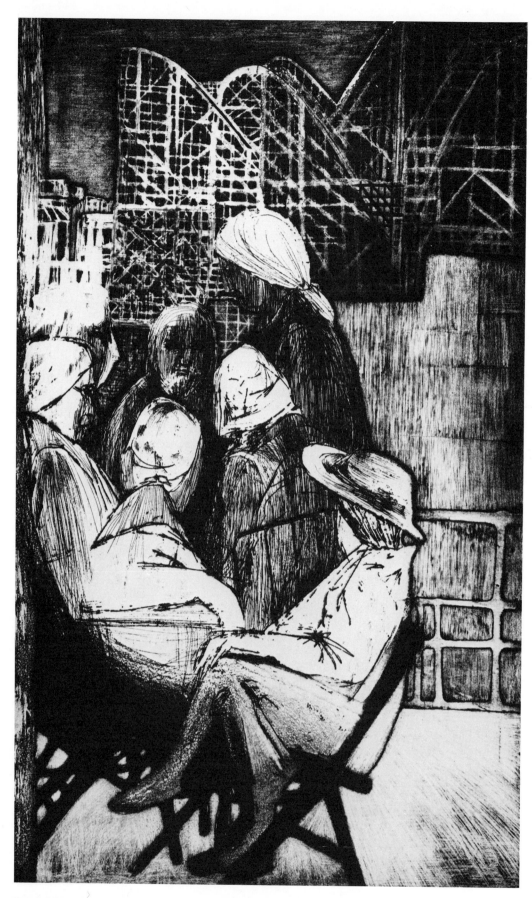

Coney Island Conversation *by Ruth Leaf. Intaglio, 29¼ x 17⅝".*

FIVE

Workshop

When planning the arrangement of a printmaking workshop, you should keep two things in mind—safety and efficiency. Your studio will contain among other things, acids, presses, electrical appliances, inks, and solvents. Not all of these materials and pieces of equipment are mutually compatible. For instance, acid fumes tend to corrode the metal on presses, and the metal dust produced by working on plates with electrical tools or files will contaminate the ink if they're used near the inking area. In general, a good plan will provide for separate work areas for different procedures, with areas for biting plates in acids far from presses, and areas for using electrical tools far from inking slabs. You'll find that there is never enough space in your studio. However, it's helpful if you arrange the different areas within the space as compactly as possible.

Most of the illustrations in this chapter are of my own studio (see Figures 1). My arrangement of space and equipment is by no means an absolute, but is simply one solution to a set of problems—Figure 2 is another solution. You'll have to make changes according to the amount of space and money at your disposal. In all cases, however, you should observe safety precautions.

FLOORING

The floor of your studio should have a surface that will be able to withstand solvents and acids without disintegrating, as even the most careful printmakers have accidents sometimes. A wooden floor is not a good idea—it will absorb all the liquid materials you spill and will create a fire hazard. You should also avoid an asbestos tile floor, since when you spill solvents on asbestos tiles they dissolve. The best flooring, therefore, is rubber or vinyl tile or linoleum—these materials are relatively impervious to acids and solvents, and they are easy to keep clean.

LIGHTING

Your studio should, of course, be well-lit. The most desirable form of lighting is daylight without sun glare. However, fluorescent light combined with incandescent light works very well also—if you're working with color, this combination gives the best approximation of daylight. Never work with glare on your plate, or you'll get eye fatigue. To avoid glare, you can fasten crates or plastic covers to fluorescent light fixtures. If sunlight comes through the windows, hang up a translucent shade.

ELECTRICITY

In addition to the electricity you'll need to light the studio, you'll need electrical plugs for hot plates, power tools, and motorized presses. Since the power tools draw a heavier amperage than ordinary household appliances, you should have a 220-volt line. Individual outlets must be especially sturdy and should be equipped with a three-pronged socket—the extra hole is for grounding the power tools.

ACID AREA

Acid should be confined to the area where it's used and stored. Ideally, this area should be adjacent to an outside wall of the building so the acid fumes can be blown outdoors—if a window is available, you can use a good fan to act as an exhaust. Keep the acid trays close to the window fan so the corrosive fumes won't permeate the studio. Acid fumes in the air will corrode metal and are detrimental to your health: take care that the exhaust fan is in use whenever plates are in the acid or when the acid baths are uncovered (see Figure 3).

If possible, the acid area should contain a large stainless steel sink with both a regu-

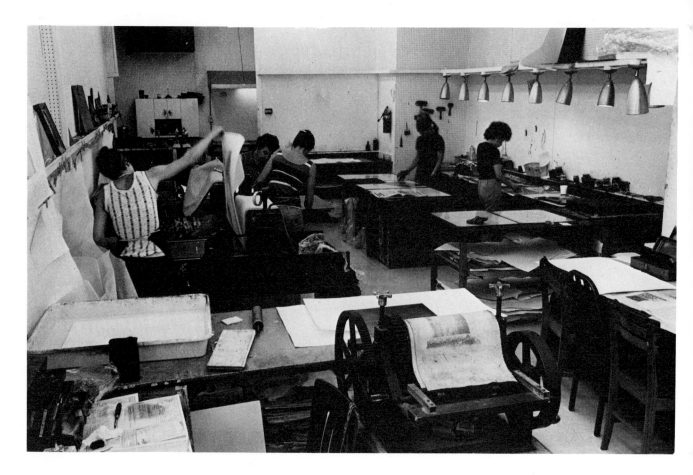

Figure 1 (above). My studio. Notice that the printing area, left, is separate from the inking area, right. The acid room is not in view.

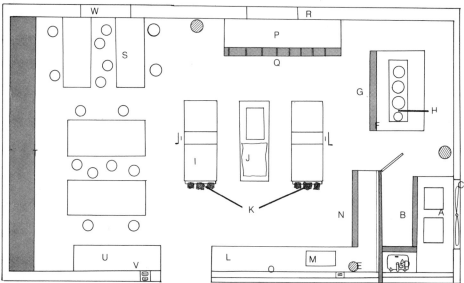

Figure 2. Diagram of a layout of a workshop. Starting with the acid room, in the lower right section, we have (A) acid trays, (B) acid storage, (C) extractor or exhaust fan, (D) sink with spray, and (E) fire extinguishers. Moving up to the area where you work with grounds, there is (F) table for applying and removing grounds, (G) enclosed metal cabinet under the table for solvents, and (H) raised platform in the center of the table to hold grounds. In the center of the room there are (I) presses, (J) table to hold a water tray to soak paper and blotters to dry paper, and (K) racks attached to the press to air-dry inky tarlatan that can be used again. Below the press area are (L) surfaces for intaglio or relief printing, (M) hot plate, (N) ink storage, and (O) pegboard for roller storage. Above the press area are (P) flat surface for drying prints and (Q) plate storage. On both sides of this area are (R) Homosote walls for tacking up prints. To the left of this area are (S) tables and stools for working on plates. Farther left is (T) storage area for papers and blotters. In the bottom left area of this workshop are (U) table for power tools and (V) heavy-duty electrical outlet for power tools and hot plates. Windows (W) line part of the room.

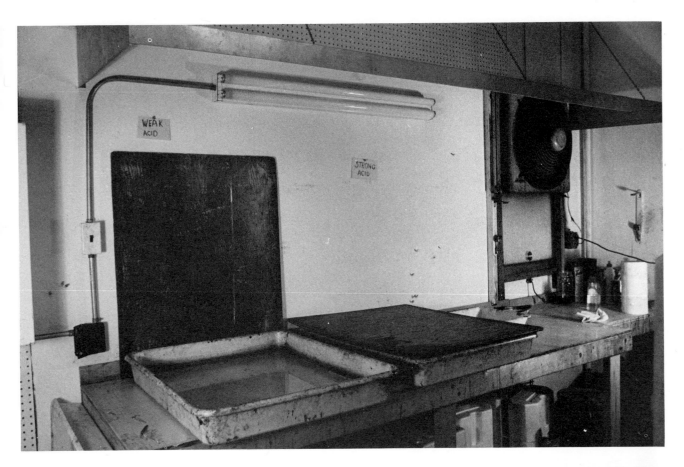

*Figure 3 (above). Acid room.
The acid is stored in plastic trays
which are covered with plywood
when not in use (like the tray on
the right). Signs above the trays
indicate the strength of the acid
bath. A fluorescent light above
the trays enables you to see the
plate clearly when it's in the
acid. The hood, high above the
acid trays and covering the extractor fan on the right, contains
the fumes so the fan can pull
them out. The undiluted acid,
under the table, is stored in
lightproof plastic boxes.*

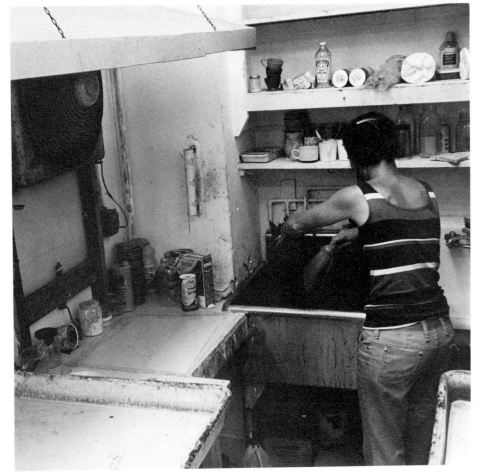

*Figure 4 (right). Acid room
showing the stainless steel sink
with spray nozzle.*

Figure 5. Table, covered with newspaper, for the application and removal of grounds. The table has a metal top with a raised rim which prevents solvents from dripping onto the floor. Above the cleaning surface is a high platform on which you can keep small cans of solvents, grounds, and brushes. Underneath the table is a metal box with doors to store larger containers of solvents.

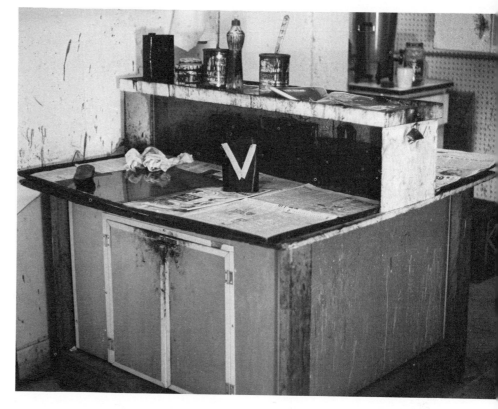

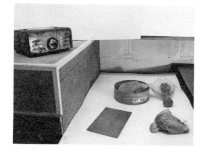

Figure 6 (above). Aquatint area. The hot plate is on the raised platform on the left; the rosin bags and the rectangular plate lie on the blotter.

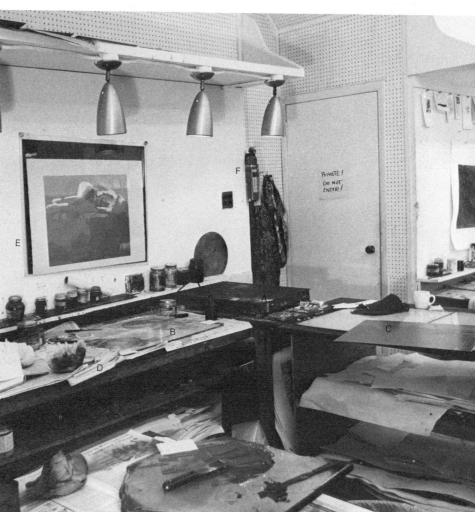

Figure 7. Part of the printing area which contains (A) large hot plate, (B) glass slabs for ink, (C) plate, (D) newspapers to absorb the ink, (E) Homosote wall for tacking up prints, and (F) fire extinguisher.

Figure 8 (right). Section of the printing area with blotters on the tabletop to remove excess water from printing paper, cardboard clips on top of the blotters to pick up the printing paper, and a water tray behind the blotters with paper soaking. All the materials can be reached easily from the press on the right.

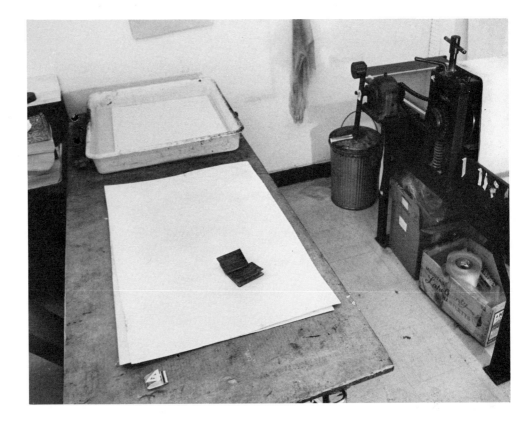

Figure 9 (below). In this small studio, gelatin rollers are hung on pegboard on the left. Inks are stored on the shelves above the work tables which hold newspaper, a water tray, and blotters. Underneath the table is a storage area for plates.

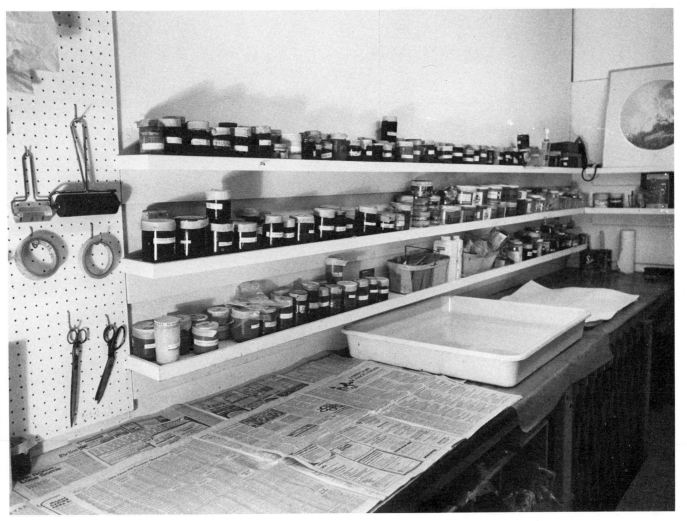

lar faucet and a spray nozzle on a hose. Place the acid trays next to the sink so when you remove plates from the acid you can wash them immediately in cold water (see Figure 4). If it isn't convenient to have the acid trays next to the sink, then place them next to a large plastic tray half-filled with cold water. When you take a plate out of the acid, plunge it into this tray with cold water to stop the biting action of the acid.

Store the acid and the trays on shelves and racks under the table where they are used. As a good safety precaution, keep a dry chemical fire extinguisher nearby, as well as a pail filled with bicarbonate of soda. If you break an acid bottle or splash acid out of a tray, throw bicarbonate of soda on the acid—it will act as a sponge and neutralizer. You can then scoop up the whole mess and throw it in the sink, flushing it down with plenty of water. In this case, the answer to pollution is dilution.

CLEANING AREA

If there's only one sink in your studio, you'll have to use it for scrubbing plates and cleaning your hands as well as for rinsing the plate off after an acid bath. Have a table top or some other flat surface near the sink for scrubbing plates—this must be done any time you apply a ground.

Store powdered cleansers, sponges, hand cleaners, paper towels, and soap for hands and brushes nearby.

AREA FOR WORKING WITH GROUNDS

To apply and remove grounds, you should have a surface that won't absorb solvents, such as a table covered with porcelain, glass, plastic, or metal. The table should be large enough to accommodate all the plates and materials you are working with. When you use the grounds, lay newspaper over the surface of this table to absorb the grounds and/or solvents. The newspaper can be removed and replaced so you always have a clean surface to work on.

Store the grounds, solvents, brushes, newspaper, and other necessary materials near this table (see Figure 5). See Chapter 1 for information on the storage of solvents.

AQUATINT AREA

Because laying an aquatint involves the use of rosin dust, a powderlike substance, you need an area that is draft-free, out-of-the-way, and contains a table and a hot plate. A small, inexpensive hot plate used only for aquatint and put away when not in use (see Figure 6) is preferable to having a single hot plate used for heating grounds and ink as well as for aquatints, since the grains of rosin might contaminate printing inks.

PRINTING AREA

The printing area is perhaps the most important part of the studio, for it's the print that determines whether all your previous efforts have been successful. It centers around the press and the inking slabs. Place a hot plate close to the inking slab and store inks, oils, gloves, and so forth under the inking table (see Figure 7). Hang inky tarlatans that are still usable under the press bed or on a clothesline strung in the studio for this purpose. Pull the tarlatans taut before you hang them up, so air can circulate through them.

Have an area to dampen and blot paper near the inking area and the press (see Figure 8). And hang small rollers for surface inking on a pegboard wall (see Figure 9) that's not too close to the hot plate—gelatin rollers will deteriorate near the heat. It's also desirable to have a wall of Homosote, cork, or some other soft material to hang prints and drawings on.

POWER TOOL AREA

You should have a separate area with a sturdy table removed from the inking area and from other working spaces for a flexible shaft, grinder, or jigsaw. It would be disastrous for the metallic dust or filings caused by the use of power tools on metal plates to come in contact with grounds or inks. If you wipe a plate with ink that contains metal particles, the scratches that result are difficult to remove, especially if they occur where there's a tone etched into the plate.

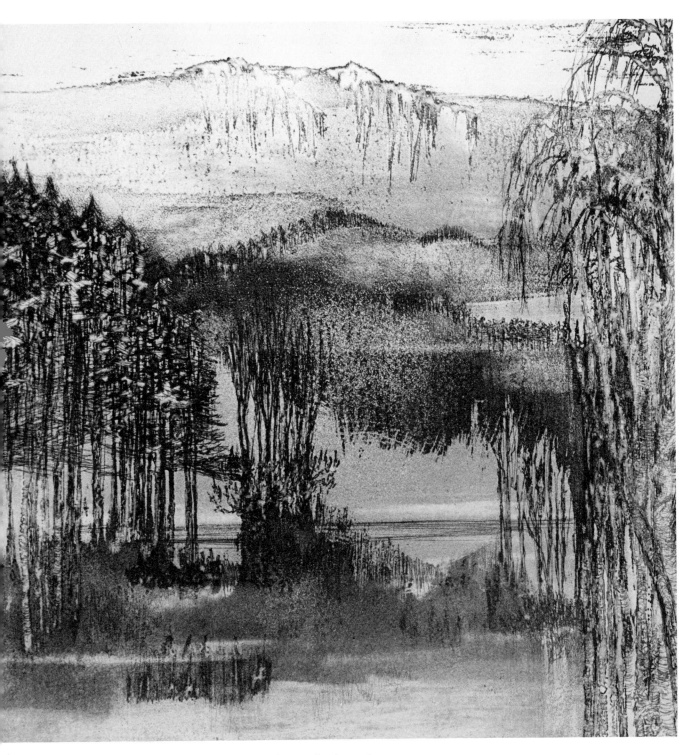

ite Mountains *by Helen Schiavo. Intaglio, 18″ x 18″. Soft ground and aquatint.*

PAPER AND PLATE STORAGE AREA

Shelves wide enough to hold blotters, proof paper, and edition paper, and standing racks tall enough to hold plates can be built very inexpensively (see Figures 10 and 11). *Don't let small plates lean against large plates*, or the larger plates will warp. Warped plates are very difficult to work with, as they tend to move on the press when you print, causing the print to have a dirty edge or a double image. It's also difficult to apply a ground evenly on, a warped plate.

The most desirable place to store prints is in a blueprint cabinet (see Figure 12). You can, however, store prints in portfolios if you don't have this kind of cabinet. See *Things Every Printmaker Should Know and Doesn't Know Whom to Ask* for further information.

Have a surface on which to dry your prints. Use the top of the blueprint cabinet, or if there's enough space, set aside a table or shelf for just this purpose. For more information on drying prints, see Chapter 13, page 144.

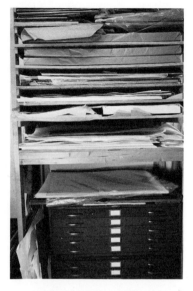

Figure 12. A lot can be stored in a small space, as this photograph shows. The blueprint filing cabinet with space left right above it to dry prints sits under shelves for storing paper.

Figure 10 (above right). Design for a workshop storage bin. Proof paper, edition paper, and blotters are stored on separate shelves, while plates or portfolios can be stored in the vertical racks underneath.

Figure 11 (right). Larger storage arrangement. The shelves are, again, used for proof paper, edition paper, and blotters—each kind of paper on its own shelf. Plate storage is in the vertical racks. In addition, the top surface of this type of storage bin can also be used for storing blotters for drying prints, left, and for stacking dried prints, right.

PART TWO
Etching Techniques

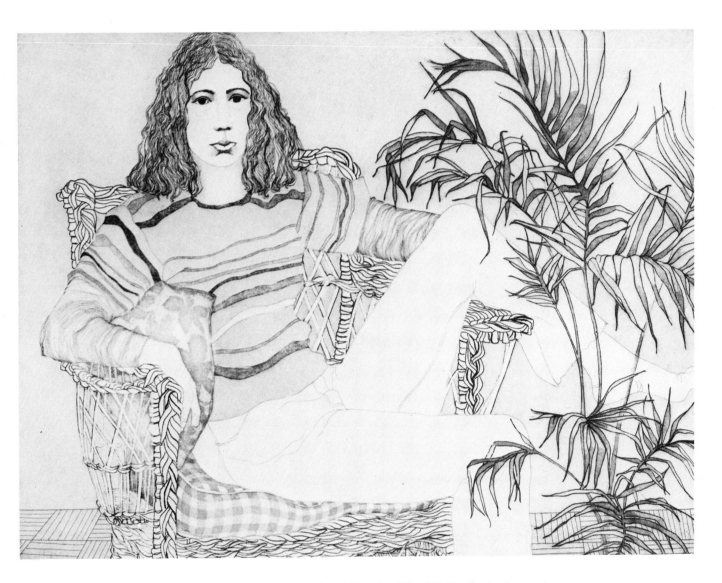

Nancy's Wicker Chair *by Elaine Simel. Intaglio, 18″ x 24″. Hard and soft grounds.*

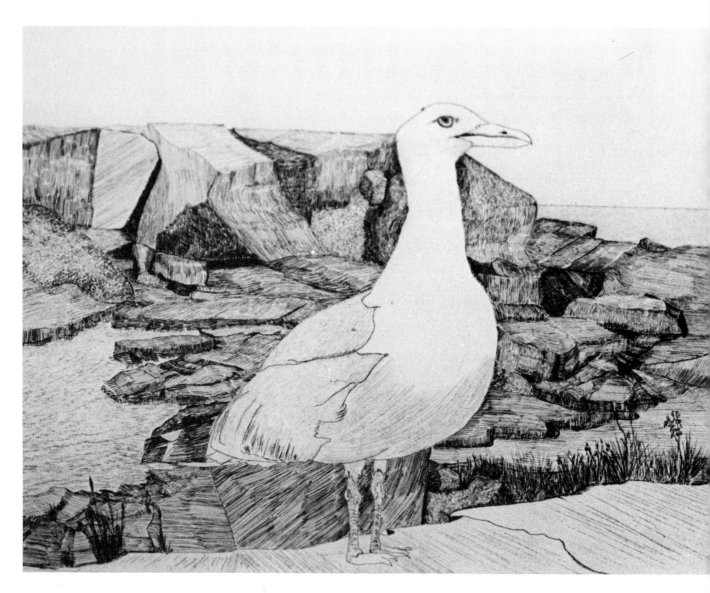

Sentry *by Richard G. Cordero. Hard ground, 12" x 18".*

SIX

Formulas for Grounds and Inks

In later chapters I'll discuss the uses of various grounds and inks. Although you can purchase some of them commercially, you can make far superior and much less expensive products in your own studio. *Always remember to label and date all cans of grounds and inks you make*, and cover the labels with waterproof tape.

See *Supplies and Suppliers* at the end of the book to learn where you can find the chemicals and materials which you'll need to make grounds and inks from the formulas that follow.

HARD GROUND

You'll need hard ground for fine line work on zinc, copper, or steel, and for coating a sugar lift ground (see Chapters 7 and 10).

Materials and Ingredients (see Figure 1)
2 lbs. pure beeswax
2 lbs. powdered asphaltum
1 lb. powdered rosin
8 oz. xylene (optional)
4 qt. enamel pot with cover, to be used *exclusively* for hard ground
You'll also need an electric hot plate, wooden spoon, garden gloves, newspaper, 4 yds. of cheesecloth cut into 4 equal pieces, varnolene or turpentine, large clean coffee or juice cans, wide-mouthed glass jars with screw tops or metal cans with covers, hammer, and fire extinguisher.

Process. Before you begin to make hard ground, make sure you're in a well-ventilated room or outdoors, since the fumes produced in the process are noxious.

The first step is to place the bars of beeswax between sheets of newspaper, break them into small pieces with a hammer, and put the pieces into the enamel pot on an electric hot plate. Stir occasionally with a wooden spoon until all the pieces of the beeswax are melted. Then remove the pot from the hot plate, and add the asphaltum, rosin, and xylene (a solvent for asphaltum and rosin). Please note that the xylene is optional, but if you make the ground without it, you'll have to heat the mixture much longer. Also, *xylene is very flammable*—be sure that none of it drips onto the outside of the pot.

After you've added the asphaltum, rosin, and xylene, replace the pot on the hot plate. Stir until all the ingredients are melted—there should be no lumps of rosin or asphaltum that break apart when you stir. Keep the cover of the pot handy in case the mixture gets too hot and flames up—you can smother the flames with the cover. Although I've made grounds for many years I've never seen this happen, but I'm told that it's possible.

When all the ingredients in the pot are melted and smooth, the ground has been cooked long enough. At this point you must pour the hot ground through a strainer made of cheesecloth into clean metal containers, such as large juice or coffee cans. *Don't pour hot ground into glass jars.*

While you strain the ground, always wear garden gloves. Place a layer of cheesecloth across the top of one of the metal cans, pour the hot ground through it. While the ground is still warm, place a fresh piece of cheesecloth over another clean can and pour the already strained ground through the second piece of cheesecloth. The ground will begin to thicken as it cools; if it becomes too thick to flow through the second piece of cheesecloth, reheat the mixture and then strain it again. You can press the cheesecloth slightly to allow the ground to flow through, but it's unwise to wring

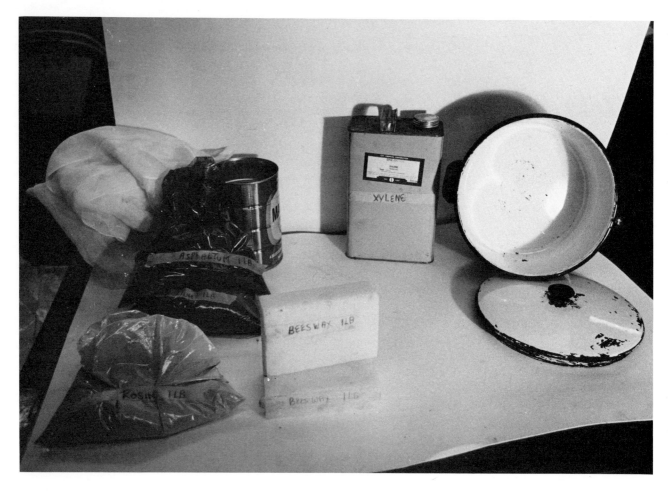

Figure 1. The ingredients and materials necessary for making hard ground, clockwise from bottom left: 1 lb. of powdered rosin; two 1 lb. bars of beeswax; two 1 lb. bags of powdered asphaltum; cheesecloth; 2 lb. coffee can for straining the ground; xylene; and a 5 qt. enamel pot with a cover.

every drop of ground out as you'll also wring out some of the impurities you're trying to remove.

Use and Storage. If you're going to use some of the ground immediately, you must add a solvent—varnolene or benzine—to give it the consistency of heavy cream. Add the solvent to the ground while it's still warm in the ratio of 1 part varnolene to 3 parts ground. Stir until the solvent becomes part of the mixture. Don't use the ground, though, until it cools.

Always cover your ground after using it, or the dust and dirt in the air will make all the straining you did while making the ground useless. Also, the jar used to hold the ground while you use it should have a mouth wide enough for a 2½″ brush to be dipped in easily.

If you intend to store the ground, then before it cools, while it's still warm enough to flow but not hot enough to crack glass, pour it into wide-mouthed glass jars with screw tops or into metal cans with covers. Tape the edges of the covers to the cans with pressure-sensitive tape like masking tape to keep air and dust out, and the ground will keep forever.

You can store the ground with or without adding varnolene. If you add varnolene, the ground will be ready to use at any time. However if you store the ground without adding varnolene, you'll have to reheat the ground to make it semi-liquid when you want to use it. To do this, place the can of ground with the cover removed into a pot with enough water to cover the can halfway. Heat the pot on a hot plate and add the varnolene when the ground is warm.

SOFT GROUND

You'll use soft ground when you draw on plates and to impress textures on a plate's surface (see Chapter 8).

Materials and Ingredients

1 can hard ground

Vaseline or axle grease

Also have a pot, two metal containers and a hot plate handy, as well as gloves, a spatula, varnolene, masking tape, and a glass jar with a screw top.

Process. To begin, take a can of hard ground which *doesn't* have varnolene or turpentine added to it. Put on the gloves and heat the can of hard ground with the cover removed in a pot of water. When the hard ground is warm, and therefore flexible, remove enough with the spatula to fill half of another container. Fill the other half of this container with Vaseline or axle grease, and stir until the two ingredients are thoroughly mixed.

Take some of this mixture and in another container add varnolene in a ratio of 1 part varnolene to 3 parts warm, soft ground. Stir the soft ground—its consistency should be like that of heavy sour cream.

Use and Storage. For immediate use keep the soft ground in a glass jar with a screw top. Make sure the jar is tightly covered except when you're working on a plate with it. For long storage keep this ground in any covered container, and seal the crack between the lid and container with masking tape.

ROSIN STOPOUT

When you coat areas of a plate's surface with rosin stopout, then those areas will be *completely* protected from the action of the acid when the plate is immersed in an acid bath. Note that a plate covered with rosin stopout can be put into acid immediately, even if the stopout is not completely dry but is still tacky.

Materials and Ingredients

8 oz. chunk rosin (powdered rosin does not work very well)

8 oz. denatured alcohol

⅛ teaspoon malachite green

Also have some newspaper and a hammer, as well as a 16 oz. jar with a screw top.

Process. Place the chunk rosin between sheets of newspaper and pulverize it with a hammer until none of the pieces are larger than a grain of barley. Then fill half a 16 oz. jar with the pulverized rosin. Add alcohol to completely fill the jar and cover. It will take a few days for the alcohol to absorb the rosin. On the second day turn the jar upside-down so the rosin which has sunk to the bottom can be absorbed.

Before using the mixture, add the malachite green, a very dark green, in order to make the stopout visible. Malachite green is soluble in both alcohol and water; without it the rosin and alcohol mixture would work very well but would be difficult to see on the plate. Be careful when you use malachite green—it's very strong and, if you spill it, you'll find green on everything.

Use and Storage. Sooner or later the moisture in the air will cause the stopout to crystalize. You can thin the solution with a few drops of alcohol; but if the mixture completely solidifies you must throw it away. It's a good idea, therefore, to pour a small amount into a jar when you use it, while keeping the larger amount always covered.

ASPHALTUM STOPOUT

Asphaltum stopout is used like rosin stopout to protect the surface of the plate from the biting action of acid. The two stopouts differ in that asphaltum is soluble in varnolene, while rosin is soluble in alcohol. Also, unlike rosin stopout, the asphaltum stopout brushed onto the plate's surface must be dry before the plate is put into the acid.

Liquid asphaltum can also be used with lift ground (see Chapter 10). Note that asphaltum can be bought ready-made in a paint or hardware store under the name of Asphaltum Paint.

Materials and Ingredients

4 oz. powdered asphaltum

4 oz. varnolene

Also have two 8 oz. jars with screw tops and extra varnolene handy.

Process. Fill half the jar with powdered asphaltum. Stir in varnolene until the jar is full. Wipe any excess asphaltum from the edges of the jar and cover tightly. Allow the asphaltum to thicken by letting it stand for a few days. If, when you open the jar the mixture is very thick, pour some off into a second jar, add more varnolene to both containers, and stir.

Use and Storage. In order to use asphaltum as a stopout, it should have the consistency of heavy sweet cream. But if it's to be used with lift ground, the asphaltum should be thinned with varnolene to the consistency of light sweet cream. Asphaltum has a tendency to thicken when it stands in a jar. Before you use it, make sure it has the proper consistency—if the asphaltum is too thick, add varnolene and stir.

SPECIAL STOPOUT

Use this stopout with any ground, in any acid, and in place of either asphaltum or rosin stopout whenever a very strong stopout is required.

Materials and Ingredients
8 oz. asphaltum (by volume)
1 tbsp. chunk rosin, pulverized to a very fine powder
1 tbsp. beeswax, cut into thin pieces
8 oz. varnolene
In addition you'll need a hot plate, measuring cup, a 1 lb. coffee can, a 2 lb. coffee can, and a jar with a screw top.

Process. Pour the 8 oz. of asphaltum into the 1 lb. coffee can. Measure the 8 oz. of varnolene and stir it into the asphaltum powder. Continue to stir until all the powder has dissolved. Then add 1 tbsp. of rosin and 1 tbsp. of beeswax to the asphaltum and varnolene.

Pour 8 oz. of water into the 2 lb. coffee can and place the 1 lb. coffee can inside it to make a double boiler. Place both cans on the hot plate, and heat and stir the mixture until it's creamy smooth. Remove the cans from the hot plate. When the mixture is cool, pour it into a jar with a screw top.

Use and Storage. In time, your special stopout may thicken. If it does, just thin it with varnolene and continue using it. Also, to remove special stopout from the plate, you'll have to use both varnolene (for the asphaltum) and alcohol (for the rosin).

SUGAR LIFT GROUND

Lift ground is brushed directly onto the plate and produces an effect similar to a pen or brush drawing (see Chapter 10). The lift ground formula that follows was published in *Artist's Proof* in an article by Misch Kohn.

Materials and Ingredients
5 oz. Karo corn syrup
4 oz. India ink
¾ oz. Tide soap or any other granulated soap (don't use detergent)
¼ oz. gum arabic
Also have a 16 oz. glass measuring cup, a glass jar with a screw top, and a stirrer.

Process. Pour 5 oz. of Karo syrup into the measuring cup. Add 4 oz. of India ink to the cup, totaling 9 oz. of liquid. Then sprinkle Tide into the mixture until the level rises to 9¾ oz. Finally, add a *pinch* of gum arabic, bringing the mixture to exactly 10 oz.

Stir until the gum arabic and Tide are mixed in. Pour the sugar lift ground into a jar with a screw top and label the jar.

Use and Storage. If you keep the sugar lift ground for a long time, it may develop a mold—if you remove the mold, the ground will still be usable. Also, if you leave the jar open, the lift ground will thicken—a few drops of water will restore the ground to its former consistency. Note that sugar lift ground is soluble in soap and water.

WHITE GROUND

When you paint white ground on your plates, you'll create unusual textural effects (see Chapter 11). The formula for this ground was invented by Frank Cassara working under Rackham Grant and was published in *Artist's Proof.*

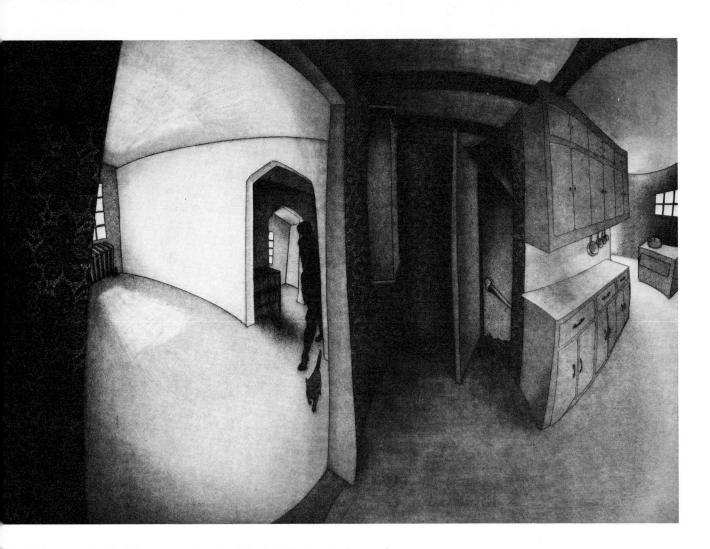

Is and Doorways *by Merle Perlmutter. Intaglio, 18" x 24". Hard and soft grounds.*

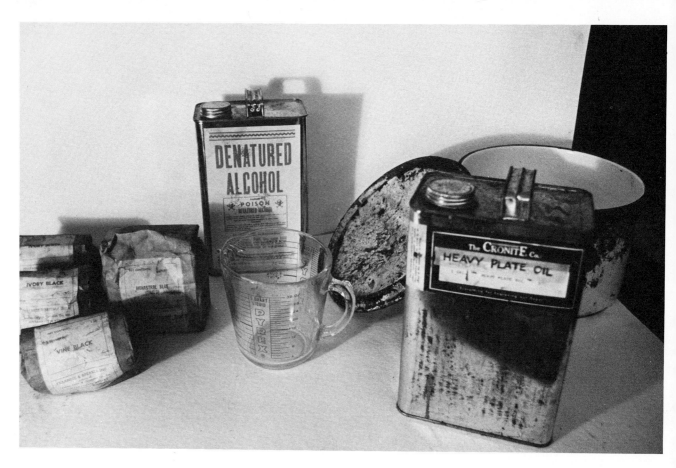

Figure 2. The ingredients and equipment used in making black ink, from left to right: four bags of pigment—one of vine black, two of ivory black, one of monastral blue; denatured alcohol, a 32 oz. measuring cup; enamel pot and cover; and heavy plate oil.

Materials and Ingredients

1 cup titanium white dry pigment
2 cups Ivory Snow, granulated
½ cup raw linseed oil
1 cup water
Also have a 16 oz. measuring cup, a plate glass or marble slab, a spatula, and a glass jar with a screw top.

Process. First measure 1 cup of titanium white in the measuring cup and pour the pigment onto the glass or marble slab. Then measure 2 cups of Ivory Snow and pour it on top of the white pigment. Mix these two ingredients together.

Now measure ½ cup of raw linseed oil. Make a small impression in the center of the mixed dry ingredients, and pour a little linseed oil into the hole. Grind the oil into the dry ingredients with the spatula until you can't see any more oil. Add the rest of the oil slowly, little by little, and continue to grind until the oil and the dry ingredients are throughly mixed into a stiff white paste.

Measure 1 cup of water and blend the water little by little into the paste with a spatula. When all of the water has been mixed in, the white ground should have the consistency of whipped cream.

Use and Storage. Keep white ground in a glass jar with a screw top. White ground cannot be kept in a metal container or the water in the ground will cause the container to rust. Please note that if you keep white ground for a long time, the oil and the pigment will tend to separate and harden—if this happens add a little water and blend it in to give the white ground the proper consistency. Also, before you apply white ground to your plate, you must thin it to the consistency of tempera paint (see Chapter 11, page 107).

BLACK INTAGLIO INK

You will need black ink for proofing and for printing editions.

Materials and Ingredients (see Figure 2)

2 lbs. ivory black powdered pigment
1 lb. vine black powdered pigment
1 tbsp. monastral or phthalo blue pigment
5 qt. enamel pot with cover, used *exclusively* for making black intaglio ink
1½ pts. denatured alcohol
1½ scant pts. Cronite heavy plate oil No. 3
You'll also need a wooden spoon, garden gloves, hot plate, putty knife, metal containers with covers or glass jars with screw tops, glass plate or marble slab, pressure-sensitive tape such as masking tape, and a fire extinguisher.

Process. To begin, put on the garden gloves and mix all the dry ingredients together in the enamel pot. Then add the alcohol and stir until all the grains of pigment are damp and the consistency of the mixture is that of a crumbly paste. Put on your gloves. Cover the pot, place it on the hot plate, and heat the pigment and alcohol. When the ingredients are quite warm, uncover the pot, and pour in the plate oil, a little at a time, stirring constantly with the wooden spoon. As you stir, you'll notice that the alcohol begins to first vaporize and then liquify at the bottom of the pot. When that happens, there's enough plate oil in the mixture—you should have only very little or no plate oil left when the alcohol separates out.

Continue to heat and stir until there's enough alcohol in the bottom of the pot to pour off. Pat the ink to one side of the pot with the spoon and put the cover back on, leaving a small opening between the cover and pot. Pour off the excess alcohol, which should be milky in color, down the sink or into an empty container—if you have a cesspool, don't use the plumbing.

Keep heating the ink and pouring off the excess alcohol until most of the alcohol is gone. The mass of ink that has been pressed against the side of the pot should now be shiny, heavy, and solid.

Use and Storage. Now put the ink into metal containers or glass jars with screw tops. Fill the containers by pressing the ink down firmly with a putty knife to remove air bubbles. You may notice some alcohol in the ink—don't worry, it won't affect the quality of the ink. If the containers aren't full, pour water on top of the ink to keep air out. When you cover the containers, tape the outside of the rims with pressure-sensitive tape to keep the contents airtight. Don't forget to date the containers, as black ink will eventually dry out no matter how many precautions you take.

After you finish cooking the ink, it's ready for storage but not for printing—before you print with it, you must add raw linseed oil. Because the linseed oil causes the ink to dry very quickly, it's a good idea to prepare only the amount of ink needed to print for a few days. To do this, remove some stiff ink from the can and place it on a marble slab. Add a little raw linseed oil and grind it into the ink with a spatula. Repeat this procedure until all the ink on the marble slab is of a smooth consistency. The ink should fall *slowly* from the spatula to the slab when you pour the ink from the spatula lifted a few inches above the slab. At this point you can print with the ink.

Store any ink that's left over after printing in a container with a cover, or in Saran Wrap if there's only a small amount—*never* put ink prepared with linseed oil back into a can of stiff ink that has no linseed oil mixed into it.

Please note that the yield for the formula for black ink given here is from 4½ to 5 lbs. of ink. Smaller amounts of the formulas can be made, of course, as long as the proportions of the ingredients are correct.

COLOR INTAGLIO INK

You can print intaglio plates in many colors, but remember that color inks are more difficult to use than the black intaglio ink since they're harder to wipe. The earth colors—ochres and umbers—are the easiest of the color intaglio inks to wipe. Other colors are more difficult to use (see chart at the end of the chapter), but they're often worth the effort.

Pigments for color intaglio inks are sold by the pound, in packets ranging in size from 4 oz. to 25 lbs. The larger amounts contain too much pigment for one printmaker, while the smaller amounts, 4 oz. and 8 oz. packets, are more expensive per ounce. A 1 lb. package of pigment is the most practical. Color pigments do not have to be cooked, and they're ground with a stiff palette knife.

Plate oil and raw linseed oil, the other two main ingredients in color inks, are sold in gallons, quarts, and pints. If you plan to mix many colors in large amounts, buy a gallon of plate oil and a gallon of raw linseed oil. If you plan to mix small amounts of few colors, a pint of each would suffice. Finally, remember that the amount of plate oil and raw linseed oil an individual color will absorb varies from color to color.

Materials and Ingredients
dry color pigment
Cronite heavy plate oil No. 3
Easy Wipe
raw linseed oil
You'll also use a spatula or heavy-duty palette knife, a plate glass or marble slab, glass jars with screw tops, paper towels, and gloves.

Process. First, put on the gloves and place a small amount of powdered pigment in the center of the glass or marble slab. Make a depression in the center of the pigment, and pour in a small amount of heavy plate oil. Wearing gloves, grind the pigment and oil with a spatula until the oil has absorbed as much pigment as possible. Add a little more oil—repeat the process until all the pigment has been absorbed by the oil. Use as little of the oil as you can—the ink should be very sticky, the consistency of a thick wallpaper paste.

Now add a little Easy Wipe. If you have used about 8 oz. of pigment, then you should add ⅛ tsp. or ⅛″ squeezed out of a tube of Easy Wipe. Easy Wipe, as its name implies, is a product which makes the ink easier to wipe. You can have too much of a good thing, however—too much Easy Wipe will puff up the ink and make your prints splotchy.

After you mix in the Easy Wipe, add raw linseed oil to the ink. Take a small amount of the ink mixed with plate oil and add enough raw linseed oil to make the ink form a puddle the consistency of heavy sweet cream—it should run off the palette knife in a long ribbon.

Use and Storage. Mix all the ink you'll need for one printing session at one time—it's better to mix too much ink rather than too little since it's distracting to have to stop printing to mix another batch of ink. And, you can never be sure that you'll get precisely the same intensity of color.

Store color ink in a jar with a screw top. Since the jar will be difficult to open if there's dried ink between the container and the lid, wipe the edge of the jar clean with varnolene or a paper towel before you cover it. Colors can last for years in these jars—even though a dry skin may form on the surface, the ink underneath remains usable. The pigments of some colors have a tendency to separate from the linseed oil: these can be ground again with the palette knife (see *Properties of Ink* below). All colors should be clearly marked by name on the jars and, as usual, the labels should be covered with waterproof tape. If you're printing an edition, you'll want to use the exact same color each time—don't count on your memory to remember which of the ten reds you used for the first prints.

PIGMENT CHART

The color chart that follows will help you to determine which colors are appropriate for different uses. The definitions of terms below help explain the pigment chart.

Density of color. A dense color means that the pigment is strong— a little bit will go a long way—and heavy in weight, as 1 lb. of dense pigment will fit into a very small package. A dense color can be made transparent by the addition of another more transparent color such as Terre Verte or Transparent Base, a surface base. Please note that a light-toned dense color ink can be used as a single intaglio in combination with a rolled surface color in a viscosity print (see Chapter 16).

Middle-range colors are neither transparent nor dense, while transparent colors are very fine, light-weight pigments that tend to float around, or fly, when they're mixed with a plate oil to make an intaglio color. A pound of transparent pigment will make a larger package than a pound of dense pigment.

Strength of color. A pigment can be very transparent and still be strong and have high saturation, i.e., great vividness or intensity. On the other hand, some transparent pigments are weak and have almost no color when they are printed—these are the inks which are used with denser color pigments to make them more transparent. Medium colors can be printed alone or over another intaglio color in a double intaglio (see Chapter 14).

Ease of wipe. Intaglio printing inks are rubbed into the grooves and crevices of the plate and wiped with tarlatan. The surfaces of the plate which aren't etched are then wiped with more tarlatan and/or tableau paper or newspaper. Some color inks tend to stick to the plate. These hard-to-wipe inks increase the difficulty of getting an even plate tone—such colors should be wiped when the plate is warm, after being heated on a hot plate.

Properties of ink. Color pigments will last indefinitely so long as they aren't mixed with plate oil. Some of them, however, separate from the oil: the heavy pigment sinks to the bottom of the container while the oil rises to the top. The pigment can be ground again in the oil which has risen to the top of the jar. Note that the whole jar of pigment should be ground at the same time, and that it's wisest to mix colors that have separated at the time you plan to use them.

Modifying. A color may be modified by mixing in either a transparent base or a small amount of a complementary color (orange is the complement of blue, green the complement of red, and so forth).

Single intaglio. When one ink, either color or black, is used to make a print, the method of printing is called single intaglio. If you use a single color intaglio for a print, you must be sure that the color is strong enough to carry the print.

Double intaglio. When one plate is printed twice with a different intaglio ink each time (the second color ink printed directly over the first) or when two different plates are printed, one over the other with different intaglio colors, the process is called double intaglio. A color which is not strong enough for a single intaglio might work very well in a double intaglio, while two dense colors printed one over the other might create a disaster, with the densities of the colors obliterating details and hiding tonal differences.

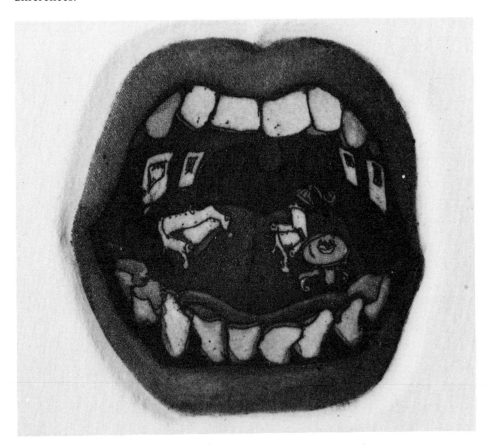

Step into My Parlor *by Merle Perlmutter. Intaglio. Hard and soft grounds.*

PIGMENT CHART

Pigment Color	Density of Color	Strength of Color	Ease of Wipe	Properties of Ink	Comments
Colbalt blue	Transparent	Medium	Easy	Tends to separate	Good for single and double intaglio
Cerulean blue	Transparent	Medium	Easy	Tends to separate	Good for single and double intaglio
Phthalo or monastral blue	Transparent	Very strong	Very difficult	Keeps well	Modify for single and double intaglio
Indigo blue	Medium to dense	Strong	Difficult	Keeps well	Good for single intaglio; modify for double intaglio with terre verte or transparent base
Milori blue	Medium	Strong	Difficult	Keeps well	Good for single and double intaglio
Ultramarine blue	Transparent	Medium	Medium	Keeps well	Good for single and double intaglio
Burnt sienna	Medium	Medium	Easy	Keeps well	Good for single and double intaglio
Burnt umber	Medium	Strong	Easy	Keeps well	Good for single intaglio
Raw umber	Medium	Strong	Easy	Keeps well	Good for single intaglio
Raw sienna	Transparent	Medium	Easy	Keeps well	Good for single or double intaglio
Van Dyke brown	Transparent	Weak	Easy	Keeps well	Good for single or double intaglio
Colbalt green	Transparent	Medium	Medium	Dries quickly in container and cannot be ground again	Good for double intaglio
Phthalo or monastral green	Transparent	Very strong	Very difficult	Keeps well	Modify for single or double intaglio
Terre Verte	Transparent	Weak	Not wiped alone —always mixed with other pigments	Keeps well	Use to modify other colors
Cadmium orange	Dense	Strong	Difficult	Keeps well	Good for single intaglio; modify for double intaglio
Mineral orange	Dense	Very strong	Difficult	Tends to dry quickly	Good for single intaglio; use with transparent base for double intaglio
Bluish pink Reddish pink Yellow pink	Transparent	Medium to weak	Medium	Tends to separate	Good for double intaglio or for mixing with dense colors to make them more transparent

Pigment Color	Density of Color	Strength of Color	Ease of Wipe	Properties of Ink	Comments
Alizarin crimson	Transparent	Very strong	Very difficult	Remains grainy in ink	Use with other colors—do not use alone
Cadmium red light, medium, and dark	Dense	Strong	Difficult	Keeps well	Good for single intaglio; modify for double intaglio
Indian red	Dense	Strong	Medium	Keeps well	Good for single intaglio
Ruby red	Transparent	Medium	Medium	Keeps well	Good for single or double intaglio
Colbalt violet	Transparent	Weak	Easy	Tends to separate and harden	Good for double intaglio
Mars violet	Medium	Medium	Medium	Tends to separate	Good for single or double intaglio; changes color when wiped on zinc
Titanium white	Dense	Strong	Difficult	Keeps well	Turns grey when wiped on a zinc plate
Transparent white	Transparent	None	Not wiped alone —always mixed with other pigments	Keeps well	Use to modify other colors
Cadmium yellow light, medium, and dark	Dense	Strong	Difficult	Keeps well	Turns green when wiped on a zinc plate; can be used in a double intaglio when added to more transparent colors or when transparent base is added to the cadmium yellow
Yellow ochre light, medium, and dark	Medium	Medium	Easy	Keeps well	Good for single intaglio; add transparent base for double intaglio
Indian yellow	Transparent	Strong	Difficult	Hardens in container; can be ground again	Good for double intaglio
Hansa yellow	Dense	Strong	Medium	Keeps well	Good for single intaglio; add transparent base for double intaglio

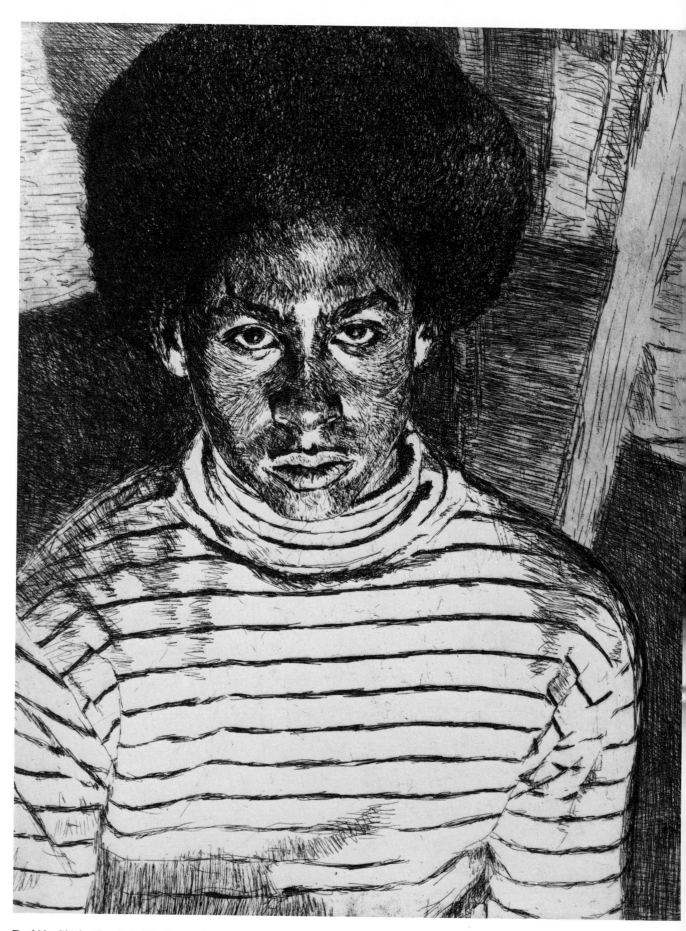

David *by Shirley Gorelick. Hard ground, 21″ x 17″.*

SEVEN

Hard Ground

In the printmaker's studio, any acid-resistant material is called a ground. Hard ground, a mixture of beeswax, asphaltum, rosin, and xylene, hardens when it dries on the plate. When the hardened ground is both cool and dry, you can draw on the plate's surface with a tool such as an etching needle that removes the protective ground. The lines and areas of the plate that are removed are thus exposed to the acid; when you put the plate into the acid they'll etch, or bite, creating a groove in the plate. At the same time the areas on the plate where the ground was left intact will remain untouched by the acid.

BEVELING THE PLATE

Metal plates have sharp edges that need to be smoothed and beveled with a file or they'll damage your printing blankets and cut the printing paper. It's a good idea to bevel the edges before you begin to work on the plate, and then to bevel them again before you print, first with a rough file, then a fine file, and finally with sandpaper wrapped around the file.

Materials and Equipment
metal plate
flat bastard file or rasp
smooth file
fine-textured sandpaper
fine crocus cloth

Process. Push the flat bastard (rough) file at an acute angle along all four top edges of the plate (see Figure 1). Try to avoid scratching the back surface of the plate if it's coated with an acid-resistant material since scratches will remove the acid-resistant backing. If this occurs, your plate will bite from the back as well as from the front surface when it's placed in the acid and you may inadvertently bite through the plate. When you're finished beveling, round off the four sharp corners (see Figure 2) with the same file. Now you're ready to begin work on your plate.

After your plate has been in the acid several times, its original bevel will become somewhat ragged. Before you print, bevel the edges and corners of the plate again, first with a rough file and then with a fine file. Next, wrap a piece of fine-textured sandpaper around the file (see Figure 3) and bevel the edges and corners once more. If you want an even smoother edge, wrap a piece of fine crocus cloth around the file and bevel the edges and corners. Remember, a beautiful bevel makes wiping the plate easier and puts a fine finishing touch on every print.

CLEANING THE PLATE

No ground will adhere properly to a plate that has any trace of grease on its surface. Always clean your plate thoroughly to remove this grease before applying hard ground or any other ground.

Materials and Equipment
metal plate
paper towels
powdered cleanser
synthetic sponge

Process. To remove the film of grease on the plate, scrub the entire surface carefully with powdered cleanser and a damp sponge, moving the sponge in a circular motion. Then rinse the plate well with warm or cold running water—make sure that all the cleanser washes off.

Figure 1. To bevel the edges of the plate, slide the file along each edge of the plate in the manner illustrated until the edge is beveled as in (A). The illustration (B) is incorrect.

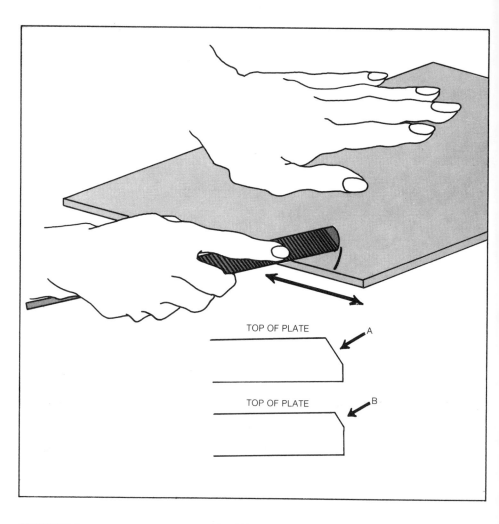

TOP OF PLATE

A

TOP OF PLATE

B

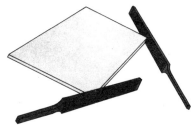

Figure 2 (above). Hold the file parallel to the edge of the plate, and push it around the corners to remove the sharp edges.

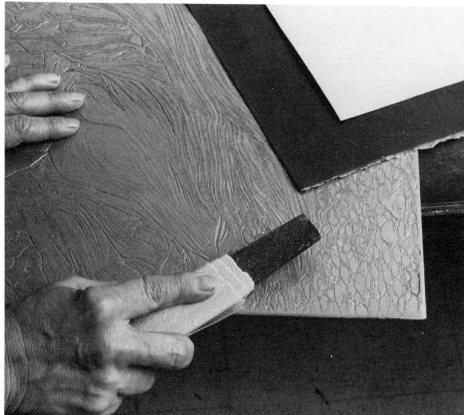

Figure 3. Wrap a piece of fine-textured sandpaper around the file and rub the edge of the plate for a smoother bevel.

Next, look closely at the plate to see if the water is drawing away from the edges or beading on the surface. If either of these are happening, there's still grease on the plate; you'll have to scrub the plate once again with cleanser. You'll know that the plate is clean when a continuous film of water remains on the surface.

At this point, blot or rub the plate with a paper towel until the surface is completely dry. Don't dry the plate with any material that contains lint, and be careful not to touch the surface of the plate with your fingertips (they're full of grease).

APPLYING A HARD GROUND

The ground is applied to coat the plate with an acid-resistant material.

Materials and Equipment
metal plate
2″ flat bristle brush stored in a can of varnolene and used only for hard ground
hard ground
hot plate
spatula
work gloves

Process. Use a brush that has been standing in a can of varnolene so its bristles are pliable. Wipe off the excess varnolene on the inner edge of the can and dip the brush into the jar of ground—touch the brush to the ground so you pick up just a little on the ends of the bristles. Hard ground is semi-liquid and has the consistency of heavy cream. The varnolene on the brush will make the ground more liquid so it can be spread with the right consistency onto the plate.

Gently stroke the loaded brush across the plate without pressing down (see Figure 4)—the weight of the brush itself should exert sufficient pressure. Brush with long strokes going the length of the plate from one end to the other. The ground should be a semi-transparent, dark golden brown and not too liquid. If your hard ground is opaque, you have too much ground and not enough varnolene on your brush; if the hard ground is too transparent, then you have too much varnolene and not enough ground.

When you have completely covered the plate with hard ground, the next step is to

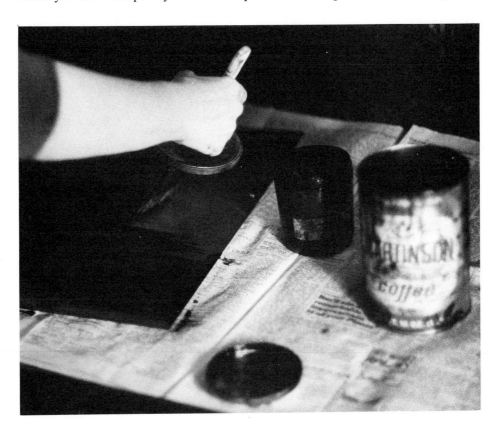

Figure 4. Holding the brush loaded with hard ground, pull it lightly across the plate. A coffee can ⅓ full of varnolene and the jar of ground stand to the right of the plate on newspaper.

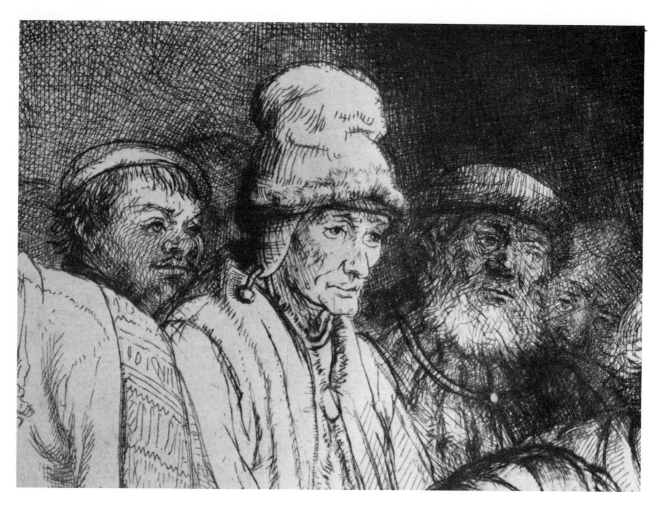

Christ with the sick around Him, receiving little children *("The Hundred Guilder Print") by Rembrandt (1606-1669). Detail, hard ground. Courtesy Metropolitan Museum of Art, New York City, The H.O. Havemeyer Collection.*

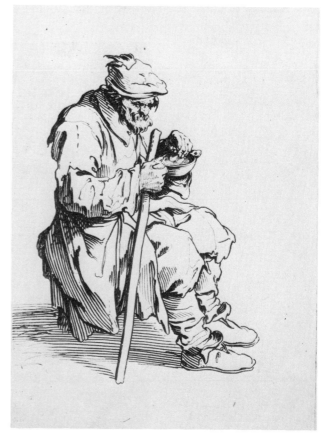

A Beggar *by Jacques Callot (1592/3-1635). Hard ground. Courtesy Metropolitan Museum of Art, New York City, Harris Brisbane Dick Fund.*

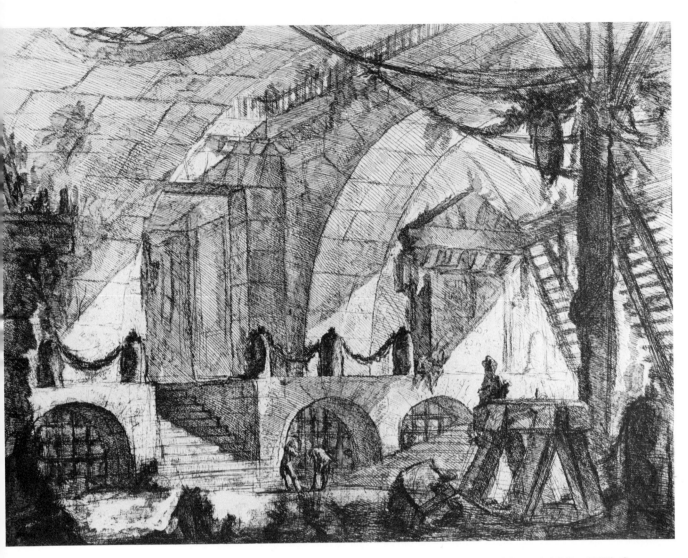

The Prisons *by Giovanni Battista Piranesi (1720-1778). Hard Ground, 16¼″ x 21⅞″. Courtesy Metropolitan Museum of Art, New York City, Harris Brisbane Dick Fund.*

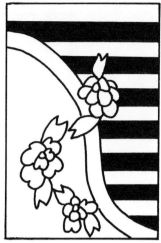

A　DRAWING

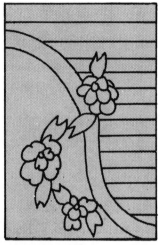

B　PLATE

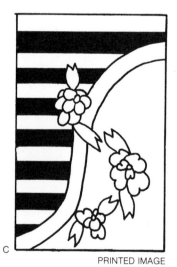

C　PRINTED IMAGE

Figure 5. The design of the drawing (A) and on the plate (B) face in the same direction. The design in the print (C) is a mirror image of the plate and the drawing.

heat the plate to evaporate the solvent—varnolene—from the moist ground. To do this, turn on the hot plate and set it at a medium temperature between 180° and 210°F.—a lower temperature than that at which water boils. When the hot plate is ready, lift the plate carefully by slipping your hands underneath it. Take the plate to the hot plate and slide it on. As the plate heats, the varnolene will begin to evaporate and you'll see vapors which look like smoke rising from the plate's surface.

When the plate stops smoking, get ready to remove it from the hot plate. Put on your gloves, lift one end of the plate up with a spatula, and push the plate halfway off the hot plate. Now take the whole plate off the heat by placing your gloved hands underneath and then lifting.

Put the plate on the bed of the press. As the plate cools, the ground will turn dull, or matte. Don't touch the surface of the plate while it's warm or you'll destroy the ground. A hard ground becomes hard only after it has cooled—then it will be sturdy enough to withstand normal hand pressure when you draw on the plate.

TRANSFERRING A DRAWING

If you don't want to draw directly on the plate, you can transfer a drawing to the plate from a piece of paper. If you follow the directions below, the image on the plate's surface and the image on the drawing will face in the same direction. A print taken from this plate will be the *mirror image* of the plate (and the drawing), i.e., the printed image will face in the opposite direction from the image on the plate (see Figure 5).

Materials and Equipment
drawing on paper
plate with hard ground
light-colored chalk
masking tape
ballpoint pen or pencil

Process. Using the flat side of the light-colored chalk, rub the chalk all over the back of the drawing. Then place the drawing chalk-side down on the plate. Use masking tape or another pressure-sensitive tape to hold the drawing in place if necessary.

Using moderate pressure, trace the lines of your drawing with a ballpoint pen or pencil. If you use a pencil, be sure that the point isn't too sharp or it will cut through the paper. Remember, too, that if you press too hard with either the pen or pencil, the ground will disintegrate. You aren't trying to cut into the ground—you just want to draw on top of it.

When you have drawn over all the lines, lift the paper off the plate. The image on the original drawing will appear in chalk lines on the plate. Both images will face in the same direction. Now begin to draw directly onto the plate with an etching or drypoint needle (see below), going over the chalk lines to expose the plate underneath.

TRANSFERRING A REVERSED DRAWING

To make an image on a plate face in the opposite direction from the original image on paper, you must transfer a reversed drawing onto the plate's surface. This is how you can make the final print identical with the paper drawing—both images will face in the same direction (see Figure 6).

Materials and Equipment
drawing on paper
plate with hard ground
pastel pencil in a light color
press set up for printing

Process. First, draw over the lines on the front of your original drawing with a light-colored pastel pencil.

Then place the plate on the bed of the press with the surface covered with ground facing up. Position the drawing face down on the plate so the chalk lines drawn over the original lines of the drawing touch the ground on the plate. Pull the blankets down over the plate and the drawing and check the pressure. *Be sure not to move the drawing.* Pull the plate and drawing through the press.

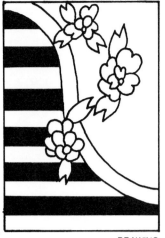

DRAWING

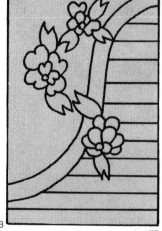

PLATE

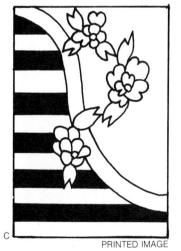

PRINTED IMAGE

Figure 6. The design of the drawing (A) is a mirror image of the design on the plate (B). The design on the print (C) is identical to that of the drawing.

Lift up the printing blankets and the edge of the paper. Remove the paper from the plate. The chalk lines of the drawing should now be transferred to the plate. The drawing on the plate will necessarily face in the opposite direction from the original drawing on the paper. The image on the print, however, will face in the same direction as the original drawing.

Now you'll have to draw directly onto the plate with an etching or drypoint needle (see below) to go over the chalk lines to expose the plate underneath.

DRAWING ON HARD GROUND

As you draw on the plate with an etching needle or another sharp instrument, the point removes the ground and exposes the plate underneath the lines or areas drawn. The exposed lines and areas appear paler than the ground, since copper, zinc, or steel plates are lighter in color than the ground. When the plate is printed after it has been etched, the lines drawn on hard ground have the quality of pen lines.

Materials and Equipment
plate with hard ground
etching needle or drypoint needle
pens—penholders and nibs of varying sizes
hard pencil
scraper
stylus, paper clip, comb (anything that will remove the ground without scratching the plate)

Process. Decide the width of the line you want and choose the proper tool. The etching and drypoint needles make fine lines; pencils produce medium-thick lines; a comb creates thick parallel lines; and a scraper makes very broad lines. As you draw with any of these tools, you'll remove the ground on the plate and expose the plate to the biting action of the acid. When you draw, be careful not to scratch the metal—you may want to stop out some of the lines to prevent them from biting, but once the plate is scratched, that scratch will print unless you scrape it out (see below).

After you've finished your drawing on the ground, you should be able to see the metal of the plate clearly where you have drawn lines. Check carefully to make sure that the lines are free of ground. If they aren't, use your hand to gently brush away pieces of the ground that were dislodged but not removed when you drew. However, don't touch the exposed areas of the plate with your fingers as you may leave grease on the plate. If the lines still aren't completely clear of ground, go over them again with the needle.

STOPPING OUT HARD GROUND

After you finish drawing, there may be areas that you don't like that you want to draw over again. In order to do this, you must stop out the unwanted areas with rosin stopout so the lines won't be bitten by the acid. Think of rosin stopout as a kind of eraser—the only difference between rosin stopout and the eraser is that you can't draw over the area coated with rosin stopout, while you can draw over an erased area.

Since you can't draw effectively through rosin stopout, you must use it in the following manner: after stopping out the unwanted lines, place the plate in the acid in order to bite the exposed lines. After the plate has been bitten and rinsed in cold water, remove the ground and stopout, brush on more ground, and draw again the areas you stopped out originally.

Materials and Equipment
plate with hard ground that has been drawn on
rosin stopout
pointed sable brush
½″ flat brush of any soft hair

Process. Identify the lines on the plate that you would like to remove whether they're part of the drawing or accidental scratches. Look also for areas where the ground looks thin or uneven where there is no drawing. Areas of thin ground are lighter in color than the rest of the plate—the unevenness in the thickness of the ground is usually caused by dirt in the ground which creates small lumps or bubbles.

After you have decided which lines and areas to coat, take a brush and paint on the stopout. Use the pointed sable brush to stop out details and a ½″ flat brush to stop out larger areas and the four edges of the plate.

All areas that are stopped out must be fully covered, with no ground or plate showing through. (The areas covered with stopout will be green, the color of rosin stopout, whether the plate is silver, copper, or steel gray.) Rosin stopout remains tacky for a long time, but you can place the plate into the acid right away.

BITING HARD GROUND

See Chapter 12 for detailed instructions on biting plates with acid.

REMOVING HARD GROUND

Before you can print your bitten plate, you must remove the ground and the stopout.

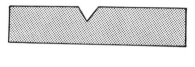
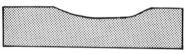
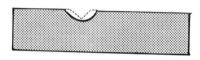

Materials and Equipment
plate with hard ground and stopout
pad of newspaper
table for removing grounds
varnolene or turpentine
denatured alcohol
scrub brush with natural bristles
paper towels or lint-free cloths

Process. After you take your plate out of the acid and rinse it off with water, dry it with paper towels. Then place your plate, ground up, on a pad of newspaper which will absorb the solvents you'll use to remove the ground from the plate.

Pour some varnolene or turpentine on the plate. If you have used rosin stopout as well as hard ground, pour alcohol on the plate at the same time. Scrub the plate gently in a circular motion with a scrub brush. The action of the brush speeds the action of the solvents that dissolve the ground and stopout. After the ground and stopout have been softened by the solvents and the brush, remove them by wiping the plate with paper towels or lint-free cloths. When the paper towels or lint-free cloths get dirty, change them for clean ones. When the front of your plate is clean, i.e., when there's no trace of ground or stopout on the metal, turn it over and clean the back with a paper towel or a rag and a few drops of varnolene. When the entire plate is clean it's ready to be printed (see Chapter 13).

Figure 7. From top to bottom: plate with line to be scraped; the plate scraped correctly; the plate scraped incorrectly—this depression will hold ink.

SCRAPING OUT A LINE

After you bite your plate and remove the hard ground, there may be some lines you wish to remove. You can do this by scraping them out and making smooth depressions in the surface of the plate that won't hold any ink (see Figure 7).

Materials and Equipment
etched plate with no ground
linseed, plate, or machine oil
scraper

Process. Hold the scraper on its taped surface so your fingers don't interfere with the scraping (see Figure 8). Place one flat side of the scraper on the plate, tilt the scraper up a little so that one edge rests on the plate, and pull the tool towards you. Scrape a small amount of metal with each pull—if you exert too much downward pressure, the metal will resist the scraper unevenly. Although you'll remove great chunks of metal, you'll also be putting a texture into the plate that will be difficult to remove.

Use a drop of oil to make scraping easier, and be sure to scrape in all directions along and across the line or lines, drawing the scraper towards you. When you've finished, you shouldn't be able to see the line. There will, however, be a tone on the plate—take it off by polishing with a burnisher and some oil.

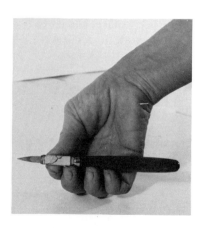

Figure 8. How to hold a scraper.

POLISHING A PLATE AFTER SCRAPING

The scraper leaves a tone on the plate that is visible when the plate is printed. The scraped area must be polished to remove this tone.

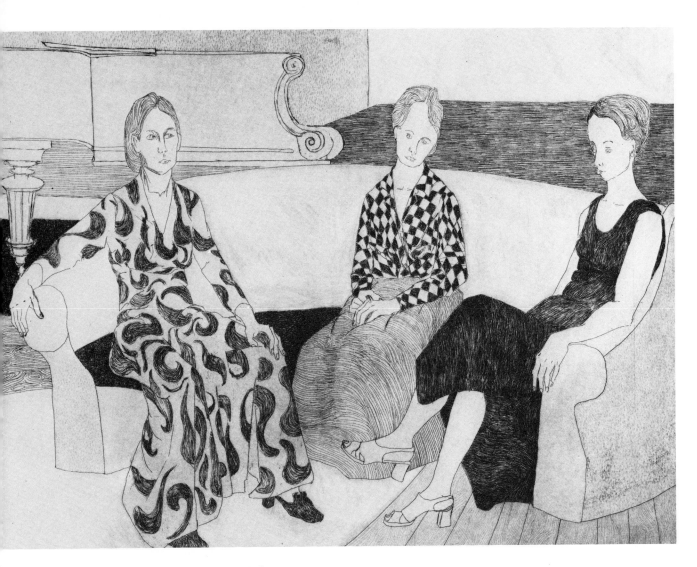

Women *by Olga Poloukhine. Hard ground, 18″ x 24″.*

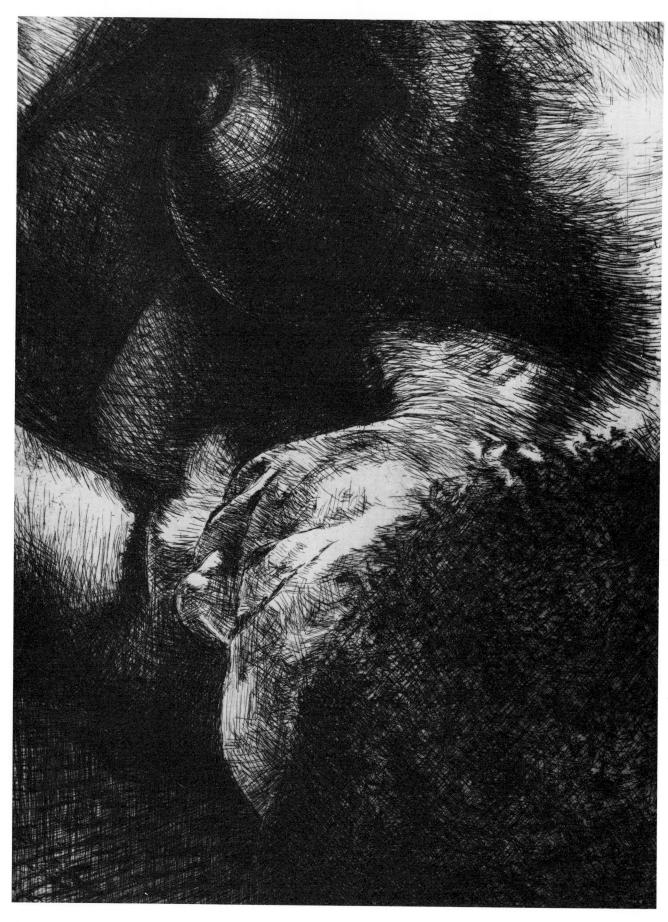

Sleep 2 *by Shirley Gorelick. Hard ground, 24″ x 18″.*

Materials and Equipment
metal plate that has been scraped
crocus cloth
0000 jeweler's steel wool
3-in-1 oil
burnisher

Process. First polish the scraped area with crocus cloth, moving the cloth back and forth. Turn the plate and continue to polish. The scraped area should have very fine striations in the directions in which it's polished.

Then polish the plate in a small circular motion with 0000 jeweler's wool. Add drops of 3-in-1 oil to cut down on friction. The jeweler's wool should remove the striations created with the crocus cloth.

Don't use jeweler's wool over etched or engraved lines that weren't scraped. The steel wool would polish inside the lines, making them too smooth to retain ink. If the area to be polished is small, wrap the jeweler's wool around a stick or a pencil for greater control.

When you're finished with the jeweler's wool, put a drop of 3-in-1 oil on the plate. Holding the burnisher as if it were a pencil (see Chapter 9, Figure 3), press down gently in the area to be polished. Excess pressure on the burnisher is undesirable, since it could create another texture. Move the burnisher back and forth in a very small space until that space gets quite shiny. Continue this procedure until the entire scraped area is polished. This highly polished area won't hold ink, even though the plate is not perfectly flat.

REGROUNDING A PLATE

After you plate has been bitten, cleaned, and printed, you may want to put another hard ground on your plate. You can apply hard ground to your plate as many times as necessary to achieve the image desired. If the image has been etched many times, it takes on a luster when printed.

Materials and Equipment
metal plate
2″ flat bristle brush stored in a can of varnolene and used only for hard ground
hard ground
heat lamp
newspaper
kitchen chair with a straight wooden back

Process. Follow the same directions given earlier in this chapter for brushing hard ground onto your plate. Please note, though, that you must heat the ground in a different manner—when you put a hard ground on a plate that has already been bitten, you can't heat it on a hot plate. Heat from underneath causes the ground on the plate's surface to break away from the etched lines, exposing the plate to the acid, and causing foul biting. To prevent this, you must either dry the plate by air or heat it from above with a heat lamp or with the heat of the sun.

To air-dry a plate after the ground has been applied, lift the plate carefully without touching the top surface and place it on a flat surface such as a table or a shelf where it won't be disturbed for 5 to 24 hours. The surface must be level so that the ground doesn't drain off to the lower side, leaving the higher side too thinly coated. You can tell that the surface is level enough if the ground doesn't move, and you can tell that the ground is too thin if it appears lighter than a golden brown.

The amount of time it will take the ground to dry depends on the moisture in and the temperature of the air. On a very warm dry day, the plate could be dry in 3 or 4 hours, while on a humid or rainy cold day the ground could take a full 24 hours to dry.

If you want to heat the hard ground on a plate that has been bitten, the heat must come from above. One way to do this is to use a heat lamp with a clamp at one end and an adjustable bulb at the other. Place the clamp on the back of a kitchen chair and put the plate on the seat of the chair (see Figure 9). It's a good idea to put a piece of newspaper on the chair under the plate to protect the chair and absorb any excess ground that might have stuck to the bottom of the plate.

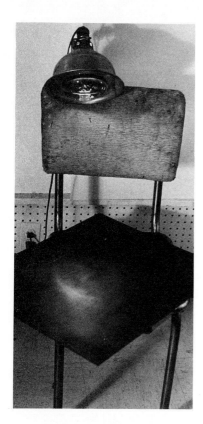

Figure 9. A heat lamp clamped to the back of the kitchen chair shines on the plate. The heat from the lamp allows the hard ground to dry without pulling it away from the lines.

The lamp should be at least 18″ from the plate. If the ground begins to look very pale near the etched lines, then the ground is pulling away from them—this means that the heat source is too close to the plate.

Another way to heat hard ground in the hot summer when the sun is shining is to place the plate on a flat surface in direct sunlight near an open window or outdoors. If it's very hot and sunny, the ground should dry in less than an hour.

Please note that a plate which was heated by a sun lamp or by the sun will be quite warm. Thus, when the ground looks matte, you must place the plate on the bed of the press to cool for a few minutes before beginning to work on the surface. If the plate has been air-dried, it will be cool and ready to work on as soon as its dry.

CLEANUP

You must always clean and put away materials, tools, and grounds used during printmaking to preserve them for future use. Remember that some materials and all solvents used in the studio are very flammable—take care to avoid spontaneous fires.

1. Put plates coated with hard ground that you're still working on into plastic bags and place them on a shelf where no one can inadvertently damage the ground. Rub plates with no ground clean with a cloth dampened with kerosene and put them into plastic bags. Tape the edges of the bags shut and put them away.

Caution: Don't leave plates uncovered or covered with newspaper. The moisture in the air and the acid in the newspapers will corrode a plate beyond recognition in a short time.

2. Dip brushes that were used with rosin stopout in alcohol to remove the stopout, and dry them with a paper towel. Then wash them with mild soap in cold water. Brushes used with the stopout and left unwashed become unusable since the stopout hardens and is difficult to remove.

3. Leave brushes used with the hard ground standing in a coffee can ⅓ full of varnolene. Keep the cover of the can closed so the brushes stay moist and ready to be used.

4. Cover the grounds in their wide-mouthed glass jars with screw covers (actually, these covers should be replaced immediately after each use). If you leave a ground uncovered, it will collect dust and particles. Also, the varnolene mixed into the ground to keep it semi-liquid will evaporate, leaving the ground hard and difficult to use.

5. Cover all solvent containers to contain the fumes and to prevent evaporation.

6. Turn off the hot plate. When it cools, remove any excess ground that might be on its surface with a cloth sprinkled with varnolene.

7. Throw out all newspaper, rags, and paper towels that contain oil, solvents, or grounds. *Don't leave flammable materials in the studio overnight unless you store them in tightly covered metal containers.* Don't use plastic bags or non-metal containers indoors to hold dirty materials. You may use plastic bags outdoors if a metal container isn't available.

WHAT WENT WRONG AND WHY

Problem	Cause	Solution
When I apply the hard ground, it doesn't go on smoothly—it seems to curdle.	Either you have grease on your plate—grease prevents the ground from going on smoothly—or you put the ground on a warm plate, and a warm plate will cause the ground to pull away, or curdle.	Remove the ground with turpentine or varnolene, and scrub the plate with cleanser and a sponge. Wash the plate with *cold* water—if you wash the plate in warm water, you must place it on the bed of the press to cool before you apply the ground.
After I applied the ground, heated the plate, and put it on the bed of the press to cool, the ground didn't become hard. It remained sticky.	You didn't heat the plate long enough to drive out the varnolene.	Heat the plate again, and put it back on the bed of the press to cool.

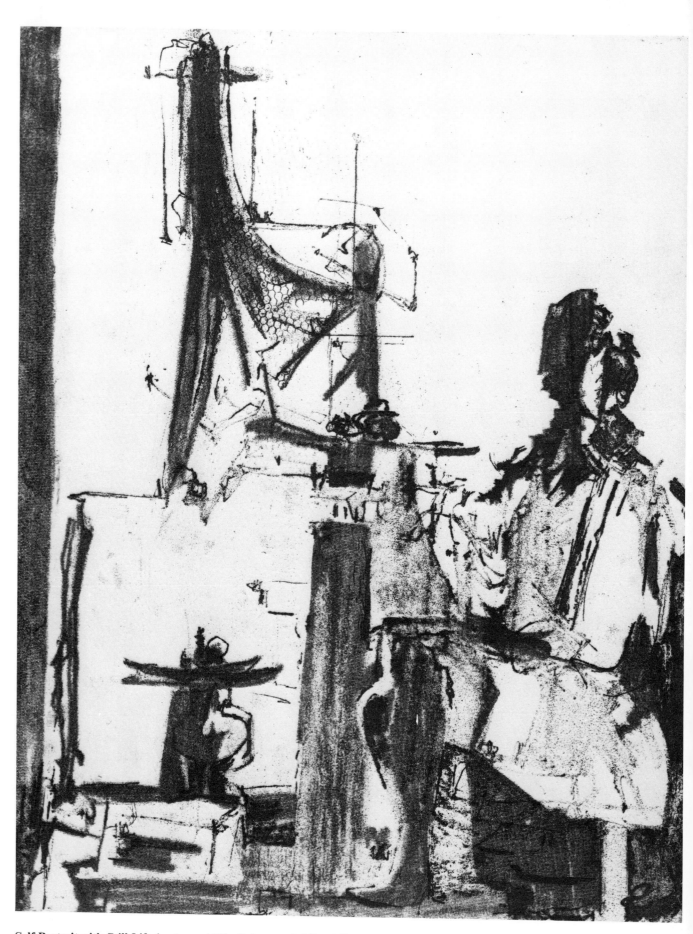

Self-Portrait with Still Life *by Agnes Mills. Soft ground, 14″ x 11″.*

EIGHT

Soft Ground

Whenever you want to coat your plate with a soft, acid-resistant material, you can brush soft ground onto the plate's surface. When you draw through a soft ground, your finished print may sometimes have the look of a soft pencil drawing on charcoal paper (see *Where did you go?—Out* by Rita Schwartz, page 83).

You can also use soft ground to apply texture to the plate. As this ground remains soft after it cools on the plate, the texture of any shape pressed to the plate's surface such as a leaf or a bit of lace will make an impression in the ground (see *Yellow Pearl* by Pearl Abrams, page 83). When you lift off the leaf or lace, some soft ground will cling to it, exposing the metal surface in the shape and with the texture of the leaf or lace. Then when you put the plate in acid, the acid will bite in the exposed areas. Please note that you can use any texture that is thin enough to be rolled through the press without damaging either the press or the plate.

APPLYING SOFT GROUND

Before you begin to brush on soft ground, make sure you plate has beveled edges (see Chapter 7). Also, scrub the plate well with a sponge and a cleanser such as Ajax so you'll get a well-bitten image after you apply the soft ground.

Materials and Equipment
metal plate with beveled edges
2½″ bristle brush (stored in a can of varnolene and use only for soft ground)
soft ground
hot plate
cloth garden gloves
spatula

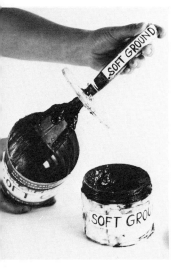

Figure 1. Labeled soft ground brush in the coffee container where it's kept, and the labeled jar of soft ground.

Process. To begin, take the brush from the can of varnolene in which it has been stored, and wipe off the excess varnolene on the inner edge of the can. Dip the brush into the jar of ground (see Figure 1). Pick up a little ground on the brush and rub the brush with a circular motion on the central surface of the plate to mix the ground and the varnolene. Take more ground with the brush and brush gently across the plate in both directions. Don't press down on the brush. The ground should be transparent, light gold-brown in color and not too liquid—the color and consistency of honey.

When the soft ground covers the plate's surface evenly and completely, you must heat the plate. Heating the plate drives the solvent out of the moist ground, and the subsequent cooling allows the ground to dry. To do this, place the grounded plate on a hot plate set at about 150° F. This temperature will allow the varnolene to vaporize slowly, leaving a smooth, even ground on the plate. Too much heat would cause the varnolene to vaporize too quickly—the melted ground would move and slide around, and the result would be an uneven density of ground across the plate.

When the varnolene vaporizes, it appears as smoke. You know the soft ground has been heated enough when the plate stops smoking. At this point, put on your gloves and remove the plate from the hot plate with a spatula (see Chapter 7, page 72, for instructions). *Without touching its surface*, place the grounded plate on the press bed and take off your gloves.

As the plate cools on the bed of the press, the soft ground will turn dull, or matte. To see if the ground is dry, *don't touch the surface of a soft ground*—you'll remove the ground and expose the plate. Instead, feel the bottom of the plate: the ground is dry when the bottom of the plate is cold.

DRAWING ON SOFT GROUND

When drawing on soft ground, you must place a piece of tracing paper between the drawing and the plate to pick up the ground—the soft ground will adhere to this paper when pressure is applied with a pencil.

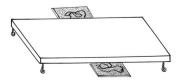

Materials and Equipment
plate with cold soft ground
drawing the same size as the plate
two sheets tracing paper at least 1″ larger on all sides than the plate (charcoal paper or a piece of silk may be substituted for one of the sheets of tracing paper)
pencil or ballpoint pen
piece of cardboard larger than the plate
masking tape, or another pressure-sensitive tape
bridge (see Figure 2)

Process. Take the drawing and trace it onto one sheet of the tracing paper. If you prefer, draw directly onto a sheet of tracing paper but remember to leave the 1″ margin on all sides.

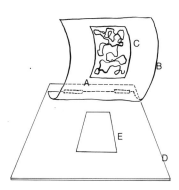

Figure 2. Bridge used to help you avoid touching a soft ground. Lean on the bridge—a wooden board with screw eyes in each corner—when you draw on the plate.

Now, put the plate with the soft ground on a large piece of cardboard, and trace the outline of the plate onto the cardboard. Leave the plate there, and place the tracing paper with the drawing carefully over the plate and cardboard. As you position the tracing paper so the edges of the drawing correspond to the edges of the plate, don't lean on the paper or you'll smudge—and ruin—the soft ground. When the drawing is in place, tape the upper edge of the tracing paper to the cardboard (see Figure 3).

Lift up the end of the drawing that isn't taped to the board and place another piece of clean tracing paper, charcoal paper, or silk carefully over the plate (see Figure 4).

Figure 3. Tape (A)) the tracing paper (B) with the drawing (C) to the cardboard (D) on which the outline of the plate (E) has been drawn.

Lower the tracing paper with the drawing to the plate, and place the bridge on top. As you draw, the pencil will lift the ground from the plate and deposit the ground to the second piece of tracing or charcoal paper or silk. This extra piece of paper (or silk) can be moved around without disturbing the drawing on top. Move it often so that you never work over an area that has already been drawn on or you'll replace ground which has already been lifted off back onto the plate.

IMPRESSING TEXTURES INTO SOFT GROUND

You can impress the textures of many kinds of materials and objects onto a plate with soft ground because of the resiliency of the soft ground. Remember, though, that textures are very seductive: use them with discretion and they can be a great tool; use them indiscriminately and they can be extremely tiresome.

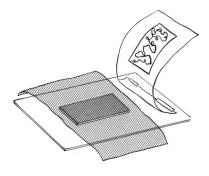

Figure 4. Place a piece of tracing paper, charcoal paper, or silk between the drawing and the plate. The texture of the paper or silk—whichever one you use— will come through on the soft ground.

Materials and Equipment
plate with cold soft ground
press set up for printing
fabrics—silk, lace, brocade, for example
tinfoil
leaves and feathers
very fine pieces of metal
paper cutouts
wax paper
blotter
drypont needle

Process. To begin, put the plate with the cold soft ground in the center of the bed of the press. Gather the various materials listed above and cut out pieces of the thin metal, fabrics, and other items. Place them gently on the plate as if you were making a collage. You can move things around as long as you don't apply any pressure.

When you're satisfied with the placement of the textures, cover them with a piece or pieces of wax paper cut larger than the plate. Then—this is optional—lay a blotter, also larger than the plate, over the wax paper (see Figure 5).

Adjust the pressure on the press to accommodate the thickness of the blotter and the textures in addition to the plate. Lay the blankets down over the plate and pull the plate covered with textures, wax paper, and a blotter through the press. Then pull up

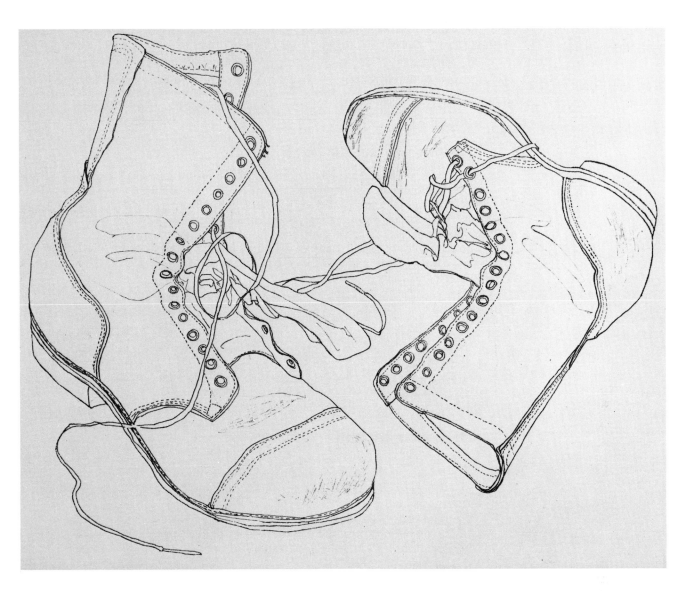

Where did you go?—Out
by Rita Schwartz.
Soft ground, 19¼″ x 23″.

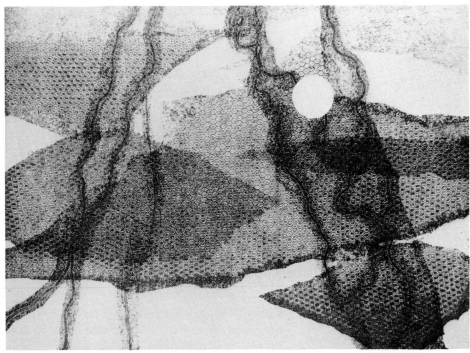

Yellow Pearl *by Pearl Abrams.*
Soft ground, 9″ x 12″.

the blankets and lift off the blotter and the wax paper. Very carefully remove the textures used to make the collage. If they stick to the plate, use a drypoint needle to pry the edges loose.

Please note that if you wish to impress on the plate the texture of an object that is too thick to run through the press, you can use hand pressure. Place the object on the plate with cold soft ground and press down firmly with your hand—just don't move the object sideways.

STOPPING OUT SOFT GROUND

Anything—hands, fingers, paper—that applies pressure to a soft ground will lift the ground off the plate and expose metal. Even the action of the press tends to make the whole soft ground porous. Before you bite the plate with soft ground, therefore, you must stop out the areas that are to appear white on the print, i.e., that aren't to be bitten. If you put the plate into the acid without stopping out some areas, the print would be all gray. *Caution:* the white shapes made by using stopout on a soft ground collage are very prominent. Apply the stopout carefully, and give a lot of thought to the shape you're painting with the brush.

Materials and Equipment
plate with textures impressed into soft ground or plate with soft ground that has been
 drawn on
rosin stopout
2 brushes, one coming to a point and one flat

Process. Brush stopout on the areas of the plate where the drawing or the textural design is not satisfactory. Use the flat brush to stop out large areas and the pointed brush to stop out details. When you're finished, stop out the edges of your plate.

BITING SOFT GROUND

Acid will bite a plate with soft ground where the drawing or texture has removed the ground. The same strength acid will bite a plate with soft ground more slowly than a plate with hard ground. For this reason, it's a good idea to use a stronger acid with a soft ground.

You can gauge how dark a printed soft ground plate will be by noting the number of times the bubbles form fully on the surface. If you want a light gray in some areas when you print with black ink, allow the plate to bubble fully once or twice. To remove the bubbles each time they form, don't feather them off—tilt the tray or the plate itself to let the acid run off and then gently lower the tray (see Chapter 12, Figure 7).

After the bubbles form fully once or twice, you may want to bite certain areas deeper to obtain a darker gray while leaving other areas light. If so, remove the plate from the acid and rinse it in cold water in preparation for applying rosin stopout. Before you apply the stopout, dry the plate thoroughly by placing a paper towel over the plate and letting it absorb the water. *Don't apply any pressure.* When the plate is completely dry, brush the stopout over the areas that are to be light gray. When the stopout is tacky, replace the plate in the acid. For further information on biting a soft ground, see Chapter 12.

REMOVING SOFT GROUND

After you finish biting the plate and before you print, you must remove the soft ground and the stopout. Varnolene or turpentine removes the soft ground, and alcohol takes off the stopout.

Materials and Equipment
plate with soft ground that has been bitten in acid
varnolene or turpentine
alcohol
newspaper
wooden scrub brush with natural bristles
paper towels or rags

Process. Place your plate on a pad of newspaper on a table. Pour on alcohol and varnolene or turpentine, and scrub the plate with a brush. Remove all of the ground, stopout, and solvents with rags or paper towels.

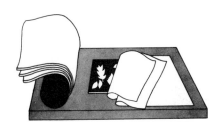

Figure 5. Plate with soft ground covered with textures lying on the press bed. Note the piece of wax paper and the blotter placed over the plate to protect the blankets which are tucked under and lying on top of the press roller on the left.

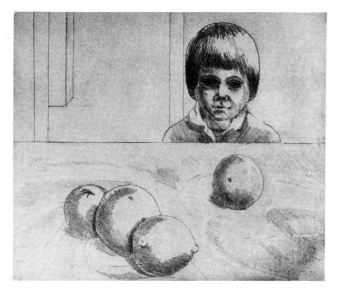

Stage 1.

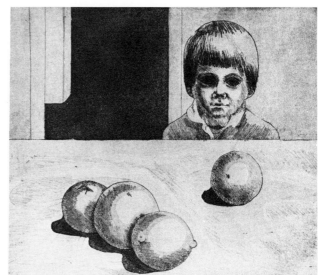

Stage 2.

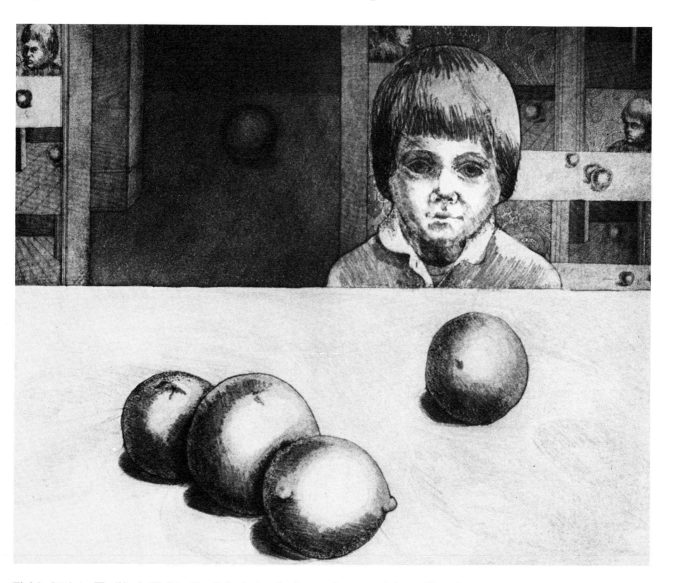

Finished Print.   The Magic Wall *by Nat Cole. Series of soft grounds on a steel plate, 18″ x 22″.*

Be sure that both sides of your plate are dry and completely free of ground. (Ground or dirt left on the back surface of the plate can show up as a raised area on the front of the plate from the pressure exerted during printing.) At this point you should pull a proof (see Chapter 13) even if you intend to put another ground on the plate, or you'll never know exactly how the acid has affected the plate.

REGROUNDING A PLATE

After printing, you may decide to put another soft ground on your plate. Apply the soft ground the same way you did it the first time, heat the plate on the hot plate, and let it cool. (The Vaseline or grease in the soft ground will cause the ground to adhere to the entire surface of the plate. Therefore, it isn't necessary to heat the plate from above as it would be if you were regrounding the plate with hard ground.) To add to a previous drawing, put the plate on cardboard again, attach the drawing, and put a clean sheet of tracing paper between the plate and the drawing before starting. With the soft ground collage plate, just add more textures in order to cause gradations in tone.

CLEANUP

1. Cover the ground—dust causes pinholes when you brush the ground on your plate.

2. Clean brushes used with rosin stopout in alcohol, then wash them with soap and water. Brushes used with the soft ground should remain upright in a can that is ⅓ full of varnolene (see Chapter 1, Figure 1).

3. Don't keep newspaper, rags, and paper towels coated with ground or soaked with solvents in the workshop overnight—they're a fire hazard.

4. Pour acid back into its container or cover it in the tray.

5. Make sure the hot plate has been turned off. When it's cold, clean it with varnolene to remove any excess ground.

6. If your plate is still covered with soft ground, put it in a safe, out-of-the-way place where it won't be touched.

WHAT WENT WRONG AND WHY

Problem	Cause	Solution
The print of the drawing on the soft ground is spotty.	1. You applied the ground too thickly.	1. Apply a thinner ground.
	2. You didn't exert enough pressure when you drew the design.	2. Apply more pressure when drawing. Lift up the unattached tracing paper and look underneath to see how much ground you're removing.
	3. When the piece of tracing paper or silk next to the plate picked up ground, you drew over the original lines and transferred the ground back onto the plate.	3. Move the second piece of tracing paper around under the drawing; wherever you're drawing, the tracing paper underneath should be clean and free of ground.
The acid bit certain areas of the plate that weren't drawn and weren't supposed to be bitten.	The pressure of your hand caused the ground to lift off the plate, exposing enough metal to allow the acid to bite in those areas. (You should have stopped out those areas before biting.)	Scrape and burnish those areas of the plate.
I used a piece of silk as texture, but when the plate was bitten no texture printed.	Using a fine silk on a soft ground results in a tone rather than a texture.	Don't use silk for texture. Note that the tone resulting from the use of silk on soft ground is often used instead of an aquatint: the tone is sturdy and will last through a great many printings.
Although I applied texture to the whole plate, the acid bit one side much more than the other side.	1. If the texture was used previously and not cleaned, it would pick up the ground unevenly.	1. Use a clean texture. You can reuse a texture if you wash it first with varnolene and then with soap and water.
	2. The pressure of the press wasn't even when the texture on the soft ground was run through the press. Therefore, the whole piece of texture didn't pick up the same amount of ground.	2. Correct the pressure of the press—make sure that both sides of the roller are the same height above the bed of the press.
There are no dark areas on the collage plate even though different areas of the plate were bitten for varying amounts of time.	If fine textures are used, even the darkest areas will appear gray.	Put another ground on the plate and apply a rougher texture in the areas where you want black. Bite the plate again and you'll get a deep velvety black in those areas when you print.
When I bite the plate a second time with textures, I get a spotty gray instead of a dark area.	If you use the same or similar textures in two bitings, you create a *crevé*, or a hole—you've actually bitten down the surface of your first bite instead of making deeper crevices.	Scrape the spotty gray area, apply another soft ground to the plate, and put on another texture.

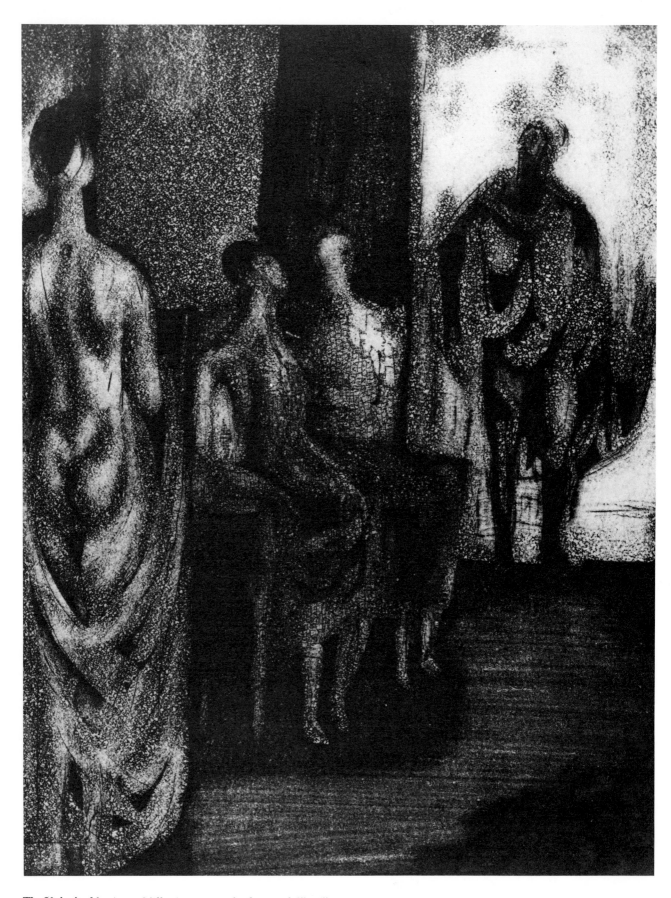

The Uninvited *by Agnes Mills. Aquatint and soft ground, 8″ x 6″.*

NINE

Aquatint

As its name suggests, an aquatint print has the look of a wash or a watercolor (see *The Uninvited* by Agnes Mills on page 88), although rosin—not water—creates the tone. The size of the grains of rosin and the depth of the acid bite determine the quality of the tone. Remember, the larger the chunks of rosin used, the coarser the acquatint and the grainier the tone; the smaller and more powdery the rosin, the finer the acquatint and the finer the tone.

You'll apply the rosin to the plate with a rosin bag. Then, when you heat the plate, the rosin will melt and adhere to the plate's surface in little dots close to each other. When you place the plate in acid the rosin grains act as a stopout and the acid bites the metal around them.

When you print your plate, the bitten areas create the tone. The smooth points between the grooves give the printed aquatint its characteristic sparkle and life. However, when you bite an aquatint deeply, the tone appears as a solid, velvety color and the smooth points aren't discernable (see *Child in a Wicker Chair* by Nat Cole, page 178).

MAKING A ROSIN BAG

To apply rosin to a plate, you must first make a container for the rosin such as a rosin bag. Use silk or nylon to make a rosin bag for a fine aquatint, tarlatan to make a coarse aquatint (tarlatan allows large pieces of rosin through its holes).

Materials and Equipment
¼ cup chunk rosin
plastic or paper bag
hammer
three 9″ squares of tarlatan, finely woven silk or nylon
rubber band
masking tape or another pressure-sensitive tape
box or jar to hold the rosin bag

Process. Place the equivalent of ¼ cup of the chunk rosin in a plastic or paper bag. Tap the chunks gently with the hammer to pulverize the rosin in the bag—be careful not to tear the bag. Leave the rosin there until you're ready to use it.

Take the three squares of whatever material you're going to use for your rosin bag—silk, nylon, or tarlatan—and place them flat on the table, one on top of the other. Put heaping tablespoonfuls of the pulverized rosin into the center of the squares. Remove any chunks of rosin that are larger than small peas, as they'll tear the bag. Gather the four corners of the material together to form a pouch with the rosin in the center. The pouch should be about ¾ full rather than tightly packed. Put a rubber band around the ends to keep them together and cover the rubber band with masking tape or another pressure-sensitive tape in case the rubber band breaks.

Storage. Store excess rosin in a closed container—it will last forever. Keep the rosin bag in a box or jar so you don't get rosin powder over all of your tools.

CLEANING AND BEVELING THE PLATE

See Chapter 7 for information on how to clean and bevel your plate. In addition, please note that you shouldn't bevel an aquatinted plate until *after* it has been bitten. The reason for this is that you should coat beveled edges with rosin stopout before you put the plate in acid. If you stop out the beveled edges of an aquatinted plate, the stopout will run over the edge and cause the aquatint to have ragged edges. You'll have to bevel the plate much more than usual when you take the plate out of the acid, and you'll lose plate surface before you obtain a smooth, straight beveled edge.

APPLYING ROSIN TO THE PLATE

You'll apply a layer of powdered rosin to a clean plate and heat the plate to melt the rosin. When the plate cools, the rosin will harden and will act as an acid-resist.

Materials and Equipment
plate
newspaper
rosin bag
hot plate heated to 212° F.
garden gloves

Process. Place the plate on top of a large piece of newspaper on a flat work surface. Make sure that the area is draft-free so the rosin won't blow away before you heat it.

Hold the rosin bag over the plate and tap it gently with your finger or with a pencil (see Figure 1). You should see the rosin falling. Move the bag back and forth over the plate, continuing to tap, until a fine dusting of aquatint covers the entire surface.

Bend down until the plate is at eye level and look across the surface of the plate to see how evenly you applied the aquatint. You should see a uniform whiteness—the grains of rosin should be very close to one another (see Figure 2). If some areas of the plate seem darker than others, shake more rosin onto those darker areas. Don't exhale onto the plate and don't shake it—the aquatint shifts very easily before it's heated.

When you've finished putting the rosin onto the plate, put on your garden gloves. Pull the newspaper under the plate to the edge of the table until part of the plate extends over the edge. Pick up the plate from underneath without disturbing the rosin, and place the plate on the hot plate. As soon as the metal becomes hot, the rosin will begin to melt. This should happen quickly—if it doesn't, then the hot plate isn't hot enough.

Bend down so that you can look across the plate at eye level—you'll see the rosin becoming transparent as it melts. If you have a small hot plate, you'll have to move the plate when the rosin becomes transparent in order to expose a new area to the heat. With the small hot plate, continue to move the plate over the hot plate until all of the rosin is transparent. With a large hot plate, you shouldn't have to move your plate around. In either case, after all of the rosin is melted, remove the plate from the hot plate, and put it on the bed of the press to cool.

Caution: Don't leave the plate on the heat once the rosin crystals become transparent. If you do, the rosin granules will begin to flow together, covering the whole plate. There will be no metal surface areas left for the acid to bite. Also, the overheated plate will begin to buckle.

ADDING TONE WITH AQUATINT

You can use aquatint to add tone to your plate after it has already been etched with hard or soft ground in a linear image. Don't apply an aquatint over an area on a plate that has been bitten with a soft ground tone—the result would be a splotchy and unpleasant gray. Of course, if you want a splotchy and unpleasant gray, go ahead.

Materials and Equipment
plate previously etched with hard or soft ground and now covered with melted rosin
    powder for an aquatint
rosin stopout solution and brushes
lithographic (grease) crayon

Process. Decide which area on your plate will remain white (unbitten) and paint those areas with stopout solution. It's a good idea to outline these areas with a lithographic, or grease, crayon since when rosin stopout is very thin, it has a tendency to run on aquatint. When you outline the area, the grease in the lithographic crayon forms a barrier between the liquid rosin stopout and the rosin aquatint. When you place the plate in acid, the acid will bite around the dots of rosin in the areas not covered with rosin stopout, creating a tone in those areas when the plate is printed.

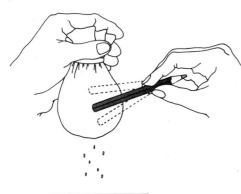

Figure 1. To tap the rosin onto the plate, hold the rosin bag in one hand and gently tap with a pencil with your other hand to release the grains of rosin

Figure 2.

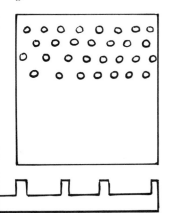

Plate with the rosin applied too sparsely and an enlarged cross section of the resulting plate after biting—the grooves are too large.

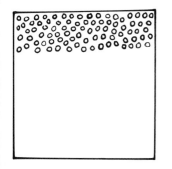

Plate with aquatint applied properly and an enlarged cross section of the plate after biting.

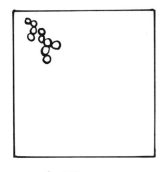

Uneven application of rosin—which would result in a spotty gray when the plate was printed with black ink—and an enlarged cross section of the plate after biting.

CREATING LIGHT TONE ON DARK GROUND

You can make a light tone or image on a dark ground by drawing over an acquatint with a lithographic pencil or rubbing ink, a block of grease crayon.

Materials and Equipment
plate covered with melted rosin powder for an acquatint
lithographic pencil
rubbing ink

Process. Take the rubbing ink or lithographic crayon and draw directly on top of the aquatint. The grease will coat the tops of the grains of melted rosin and will make them larger. Less of the plate will be exposed to the acid, creating a lighter area against the untouched aquatint background when the plate is bitten. If you use the crayon with much pressure in any area and coat the plate solidly, the grease will act as a stopout and cause that area to remain completely white.

To get a graded tone from very light to dark, use the rubbing ink. Press down with the side of the piece of rubbing ink on the areas of your plate that are to be light. Move the ink with less and less pressure toward the area that you want to print darker. Where the rubbing ink is thick and dark your etching will print light.

Before you put the plate in acid, brush stopout on those areas that you want to be completely white. Don't stopout the edges of the plates—the stopout solution would run over the melted rosin and would ruin your aquatint.

BITING AN AQUATINT

Put any plate with aquatint into a weak acid since aquatint bites more quickly than other grounds. Before you proceed, look at Chapter 12 for general information about acids and acid baths.

Materials and Equipment
weak nitric acid bath or Dutch mordant in a tray
copper or zinc plate with aquatint
feather
water
drypoint needle (optional)

Process. Place your plate into the acid and then rinse your hands in cold water. If you're using nitric acid to bite a zinc plate, use the bubbles to time the depth of the bite. Watch the plate closely—when bubbles have formed thickly all over the plate, remove them gently with the feather. Do this once or twice and remove the plate from the acid if you want a light tone in your print. Wash the plate in cold water, and dry it gently by patting a paper towel over the surface.

If you want a light tone in only one area of the print, paint the area that is to be a light tone with stopout, and then replace the plate in the acid for further biting. At this point if you want a tone that is visibly darker than the first one, you must leave the plate in the acid twice as long as the first time. In other words, if the acid bubbled fully two times for the light tone, it would have to bubble fully four times for the darker one. If you want a still darker tone let the acid bubble fully eight times, and so on.

For a solid, dark aquatint on a zinc plate, you should leave the plate in the acid for as long as you can see the aquatint texture after you've feathered the bubbles away from the plate. If at any time the texture should disappear, then remove the plate from the acid immediately—the aquatint has broken down.

In order to determine the depth of the bite of an aquatint when you put a copper plate in Dutch mordant, you have to observe the tone of the plate—it becomes darker the longer the plate is in the acid. Or, you can remove the plate from the acid, wash it in cold water, and insert a drypoint needle gently into the grooves that surround the aquatint grains to feel the depth of the bite.

When you've finished biting your plate, remove it from the acid and rinse it in cold water. Wipe the plate dry with a paper towel—you'll have difficulty removing the melted rosin if your plate is wet.

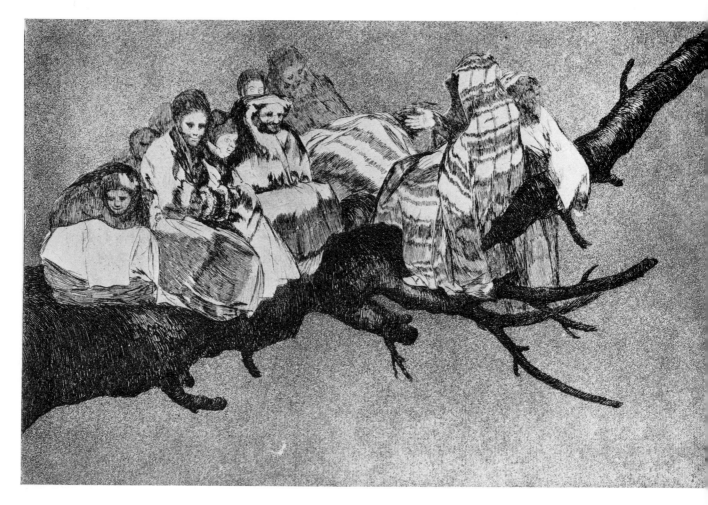

Disparate Ridicule, Los Proverbios, *pl. 3, by Francisco de Goya (1746-1828). Aquatint, 14 1/16″ x 18⅛″. Courtesy Metropolitan Museum of Art, New York City, Harris Brisbane Dick Fund.*

Caprichos *by Francisco de Goya (1746-1828). Aquatint, 8 7/16″ x 5⅞″. Courtesy Metropolitan Museum of Art, New York City.*

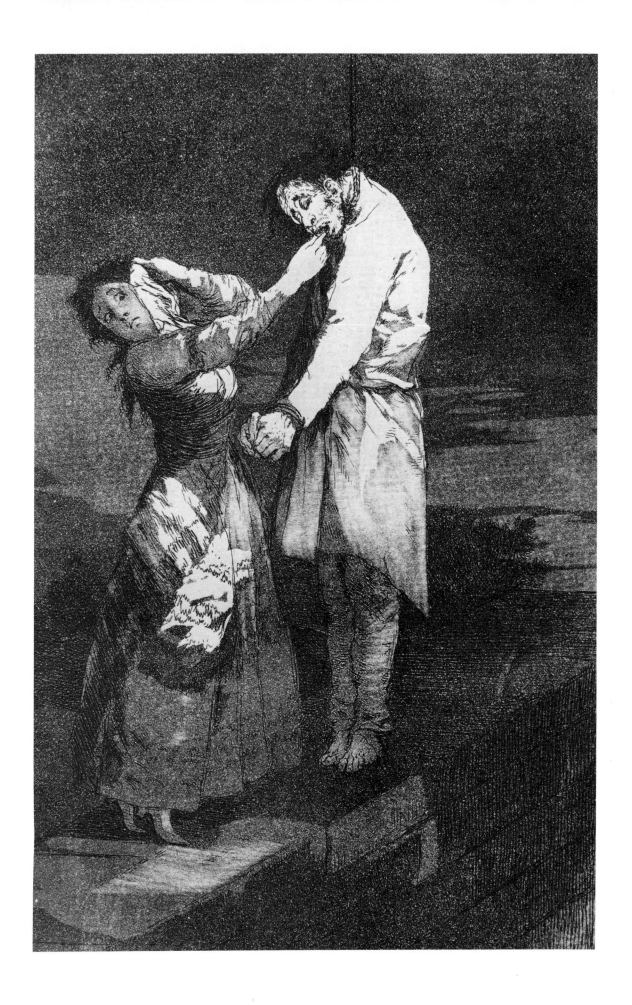

REMOVING ROSIN

You must remove the melted rosin from the plate before you do any more work on it and before you print the plate.

Materials and Equipment
dry plate with aquatint that has been bitten in acid
newspaper
alcohol
varnolene
scrubbing brush
rags or paper towels

Process. Place your dry plate on newspaper. Pour on alcohol—if you've used rubbing ink, you'll need to pour on varnolene also—and scrub vigorously with a scrub brush. You'll see that the rosin is difficult to remove. When it has dissolved in the alcohol, wipe the plate with rags or paper towels.

After the plate dries, run your hand over the surface—you shouldn't feel any grit. If you do, rosin is still adhered to the plate. Pour more alcohol on and scrub again.

BEVELING THE PLATE

Now it's time to bevel the edges of your aquatinted plate. For directions see Chapter 7.

PRINTING AN AQUATINT

Look at Chapter 13 for general printing information. There are, however, a few special directions for printing an aquatint. First, a plate with an aquatint ground doesn't require as much pressure as a deeply bitten intaglio plate when you pull a print. Excess pressure on an aquatint will wear the plate down quickly. Also, the ink used for aquatint should be stiff rather than oily, so when you wipe the plate well, you don't wipe out all of the ink. (Stiff ink sticks to the plate more than oily ink.) Your ink is stiff if, when held on a palette knife raised above a mixing slab, it falls very slowly back onto the slab.

AQUATINT USED AS A MEZZOTINT

A mezzotint is made by darkening a plate with a rocker—you rock this tool back and forth all over the plate for a great amount of time to create an infinite number of tiny ink-holding dots. Then you scrape and burnish an image out of the darkened plate. It's far easier to use an aquatint for the first step, i.e., to darken the plate. The mezzotint and the bitten aquatint plates don't look alike, but the method of working from dark to light to create the image is the same. To use an aquatint in this way, you must first lay a medium to fine aquatint on the plate. When you put the plate into the acid, bite it deeply—until the aquatint will print a dark gray or black when you use black ink (this applies to both zinc and copper plates).

Materials and Equipment
plate with a deeply bitten aquatint
lithographic crayon
drypoint needle
cloth
scraper
burnisher
machine oil

Process. Draw the outline of your image on the plate with a lithographic crayon. If you decide to change the drawing, simply rub off the crayon mark with your finger or with a cloth. Don't make the image too detailed: remember that all the light and white areas must be scraped out.

When you're satisfied with your drawing, take a drypoint needle, press down, and outline the lithographic crayon drawing. Hold the needle as perpendicular to the plate as you comfortably can. What you're doing, actually, is reinforcing the drawing so when you begin to scrape and remove the crayon marks you don't lose the image.

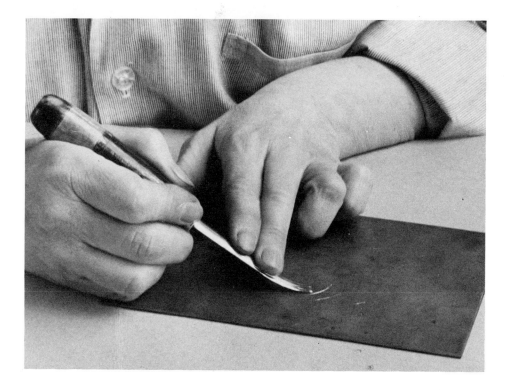

Figure 3. The burnisher held like a pencil. The two fingers placed on the shank are pressing down and guiding the tool.

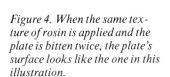

Figure 4. When the same texture of rosin is applied and the plate is bitten twice, the plate's surface looks like the one in this illustration.

Pick the scraper up and hold its taped section (see Chapter 7, Figure 8). Scrape the same way you would if you were scraping out a line (see Chapter 7).

Scrape the texture away completely in any area that's to be totally white. If you want a light tone, scrape only until the texture is smoother than the rest of the aquatint.

The next step is to polish the scraped areas of the plate with a burnisher and a drop of machine oil. The burnisher will make the white areas shine so they'll print clean and leave the gray areas smooth. Hold the burnisher in your right hand and press the rounded end down with the second and third fingers of your left hand (see Figure 3). With strokes that are close together, move the burnisher back and forth in the area you're polishing. Use firm, light pressure—heavy pressure is unnecessary and can cause damage to the plate.

When you feel you've scraped and burnished enough, pull a proof (see Chapter 13). You'll probably find that you haven't scraped enough, but the proof will give you an idea of how much more scraping is necessary.

Continue to scrape, burnish, and pull proofs until your plate is finished. At this point you can put other grounds on the plate to change the image if you wish to go further.

PUTTING ONE AQUATINT OVER ANOTHER

You apply a second aquatint ground the same way you apply the first. But remember, if your first aquatint was very fine, the second should be coarse and vice versa. If the two aquatints were of the same grain, they would tend to cancel each other out. The texture of an aquatint depends on the smooth dots in between the grooves—should these disappear, you'll end up with an unpleasant tone, called a *crevé* (see Figure 4).

When applying a coarse-grain aquatint, it's sometimes easier to put on the stopout before you lay the aquatint. Immediately after brushing on the stopout, dust the aquatint on over it—don't wait for the stopout to dry since it will dry when you heat the plate to melt the rosin. When the plate cools after heating, check the stopout for little bubbles and if there are any, cover them with fresh stopout before immersing the plate in acid. If there aren't any bubbles, place the plate in acid as soon as it's cool.

Caution: You should apply stopout before putting on aquatint only when you use an electric hot plate as a source of heat. Never do this if you're using an open gas flame for heat. If flame touches any stopout, the stopout will catch fire.

USING SPRAY ENAMEL

Another way to get a fine aquatint texture is to spray on color enamel. This process comes in handy when you can't heat the plate, such as when you have a deeply bitten plate with ground still on it, and you want to put an aquatint on a large open area. Spray enamel doesn't last as long in acid as rosin does, nor will its aquatint last as long in printing. Before you begin to use the spray enamel, be sure that you have adequate ventilation.

Materials and Equipment
plate
newspaper
spray can of color enamel
varnolene or turpentine
alcohol

Process. To begin, make sure that if your plate has no ground on it, its surface is clean. If your plate does have a ground on it and has already been bitten, be sure that the area to be sprayed is dry. Tack newspaper on the wall against which the plate will be leaning, and spread them on the table or floor below that part of the wall.

Take the spray can and practice spraying on some of the newspaper on the wall. Then lean the plate against the wall on the newspaper. Holding the can about 18″ away from the plate, spray the plate. Move the can back and forth across the surface with a slow sweeping motion, beginning at the top and working slowly down.

Stop spraying when the sprayed particles are close together—some of the metal surface should still show through the enamel. If the enamel drips anywhere, you've either sprayed on too much enamel, or you've held the can too close to the plate. You'll have to clean the plate and start again.

The enamel dries quickly—you can put the plate into the acid almost as soon as you finish spraying. Don't feather a plate with enamel spray paint while it's in acid. To clear off the bubbles, tilt the tray and allow the acid to roll off the plate (make sure that the tray is less than half full of acid). Or you can pick up the plate, allow the acid to run off it, replace the plate in the acid, and wash your fingers in cold water.

If you see that the enamel is wearing away in certain areas, remove the plate from the acid, rinse it with water, dry it well, and spray those areas again before replacing the plate in the acid. When you're completely finished biting the plate, remove the enamel with alcohol and varnolene or turpentine.

CLEANUP

1. Rub the scraper and burnisher with a little machine oil or kerosene. Store them in a box—if moisture attacks these tools, they'll rust.

2. Put used rosin bags in a dust-free container.

3. Wrap the rubbing ink in waxed paper or a polyethylene bag. You can use it until it becomes gritty.

4. Wash the brushes used for stopout first in alcohol and then in soap and water.

5. Turn off the hot plate. When it's cold, clean it with varnolene to remove the excess rosin.

6. Throw away any newspaper, rags, or paper towels that have rosin or solvents on them. them.

7. Store all solvents in covered metal containers.

8. Pour the acid back into its container or cover its tray.

WHAT WENT WRONG AND WHY

Problem	Cause	Solution
The aquatint has a strange texture consisting of little curly lines on a smooth background.	1. You applied too much rosin.	1. Scrape and burnish the plate until it's smooth, and apply the rosin again. Next time, shake less rosin onto the plate.
	2. You overheated the rosin, and the particles ran together when they melted.	2. Remove the rosin and start again. Take care to remove the plate from the heat *as soon as the aquatint becomes transparent.*
The aquatint prints as a splotchy gray spotted with little white dots lying quite far apart.	1. You didn't apply enough rosin.	1. Scrape and burnish the plate. When you shake the rosin on again, make sure it has a white rather than a gray appearance at eye level before you heat it.
	2. You didn't heat the plate sufficiently—the rosin didn't adhere properly to the plate, and it came off in the acid.	2. Scrape and burnish the plate and shake on more rosin. When you heat the plate covered with rosin a second time, make sure the rosin is transparent before you remove the plate from the heat. If the rosin appears white in places, it hasn't been heated enough.
The image of the drawing made with the lithographic crayon isn't visible in the print.	In order to be seen as a light or white area, you have to apply a lot of pressure with the lithographic crayon so the grease can act as an acid-resist.	Scrape the area where the lithographic crayon was used—this will have almost the same effect as the crayon applied with pressure.
One area of the aquatint is lighter than the rest, although it seemed to be biting evenly in the acid.	There may be a film of oil on the plate if you didn't scrub it properly or if you touched the plate after cleaning it. This oil film protects the plate for a short while after you put it in acid, and it takes time for the acid to break through to the metal. Therefore, that area of the plate will be underbitten.	If you want an even tone over the entire plate, you'll have to scrape the surface and put on another aquatint. If the aquatint texture isn't important, you can put on a soft ground to darken that area (see Chapter 8).
The rosin stopout ran when I brushed it over the melted rosin.	Rosin is soluble in alcohol. Since rosin stopout is made with alcohol, it tends to spread on the aquatint.	The rosin stopout won't spread if you outline the area to be stopped out with a lithographic pencil. The grease in the pencil will act as a barrier and contain the stopout. Or you can use asphaltum stopout on an aquatint, although remember that you must air-dry it and that might take an hour or more.

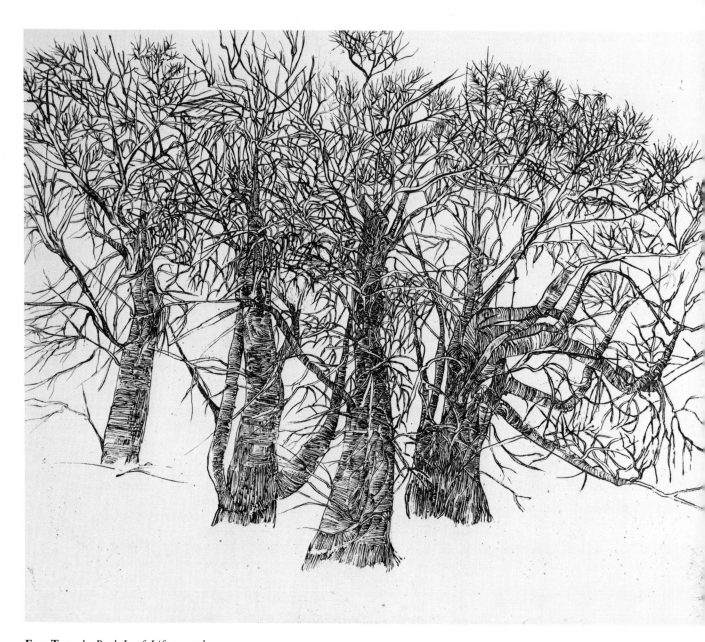

Four Trees *by Ruth Leaf. Lift ground.*

TEN

Sugar Lift

To draw an image directly onto a plate with a brush or pen and to have a finished print with the spontaneity of a brush or pen drawing, use sugar lift ground. Briefly, the process is to create your drawing on the plate with a ground made with sugar that is soluble in water. When the drawing is dry, coat the plate with asphaltum or hard ground—neither of which is soluble in water. After the asphaltum or hard ground dries, place the plate in hot, but not boiling, water. This will cause the sugar in the lift ground to dissolve and lift, exposing the metal under the drawing and leaving the rest of the plate coated with hard ground or asphaltum. You'll then place the plate in acid to bite the exposed areas.

DRAWING WITH LIFT GROUND

Use the lift ground as if it were India ink, and remember that the drawing you make directly on the plate will be the printed image. Make sure that the plate you're working on is clean and has beveled edges (see Chapter 7).

Materials and Equipment
beveled and cleaned plate
sugar lift ground made according to the formula given in Chapter 6
brush or pen
stick or pencil
toothbrush
paper towels

Process. Use the lift ground with a brush or pen and draw on the plate as you would draw on paper. Keep a paper towel under your hand so your hand doesn't rest on the plate, leaving traces of oil.

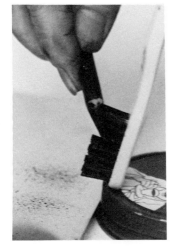

Figure 1. Splatter technique with lift ground and a toothbrush.

Another way of applying sugar lift ground to the plate is to splatter it on with a toothbrush. First, dip the toothbrush into the lift ground. Hold the brush close to and perpendicular to the plate, with the bristles facing *away* from you. Run a stick or pencil across the bristles, starting from the end of the brush which nearly touches the plate (see Figure 1). It's a good idea to practice on a piece of paper for a while until you're adept at this technique.

If you're unhappy with sections of the image once the lift ground is on the plate, don't try to remove them. You can eliminate any undesirable areas with rosin stopout after the ground has lifted. However, if you find the drawing completely unsatisfactory, scrub the plate with powdered cleanser, rinse it off, and start all over again.

When you're finished with the drawing, let the lift ground dry thoroughly. To be sure that it's dry, touch the surface of the lift ground gently—it should feel hard. Avoid touching the plate itself.

COATING THE LIFT GROUND

You must coat all sections of the plate that don't hold lift ground—the negative spaces—with asphaltum before the lift ground can be lifted. If you don't do this, there won't be an image to bite and print.

Materials and Equipment
plate on which you've drawn with lift ground
asphaltum in a squeeze bottle or hard ground and a brush
newspaper
gloves

Process. To start, put on your gloves and pour the asphaltum into a squeeze bottle if it isn't already in one. Be sure that the asphaltum contains enough varnolene to make it very liquid—test its consistency on an old plate.

When you're satisfied with the consistency of the asphaltum, stand the plate with dry lift ground on one end on top of newspaper with the surface with the drawing facing you. Holding a top corner of the plate with one hand without touching the surface, squeeze the asphaltum out of the bottle at the top of the plate with your other hand. As you squeeze, move your hand across the top of the plate (see Figure 2). The asphaltum will run down the plate quickly, covering the drawing or parts of the drawing and leaving a puddle of asphaltum on the newspaper. Turn the plate from side to side if necessary to cover the entire surface with asphaltum (see Figure 3).

Always try to hold the plate in an upright position as you apply the asphaltum so a lot of it drips off. You should be able to see the lift ground drawing through the dark but transparent brown asphaltum, which should cover the *whole* plate (see Figure 4).

Allow the plate to dry by leaning it against the wall—be sure there's newspaper underneath to catch the asphaltum drippings.

If you're using hard ground rather than asphaltum, then brush it lightly over the plate with the dry sugar lift drawing. Cover the *entire* plate and then allow the plate to air-dry—don't dry it on a hot plate.

LIFTING A LIFT GROUND

You must remove the lift ground from the plate's surface in order to expose the metal under the drawing.

Materials and Equipment
plate with lift ground drawing coated with asphaltum or hard ground
water tray
hot water
rosin stopout and brush
feather
paper towels

Process. Fill the water tray half full of very hot tap water. Place the plate in the tray (see Figure 5) and let it sit in the water for a few minutes. Soon you'll notice cracks appearing in the drawing. Gently rock the tray so the hot water washes back and forth over the plate—the drawing will begin to lift.

As the sugar lift rises little by little, it may expose the metal in an interesting textured design. You can keep this texture and incorporate it into your drawing. When the texture seems most exciting to you, just take the plate out of the water. Blot any area on the plate with a paper towel *gently* where you don't want the acid to bite. Try not to disturb the drawing. Coat these areas and the edges of the plate with rosin stopout. When the stopout is tacky, place the plate in acid—as the plate bites, the lift ground protects the plate for a short time and then continues to lift. Thus the plate bites at different levels, and an exciting textural effect results.

If you plan to lift all of the lift ground, pour the water out of the tray after it's cool, but don't remove the plate from the tray. Pour more hot water into the tray without pouring it directly onto the plate. Repeat this process until the ground lifts completely (see Figure 6).

If your asphaltum is too thick, the sugar lift may have difficulty lifting. If this happens, try stroking the drawing with a feather while the plate is under water to expedite the lifting process.

When the sugar lift has fully lifted, remove the plate from the water and pat the surface dry with paper towels. Use stopout to coat the edges of the plate and any other exposed areas that you don't want the acid to bite. You can add more lines to the plate by drawing through the asphaltum or hard ground with an etching needle before you bite the plate with acid. Please note that asphaltum is brittle—lines drawn through it have a ragged look.

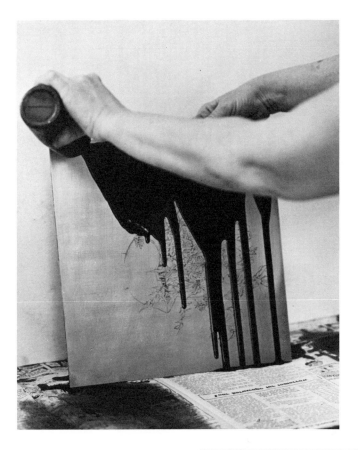

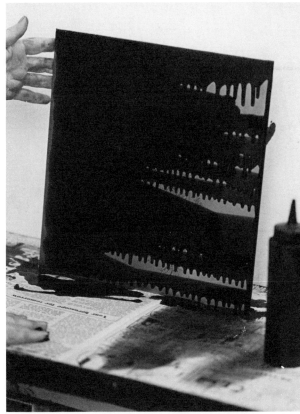

Figure 2 (above). Asphaltum applied by squeezing a bottle while pulling your hand slowly across the plate.

Figure 3 (above right). When you turn the plate, the asphaltum runs down to cover the open spaces.

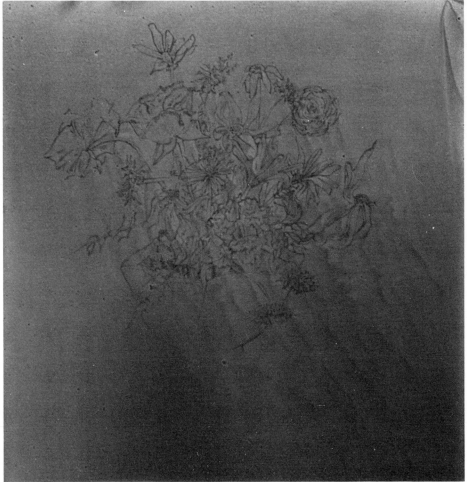

Figure 4 (right). Lift ground covered by asphaltum. Note that the asphaltum is thin—you can see the drawing underneath.

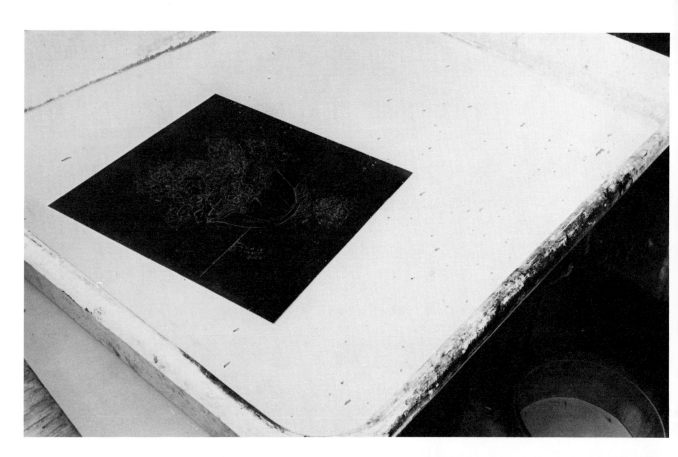

Figure 5 (above). The plate with lift ground and asphaltum placed in a tray of hot water.

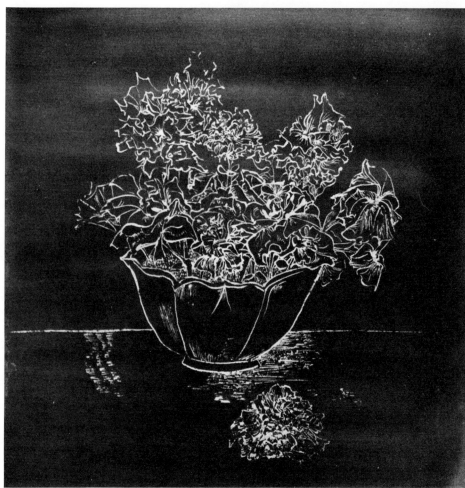

Figure 6 (right). The plate after hot water lifted the lift ground.

BITING THE LIFT GROUND

If you bite a zinc plate after the sugar lift has lifted and print it in black ink, the wide lines or areas of exposed metal will appear gray with a dark line around the edges of the forms; the narrow lines will be black. If you do the same with a steel plate, all bitten areas will appear black. See Chapter 12 for general information on biting plates. There are, however, a few rules pertaining mainly to biting a sugar lift.

First of all, remember that the wider areas of exposed metal will bite deeper and faster than the more narrow lines. If you're satisfied with the depth of the wide areas but not with the depth of the narrow lines, remove the plate from the acid, wash it in cold water, dry it gently with paper towels, and stop out the wide areas before replacing the plate in the acid.

If you wish to apply an aquatint on top of the lifted sugar lift, first bite the plate for a few minutes until you can feel the depression when you pass a drypoint needle across the lines. Remove the plate from the acid, pat it dry with a paper towel, and stop out any areas you don't want to aquatint. *Don't remove the ground.* Please note that there's no need to aquatint the lifted areas on a steel plate—they'll appear dark on the print without any help.

APPLYING ROSIN AQUATINT TO A LIFT GROUND

You'll apply aquatint to a lift ground on a zinc plate if you want to darken the large open areas of the image. You may use rosin aquatint if you used asphaltum to coat the lift ground. If you used a hard ground, use spray enamel as aquatint (see Chapter 9).

Materials and Equipment
plate lifted with asphaltum, slightly bitten
aquatint bag
gloves
hot plate
slow nitric acid or Dutch mordant
asphaltum
stopout

Process. Turn on the hot plate. Next, shake aquatint over the entire plate by tapping the rosin bag (see Chapter 9). Then, put your gloves on, lift the plate carefully from underneath, and place it on the hot plate. Heat the plate until the rosin melts and becomes transparent, and then place the plate on the bed of the press to cool.

Look at the plate carefully to see if there are any unwanted scratches in the asphaltum—stop out any suspicious areas. Place the plate in a slow nitric acid or Dutch mordant. Treat the plate from now on as an aquatint plate (see Chapter 9).

SPRAYING ENAMEL ON A LIFT GROUND

If you used hard ground to coat the sugar lift, you must use spray enamel to create an aquatint effect. If you used rosin, you would have to heat the plate to melt the grains—the hard ground would become porous and would no longer protect the plate from the acid. See Chapter 9, page 96, for instructions on how to spray enamel onto a plate.

REMOVING THE GROUND

See Chapter 7 for instructions on removing ground from the plate. Just remember that hard ground and asphaltum are soluble in varnolene; rosin and rosin stopout in alcohol; spray enamel in alcohol and varnolene. If there's any lift ground left on the plate, it would be soluble in soap and water.

PRINTING THE LIFT GROUND

If areas of the lift ground have been bitten very deeply, place a damp blotter over the printing paper for added pressure when you print. If you applied aquatint, less pressure is necessary. For basic printing information, see Chapter 13.

LIFT GROUND AS THE SECOND GROUND

You can apply a second lift ground, if necessary, to the plate—follow the same process as you did the first time. You can also apply a lift ground to a plate that has been bitten with another ground. You'll be able to make a deeper and wider line by applying sugar lift rather than hard ground to a plate that has already been bitten. Take care that the hard ground or asphaltum completely covers the previously bitten areas of the plate that aren't to be bitten again.

CLEANUP

1. Wash brushes used for lift ground in soap and water. Wash brushes used with asphaltum stopout in varnolene, dry them with paper towels, and then wash them in soap and water. Brushes used for rosin stopout should be washed in alcohol, dried, and then washed in soap and water.

2. Store rosin bags in dust-free containers.

3. Turn off the hot plate—when it cools, wipe the surface with a rag dipped in varnolene to clean off grounds or aquatint.

4. Cover the lift ground and the rosin stopout, if used.

5. Store the asphaltum you use for lift grounds in the squeeze bottle. Remember to tape the hole in the bottle cap to prevent evaporation of the solvent. Before you use the asphaltum again, test it on an old plate. If it has thickened, add more varnolene and shake the bottle until the asphaltum is smooth.

6. Throw out any newspaper and rags soaked in solvent or coated with asphaltum. Please note that if you allow asphaltum to dry on newspaper, the asphaltum will glue the newspaper to any surface it happens to be resting on.

7. If you used acids, pour them back into their containers or, if you're leaving them in the trays, cover the trays. If there are pieces of lift ground in the acid, you can strain them out by pouring the acid back into a bottle through a funnel that has cheesecloth stretched across its wide opening.

WHAT WENT WRONG AND WHY

Problem	Cause	Solution
When I put the plate into the warm water, areas of the asphaltum lift where there is no lift ground drawing.	If the plate isn't completely grease-free when you begin, the asphaltum or hard ground will lift in the hot water.	Be sure that you scrub your plate properly. And when you're drawing on the plate, be sure that your hand doesn't touch the plate's surface.
The lift ground won't lift in the warm water.	You applied the asphaltum or hard ground too heavily.	Place the plate in hot water. Break the surface of the asphaltum or hard ground with a drypoint needle over the areas in the drawing—this will sometimes start the lifting process.
The ground lifted well and the exposed areas were bitten in acid. The print, however, has large light areas surrounded by dark edges.	When a large area of the plate is bitten without a texture such as soft ground or aquatint, that area will only hold ink at the edges of the depression. (You may want this effect when you make color prints.)	1. After the plate is in the acid for a while, put on a rosin aquatint or spray on enamel paint. 2. Put on a soft ground texture to darken the light areas after you remove the sugar lift and asphaltum or hard ground.

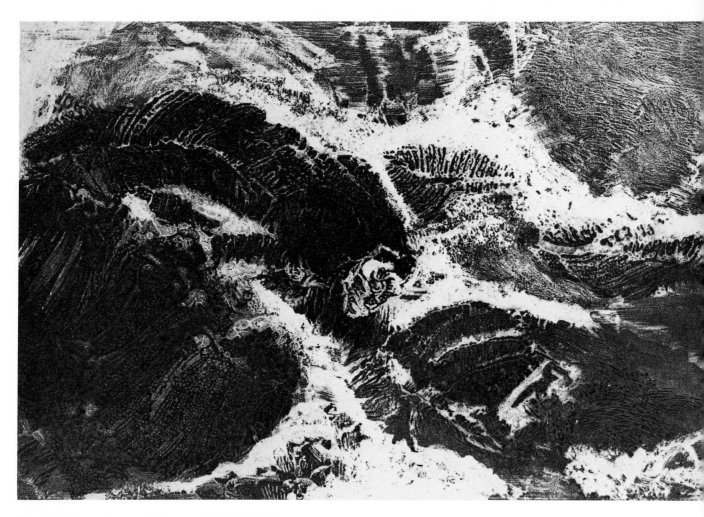

Waves *by Shirley Roman. White ground, 11½″ x 17¼″.*

ELEVEN

White Ground

White ground is a mixture of white pigment, soap flakes, and linseed oil. It isn't completely acid-resistant and acts as a timed stopout in acid when applied to the plate. White ground resists the acid longer where it's applied heavily and bites faster in those areas where it's thinly applied. Thus you can get variation in tone from light to dark. You can use white ground by itself and produce a completed plate with one application, or you can use it as an underpainting and apply other grounds on top.

PREPARING WHITE GROUND

White ground as prepared according to the formula given in Chapter 6 is too thick to be applied to the plate with a brush. You must add water in order to make the ground liquid enough for use.

Materials and Equipment
white ground made according to the formula given in Chapter 6
tinfoil or plastic plate
water
palette knife

Process. If the oil in the white ground has risen to the top, stir the ground in the container with a palette knife until all of the ingredients are mixed.

Remove approximately 1 tsp. of ground from the jar with the palette knife, and put it on the tinfoil or plastic plate (see Figure 1). Pour a few drops of water over the ground, and mix thoroughly with the palette knife until the ground has reached the consistency of tempera paint. You can add more water at any time as needed.

APPLYING WHITE GROUND WITH A BRUSH

You'll use a brush to paint the white ground onto the plate. After the ground is on the plate, you can use other brushes, pieces of cardboard, sticks, sponges, or textures to create your image. Before you begin, make sure your plate is clean and its edges are beveled (see Chapter 7 for instructions).

Materials and Equipment
zinc or steel plate
prepared white ground in a tinfoil dish
2½″ camel's hair brush, or any 2½″ brush made of hair
pointed sable brush
hot plate
sharpened wooden stick
textures such as tinfoil, sponges, lace
pieces of cut cardboard

Process. With the 2½″ camel's hair brush, paint a thin layer of white ground over the entire plate. Don't worry if the coat of ground isn't smooth.

Heat the hot plate and when it becomes warm enough to cause water to evaporate, place the plate on its surface. You should be able to watch the plate's surface dry. Try not to overheat the ground—if you do it will turn yellow, the oil will harden, and further manipulation of the ground will be difficult.

When the first layer of white ground dries, remove the plate from the heat. Brush on a second thin coat of white ground over the first, and warm the plate again as you did before to allow the water to evaporate.

At this point, the plate looks gray. And if you bit the plate in acid now, cleaned it, and printed it in black, you would end up with a medium gray tone. To create lighter tones

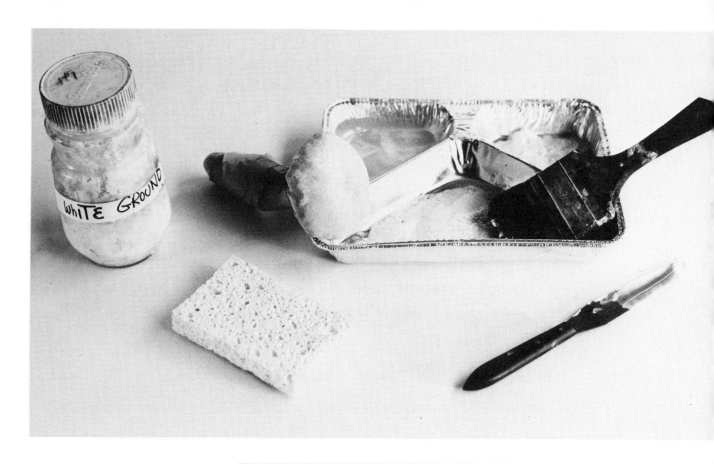

Figure 1 (above). Some of the materials and equipment used to apply a white ground. Top row, from left to right: jar of white ground, dauber, aluminum dish, and large soft brush. In the foreground: sponge and palette knife.

Figure 2 (right). Plate with a white ground applied. The texture that will appear in the print is visible on the plate.

or white areas, add more white ground. The more ground you apply, the whiter it will look, the longer it will take the acid to bite through to the plate, and the lighter the plate (or area of the plate) will print.

To create darker images, draw into the ground with a sharpened stick. Don't draw with very sharp tools such as drypoint needles—they may scratch the plate without making a line in the white ground wide enough to be noticeable. To create a very dark line, draw with the edge of a cut cardboard. To add texture, press crumpled tinfoil, a sponge, or a piece of lace into the ground.

Keep on manipulating the white ground until you're satisfied with your image. To see the image, place the plate in indirect light—the image you see (see Figure 2) will be the same image that will appear on the finished print.

Dry the plate for 24 hours before you place it in the acid or before you add an aquatint or another ground.

APPLYING WHITE GROUND WITH A DAUBER

When you apply white ground to the plate with a dauber, you create a tone that is similar to that made by pressing silk evenly over an entire plate covered with soft ground.

Materials and Equipment
dauber made of lamb's wool or cotton wrapped in silk or nylon (see Figure 3)
¼″ glass plate
white ground
clean beveled zinc plate
tracing paper
brushes
pieces of cut cardboard, sticks, combs (anything you can draw through the ground without scratching the plate)

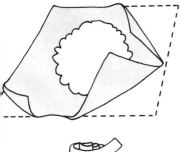
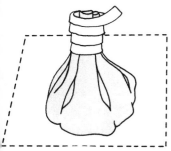

Figure 3. When you make a dauber, wrap a piece of lamb's wool or absorbent cotton in finely textured silk or nylon, top, and tape the fabric at the top, bottom.

Process. After you make the dauber, put a small amount of white ground onto the ¼″ glass plate. Make sure that the ground has the consistency of paste—it shouldn't run together when applied. Don't add as much water as you would if you were using a brush. Pick up a small amount of ground on the bottom of the dauber and rock the dauber on the glass plate until the white ground is evenly distributed over its bottom. Next, rock the dauber on a clean piece of glass to see if the ground comes off evenly. When you look closely, the ground should appear to have little holes distributed evenly throughout it. If there aren't any small holes, then the gound is too liquid. In this case, you must add thicker ground to the ground already on the glass plate. Then remove the ground from the bottom of the dauber with a clean cloth and repeat the last step.

When you're satisfied with the white ground on the dauber, apply it to the plate with a rocking motion until the entire plate is covered.

Warm the plate to dry the white ground the same way you would if you had brushed it on (see above). When the plate is dry, you can either draw directly into the ground or place a piece of tracing paper with or without a drawing over the ground and draw on it as you would with a traditional soft ground (see Chapter 8).

When you've completed the drawing on the plate, there may be areas that you want to stop out. To do this, apply thin coats of white ground to these areas with a brush until the ground looks opaque—remember to heat the plate between coats. Opaque white ground is an effective stopout. Note that rosin or asphaltum stopout can't be used *over* white ground, although they can be used *under* it.

Dry the plate for 24 hours before you put it in acid. If, however, you want to add an aquatint, you can do it immediately, before the plate dries for 24 hours.

APPLYING AQUATINT TO WHITE GROUND

If you bite a white ground by itself without adding an aquatint, the result is a very shallow bite. You have to apply other grounds and bite the plate again to give the intaglio any depth. However, when you apply an aquatint over the white ground, the intaglio in the plate should be deep enough to last through many printings. You can

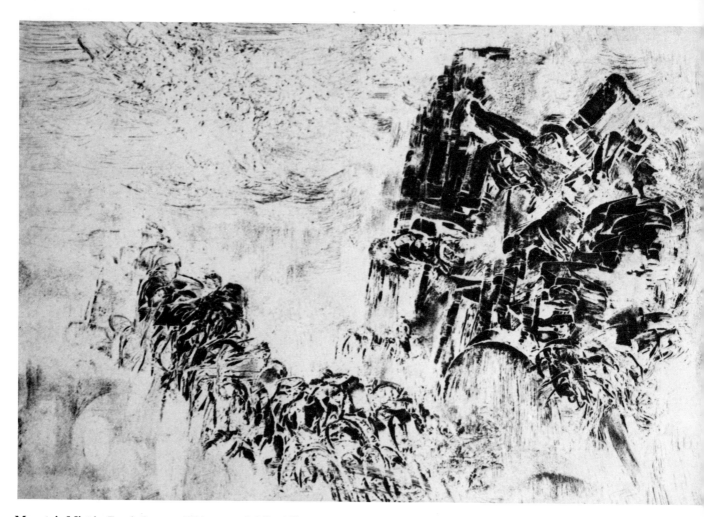

Mountain Mist *by Frank Cassara. White ground, 14″ x 21″.*

always scrape areas that are too dark or apply additional grounds if the plate is not esthetically satisfying.

Materials and Equipment
plate with white ground
rosin bag
¼″ plate glass or clean zinc plate
hot plate
garden gloves
press bed

Process. The technique of applying aquatint to a plate covered with white ground is a little more difficult than that of aquatinting a clean plate, because you can't see the rosin clearly on the white ground. You should begin, therefore, by testing your aquatint—shake the rosin onto a clean piece of glass or a clean zinc plate, so that the grains are evenly but thinly spaced. Then shake the rosin onto the plate with white ground in the same manner to get the same even-but-thinly spaced effect.

Now turn on the hot plate and put on garden gloves. Place one section of the plate on the heated hot plate, and holding the other end of the plate, heat one section at a time. You'll notice that it's difficult to see the aquatint on the white ground, but you'll know when the rosin is melting because the white ground will turn yellow from the heat. As the ground becomes slightly yellowed, move the plate so a new area is on the hot plate. Heat the whole plate until the color is uniform throughout.

Place the plate on the press bed to cool. You can place it in weak acid as soon as it's cold. Don't feather the plate while it's biting—the feather will remove the white ground.

APPLYING WHITE GROUND TO AN ETCHED PLATE

You can apply a white ground texture to an etched plate—that has already been bitten—using other techniques and grounds.

Materials and Equipment
scrubbed plate that has already been bitten
rosin stopout and brush
white ground
2½″ brush or dauber for white ground
hot plate

Process. Brush stopout onto those areas of the plate that are to remain unbitten. Allow the plate to stand until the stopout is tacky. Please note that for a more effective and safer stopout, you can first apply asphaltum, heat it, cool it, and then brush rosin stopout over the asphaltum. Or you can use special stopout.

Apply the white ground with a dauber or a wide brush, as described earlier in this chapter, covering the plate where there is no stopout. It doesn't matter if the white ground covers the stopout in places—the stopout will still be effective.

You can work with the white ground in any of the ways described in this chapter except one—if there's a texture on the plate already when you apply the white ground, don't put an aquatint over the white ground. The texture will cancel out the white dots of the aquatint which create its characteristic sparkle. When you finish working, allow the plate to dry for 24 hours before you put it in acid.

BITING WHITE GROUND

See Chapter 12 for instructions on biting a plate.

REMOVING WHITE GROUND

After the plate has finished biting in acid, rinse it off in cold water. Now you must remove the ground in order to print the plate.

Materials and Equipment
bitten plate with white ground
newspaper
varnolene
alcohol

scrub brush
paper towels or lint-free cloths

Process. Place the plate on a pad of newspaper on the table that's used for applying and removing grounds. Pour a small amount of varnolene onto the plate and add some alcohol if you used rosin stopout under the white ground. Scrub the plate with a scrub brush to loosen the ground.

When you're finished scrubbing, wipe up the ground with paper towels or lint-free rags. Wipe both the front and back of the plate, changing the paper towels or cloths when they absorb too much ground. Wipe the plate until it's completely free of ground and stopout—then the plate is ready to be printed.

CLEANUP

1. Place any plate with drying white ground on a shelf where it won't be disturbed until it's ready to be put into the acid.

2. Wipe any plate that's free of ground with kerosene and cover it with a plastic bag.

3. Rinse the brushes used for stopout in alcohol, wipe them with a paper towel, and then wash them in soap and cool water. Wash the brush used for the white ground and the palette knives in soap and cool water.

4. Scrape the dauber with a palette knife and put it into a plastic bag to keep it clean.

5. Pour any white ground left in the tinfoil plate into the container of white ground.

6. Turn off the hot plate. When it's cool, wipe the surface with a cloth dipped in varnolene to remove any excess white ground.

7. Return the rosin bag to its container.

8. Throw away any newspaper, rags, or paper towels that contain oil, solvents, or grounds. Don't leave flammable materials in the studio overnight unless they're in tightly covered *metal* containers.

WHAT WENT WRONG AND WHY

Problem	Cause	Solution
When I brush white ground over white ground that has already been heated, my brush picks up the ground underneath.	1. The ground on your brush is too liquid.	1. Add thicker white ground to the ground that is too liquid, and pick up only a little white ground on the brush when you put on a second coat.
	2. The ground underneath isn't sufficiently dry.	2. Reheat the plate—the ground is heated sufficiently when it appears matte.
When I put my plate with white ground in the acid, the ground lifted off the plate very quickly and the bite was shallow.	1. You didn't dry the ground long enough before putting the plate in acid.	1. Be sure that the ground dries for at least 24 hours before you put the plate in acid. That way you can be sure that the ground has set.
	2. The plate wasn't clean and free of grease when you applied the ground.	2. Scrub the plate before you apply the ground.
When I printed the plate, none of the white ground texture appeared—only the aquatint.	You shook too much rosin onto the plate.	When you shake rosin onto a white ground, there should be fewer grains of rosin per square inch than when you're shaking rosin onto a clean plate.
After I etched and printed a white ground, the print showed some very deep, dark areas, but many of the other textures and shapes weren't bitten at all.	White ground acts as a stopout if it's too thick, and it bites deeply and quickly if it's very thin. The acid also bites quickly where you have drawn into the white ground and removed the ground.	Apply the white ground thickly only in those areas where you want a pure white. When the plate is in the acid, you can easily see which areas are biting. If only small areas of the plate are biting, take an old brush and gently disturb the opaque areas to remove some of the ground. Be careful not to remove too much ground.

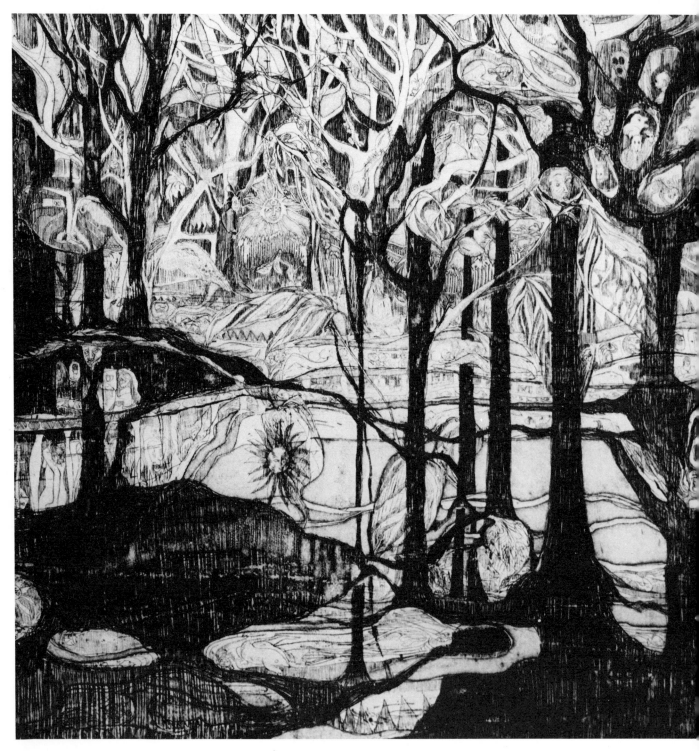

Forest People *by Diane C. Bolhagen. Hard ground, 18″ x 18″.*

TWELVE

Acids

Acids etch, or bite, metal plates. The stronger the acid bath, the faster the acid will bite the plate. Bite steel or zinc plates with nitric acid diluted with water; bite copper with Dutch mordant, a solution of hydrochloric acid, potassium chlorate crystals, and water. You can also use nitric acid instead of Dutch mordant to bite copper if you want a ragged, deep bite.

Never bite two different metals with the same acid solution. If you bite a copper plate in a nitric acid bath, for instance, the action of the acid on the metal dissolves some of the copper which goes into the solution. If you then put a zinc plate in this acid bath, the zinc plate and the copper in the solution together with the acid itself will set up an electrolytic action. The result will be copper particles deposited on a zinc plate and no biting action, rather than an etched plate. To avoid this, keep all acid solutions in separate containers that are labeled clearly, indicating the type and strength of acid *and* the metal on which it has been used. See the acid chart at the end of the chapter to determine which acid solutions you need for a particular metal and/or technique.

Finally, a word of caution. When you make an acid bath, *always pour pure acid into water—never pour water into pure acid.* Water poured into acid will fume violently and the fumes are noxious. Also, if your skin is particularly sensitive or if you have allergies, wear rubber gloves whenever you work with acid.

MAKING NITRIC ACID BATHS

You'll want to use nitric acid in three strengths—weak, medium, and strong. Once you mix each of them, label them.

Materials and Equipment
nitric acid, ACS commercial grade
three 1 gallon bottles of dark glass or plastic with plastic acid-proof caps
large plastic funnel
cold running water
extractor fan
grease pencil
rubber gloves (optional)

Process For the weak nitric acid bath, divide the first container or bottle into 10 equal parts by marking with a grease pencil (see Figure 1). Mark the second container into 7 equal parts for the medium nitric acid bath (see Figure 2). Use the last bottle for the strong nitric acid bath, marking the container into 5 equal parts (see Figure 3).

Place the container in the sink and fill each one with water: fill the bottle for the weak acid to the ninth mark, the one for the medium acid to the sixth mark, and the last for the strong acid to the fourth mark (see Figures 1, 2, and 3).

Now add the acid to each container in the sink. Please note that whenever you pour acid, you should turn your extractor fan on to draw the fumes away from you. Also, you should keep cold water running to dilute any acid that accidentally spills into the sink and to douse any area of your skin or clothing that the acid accidentally touches.

To pour the acid, place the funnel in each container consecutively and pour the acid slowly into the funnel. Always tilt the bottle of acid gently and pour slowly and steadily. Add enough acid so the acid solution reaches the highest mark on each bottle. In other words, the acid will bring the solution level in the bottle for weak acid up to the tenth mark; in the bottle for the medium acid bath, to the seventh mark; and in the bottle for the strong acid bath, to the fifth mark. There's no need to stir or shake the acid mixture. When you use the acid later, the action of pouring the acid into the tray will be enough to integrate the acid and water.

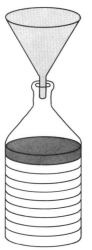

Figure 1. Container marked in 10 equal parts with a grease pencil. To make a weak nitric acid bath, mix 9 parts water with 1 part acid.

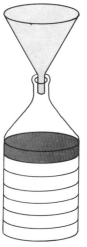

Figure 2. Container divided into 7 equal parts. For a medium acid bath, combine 6 parts of water and 1 part of acid.

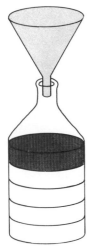

Figure 3. Container divided into 5 equal parts. To make a strong nitric acid, mix 4 parts of water with 1 part nitric acid.

After you finish making the acid solutions, rinse your hands and everything that has come into contact with the acid—the funnel, the sink, etc.—with cold water. Acid left on your skin will itch or burn. If acid should accidentally splash into your eyes, flush them immediately with cold water *for at least 20 minutes*. If any irritation persists after flushing with cold water, see a doctor.

Storage. Store the solutions of nitric acid in capped bottles or in covered plastic trays after use—don't use rubber trays as they'll deteriorate. Please note that if you don't cover the trays, the water will evaporate and the acid solution will become stronger. The covers don't have to be airtight—a ¼″ plywood board slightly larger than the size of the tray is sufficient. Make a sign to keep on the wall above each tray or make a label for the bottle stating the strength of the acid and the metal used or to be used. A typical sign would say "Weak Nitric for Zinc."

MAKING DUTCH MORDANT

You'll want to use Dutch mordant for biting copper plates when you need a fine, accurate, or delicate line.

Materials and Equipment
2 oz. potassium chlorate crystals (or more if needed)
88 oz. tap water hot enough to dissolve the crystals
10 oz. hydrochloric acid
2 oz. old (used) Dutch mordant or a copper penny
32 oz. glass measuring cup
plastic funnel
glass or plastic 1 gallon bottle with acid-proof cap
cold running water
extractor fan
pencil or thin wooden stick
rubber gloves (optional)

Process. To begin, measure 2 oz. of potassium chlorate crystals in the measuring cup. Place the funnel in the gallon bottle and pour the crystals through. If they stick in the funnel, push them into the bottle with a pencil or a thin stick. Then, using the measuring cup, pour 88 oz. of hot tap water through the funnel into the bottle with the crystals. Remove the funnel and cap the bottle. Swirl the water around until the crystals are completely dissolved. Allow this mixture to cool.

When the mixture of water and crystals is cold, you should see some crystals left in the bottom of the bottle. If there aren't any, add more crystals until some do remain undissolved. They won't affect the action of the Dutch mordant, and their presence indicates that you have a saturated solution.

Now turn your extractor fan on to draw air away from you, and measure 10 oz. of hydrochloric acid in the measuring cup. Pour the acid into the cold water and potassium chlorate. Avoid breathing the acid fumes as much as possible since they're noxious.

When you finish pouring in the acid, either drop a copper penny or any small piece of copper into the acid bath or add 2 oz. of old, used Dutch mordant and leave overnight. If you use Dutch mordant without adding old mordant or a piece of copper, the acid could lift the ground off the plate.

Storage. Keep this acid solution in a labeled glass or plastic bottle with a plastic, acid-resistant cover.

BITING PLATES WITH NITRIC ACID

The acid will bite all areas of any plate—zinc, steel, or copper—that are exposed (not covered with ground). When you use nitric acid to bite metal such as zinc and steel, the acid bites sideways and down (see Figure 4). This type of biting action causes the lines you've drawn through the ground to become wider than those in your original drawing. When the nitric acid solution is weak, though, the lines widen more slowly than when the acid is strong.

You can bite copper in nitric acid also—the effect is the same as on zinc or steel. The lines resulting will be rough and wide if the nitric acid bath is strong. (To obtain fine,

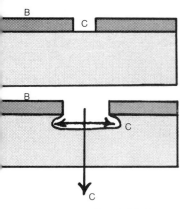

Figure 4. Top, plate (A) before biting, coated with ground (B) leaving exposed metal (C). Bottom, the same plate (A) after biting. Note how the acid bit the exposed metal (C) sideways as well as down.

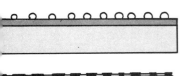

Figure 5. If the bubbles were allowed to remain on the plate during the biting, top, the line would look spotty and uneven when printed, bottom.

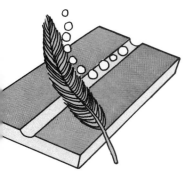

Figure 6. Use a feather to gently brush the bubbles off a plate immersed in an acid bath.

delicate lines on copper, bite the plate in Dutch mordant.)

Caution: Please note that nitric acid used on zinc will heat up in proportion to the amount of metal being bitten. The heat of the acid will heat the plate, which will in turn add more heat to the acid, starting a cycle which can be quite dangerous. If you're biting large sections of metal in strong acid, the acid can get hot enough to cause the ground on the plate to catch fire. The danger signal to watch for is hydrogen gas bubbles forming so quickly that they appear to fume and cover the plate so it's no longer visible. Wearing protective gloves, pick up the tray slowly and allow the acid to run off the plate. Prop the tray up if you have to and remove the plate. If the plate isn't hot, replace it in the acid. If the plate is hot to the touch, rinse it off in cold water and place it in a weaker bath for further biting. If the fumes begin to change color (orange, for example) pour baking soda into the tray until the biting action stops. These fumes are extremely noxious—don't inhale them, and wear a mask to filter them if you have one. Using ordinary safety precautions, however, the above need never occur.

Materials and Equipment
zinc, steel, or copper plate
tray for acid
tray of water or running water
nitric acid bath
gull feathers
drypoint needle
stopout
natural hair brushes such as pointed sable
roll of paper towels
rubber gloves (optional)

Process. Rinse the tray you intend to use with cold water before pouring in an acid solution. Any traces of Dutch mordant in the tray could ruin your nitric acid. After you've done this, pour the acid solution into the tray, tilting the bottle at an angle that permits the acid mixture to pour out slowly, without splashing.

To place the plate in the acid bath, hold the plate at the edges or underneath and lower it gently into the acid. Be very careful—dropping a plate heavily into the acid is a sure way of getting acid splashed into your eyes. After the plate is in the acid, make sure the acid completely covers the plate. If you aren't wearing gloves, wash your hands immediately with cold water.

Look at the plate in the acid closely. You'll notice bubbles appearing on the exposed metal. The bubbles are liberated hydrogen gas. If they're allowed to remain, they'll retard the action of the acid on the plate (see Figure 5). To remove the bubbles from a plate coated with any ground *except* soft ground or white ground, brush a feather over the plate (see Figure 6).

Don't use a feather to remove bubbles on a plate with soft ground or white ground—the feather will pull the ground across the plate and disturb the image. You'll expose metal not intended to be exposed and cause foul biting, i.e., unplanned biting. To remove the bubbles from a soft ground, pick up one side of the plate and let the acid run off back into the tray. After all the acid has run off, lower the plate gently into the acid and immediately rinse your fingers in cold water. Another way of removing the bubbles on a soft ground is to tilt the tray if the tray is less than half full of acid (see Figure 7). Raise the tray gently until the acid no longer covers the plate. Carefully put the tray down again—the acid will run back over the plate and remove the bubbles.

White ground is unique because the ground itself is penetrated by the acid: in the areas where the ground is thin, the acid penetrates and bites quickly; in the areas where the ground is heavily applied, the acid doesn't penetrate enough to affect the plate and therefore some areas of the plate remain unbitten. Leave a plate with white ground in the acid as long as the bubbles are evenly distributed. Allow the biting to progress undisturbed until the acid fumes in one or more areas of the plate. Then lift the plate from the tray. Once you remove the plate from the acid, you can't replace it in the acid—the movement of the acid as the plate is lifted destroys the surface of the ground.

The steel plate will bubble in the nitric acid bath just as the zinc plate will— treat both plates the same way. However, you'll notice a brown residue when the bubbles are removed from a steel plate. Avoid breathing these fumes—they're more noxious than hydrogen gas. When the entire bath appears brown, make a new acid solution for steel.

After you've noticed and removed the bubbles from your plate, study the progress of the biting. Remember that acid bites quickly when the day is warm—the same acid will bite more slowly on a cold day. Furthermore, every time a plate is put into the acid, the acid becomes weaker—timing a plate for the depth of the bite is useless. After a while you'll see that when nitric acid is bubbling quickly, the plate is biting faster than when the bubbles form more slowly.

As the plate bites, make sure that there aren't any areas that are bubbling or biting that weren't planned to do so. This is foul biting, or false biting, the same kind of unwanted biting you would get if you brushed soft ground with a feather. If foul biting occurs, remove the plate from the acid, rinse it off, and blot it dry with a paper towel. Stop out the areas that shouldn't be bitten (see Chapter 7), and replace the plate in the acid. Let the acid bite until the lines are as deep as you want them to be.

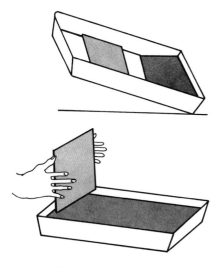

Figure 7. Tilt the tray, top, or lift the plate out of the acid, bottom, to remove the bubbles.

When you're satisfied, or think you're satisfied, with the depth of the bite, remove the plate from the acid. Put your hands into the acid, grasp opposite sides of the plate firmly, and lift it up. Tilt the plate so that all of the acid runs back into the tray. Then place the plate immediately in the tray filled with water or wash the plate under running water, and wash your hands also. Never allow acid to remain on your hands or on the plate after you remove the plate from the acid tray. Acid dripped around a studio is destructive to tools, paper, and other plates; if you leave it on your skin, it will burn. Remove acid from any surface—clothing, plates, or skin—by washing with cold water.

To test the depth of the bite, insert a drypoint needle into the bitten area. You can feel the depth of the bite by pressing the needle gently against the side of the depression made by the acid. The needle will catch in the roughened plate. Note that while a zinc plate appears silvery when bitten, the lines in a steel plate appear very dark.

You may not have to remove a plate with aquatint from the acid at all to test for depth. If you regard the plate as a mirror which catches the reflection of the light in the room (see Figure 8), you can see the texture clearly with practice. You'll be able to judge the degree of darkness of the area you're biting by comparing it with the tone of the area already bitten.

Please note that before you place a copper plate in a nitric acid bath, you should immerse a small piece of copper or a copper penny in the solution until the acid turns slightly blue. Dispose of this bath for copper when the color turns dense blue.

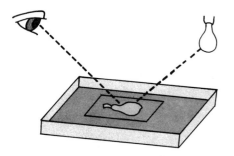

Figure 8. If you catch the reflection of the light on the aquatinted plate when it's in the acid, you can see the texture clearly.

PREPARING THE PLATE WITH CONTACT PAPER

You can use a strong nitric acid bath to bite shapes out of a zinc plate if you cover the plate with contact paper. You can either bite shapes out of already bitten plates—if you want to isolate a certain area—or you can bite new plates into round, oval, or freeform shapes (see Figures 9 and 10). These plates can be printed just as though they were square. The basic method is to cover the plate with contact paper, cut a line with a razor blade around the area you want to isolate or the shape you want to create, and bite that line all the way through in strong acid. Should you want to print different areas of a plate in different colors, one area could be separated from another this way.

Materials and Equipment
zinc plate
powdered cleanser
sponge
scissors
transparent, white, or solid color contact paper
single-edged razor blade or X-acto knife
press set up for printing
drypoint needle
rosin stopout and brush
pencil

Process. Scrub the plate with cleanser and a sponge, rinse the cleanser off completely, and dry the plate thoroughly. Cut the contact paper 1″ larger than the plate on all

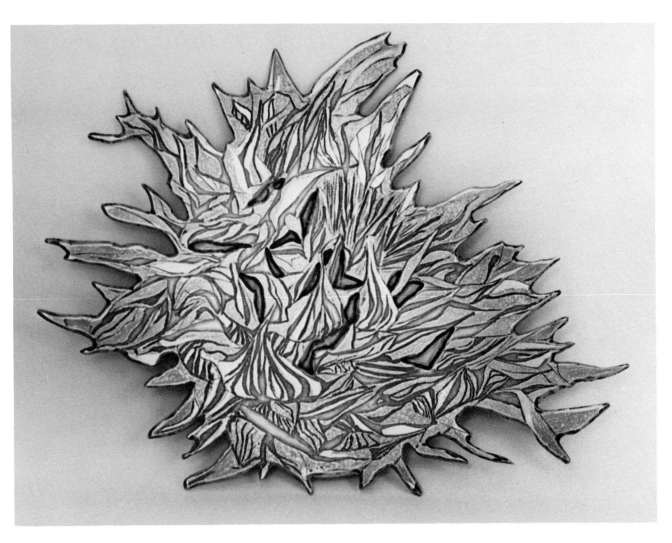

Figure 9 (above). Plate that was bitten in acid to form the shape.

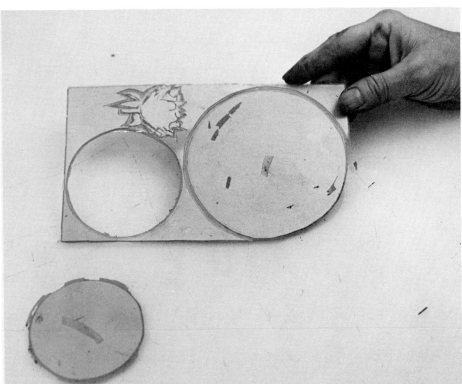

Figure 10 (right). Several shapes can be bitten from one plate. Each shape is then treated as an individual plate or combined with other plates to make a print.

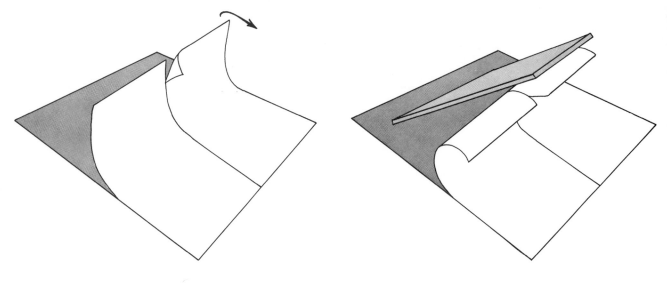

Figure 11. Protective paper pulled half the way down, away from the sticky side of the contact paper.

Figure 12. One edge of the plate placed surface down on the sticky side of the contact paper.

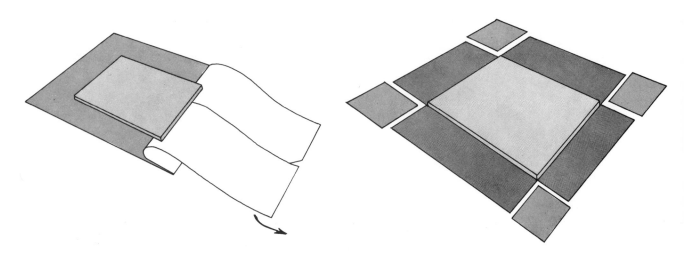

Figure 13. While the plate rests on the contact paper, you pull the rest of the protective paper away.

Figure 14. When the plate lies face down on the sticky side of the contact paper, use a single-edged razor blade to cut a square out of each corner.

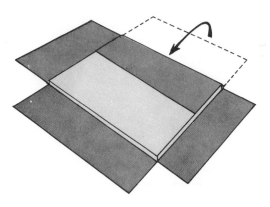

Figure 15. Bend each flap over the back of the plate.

sides. For example, if your plate is 9″ x 12″, cut the contact paper 11″ x 14″. Please note that if you're biting an area out of an already bitten plate, use transparent contact paper. If you're biting shapes out of an unbitten plate, solid color contact paper will suffice.

Place the contact paper, with the protective paper face up, on a flat surface. Peel the protective paper half the way down (see Figure 11). Then place the plate, with its surface facing down, on top of the contact paper 1″ from the top and from either side (see Figure 12). With the plate on top of the contact paper, pull the protective paper down further so that the plate makes contact with the glue on the contact paper (see Figure 13). Finish pulling off the protective paper—the plate should then be lying flat on the sticky side of the contact paper.

Now cut a square out of each corner with a single-edged razor blade (see Figure 14). Bend each flap down so that it wraps around the edges of the plate (see Figure 15).

Place the plate on the bed of the press, with the contact paper facing up. Roll the plate through the press—use as much pressure as if you were printing. When you remove the plate from the press bed, look at the surface to see if there are bubbles in the contact paper. If there are, prick them with a drypoint needle *without touching the plate.* Rub the contact paper with your finger over the holes to remove the air trapped by the bubbles. Then stop out the holes made in the contact paper by the drypoint needle unless they're in the area that will be bitten away by the acid.

Take a pencil and draw the shape that you wish to bite on the surface of the contact paper. Use the single-edged razor blade or the X-acto knife to cut along the line you have drawn. Then cut another line ¼″ outside the first line (see Figure 16). Peel off the ¼″ strip of contact paper surrounding the shape (see Figure 17). This will leave a ribbon of unprotected plate for the acid to bite.

BITING THE SHAPED PLATE

You'll put the zinc plate covered with contact paper in a *strong* nitric acid bath to bite an odd shape (see previous section). The acid will eventually bite down to the protective coating on the back of the plate—this may take 8 hours or even longer, depending on the temperature of the acid, the temperature of the air, and how much the acid has been used previously. (The warmer the acid and the air and the less the acid has been used, the faster the biting action.)

Materials and Equipment
zinc plate prepared with contact paper (see previous section)
strong nitric acid bath
tray of cold water or running water
gull feather
rosin stopout and brush
pliers
garden gloves
tin shears
fine and rough bastard files
denatured alcohol

Process. Place the prepared plate in the strong nitric acid bath. Feather it every ½ hour or so to remove the bubbles and the residue that will form on the plate.

Remove the plate from the acid from time to time to see that the acid isn't biting under the contact paper and to see if there are any scratches in the acid-resistant backcoat that may be biting. If you don't stop out these scratches, you may bite your plate through in the wrong spot. Rinse the plate in cold water and dry it thoroughly before you apply stopout to any area where there's unwanted biting—stopout won't adhere to a wet plate.

When the color of the back coat of the plate begins to appear in some areas, the acid has sufficiently bitten through the plate. This doesn't necessarily happen evenly all over the plate at once, but when you see a fairly large area of backcoat showing through, put on gloves, remove the plate, and place it in cold water. *Always wear gloves when you do this*—plates that are bitten through in acid have razor-sharp edges.

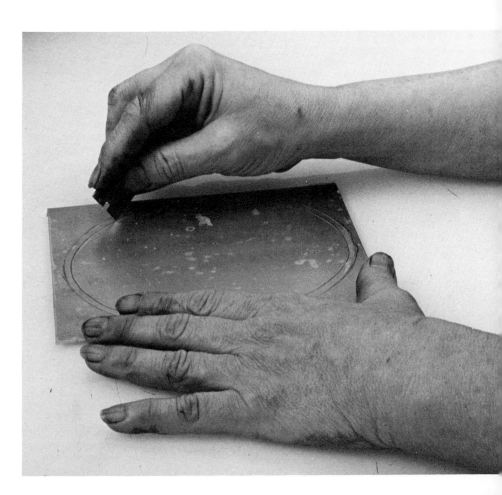

Figure 16. Cut a ¼" wide strip around the shape to be bitten in the acid.

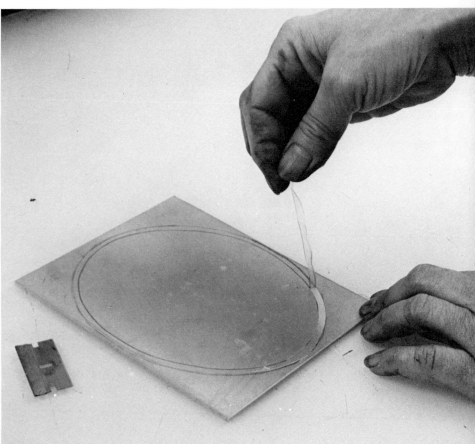

Figure 17. Peel the ¼" strip of contact paper away from the plate.

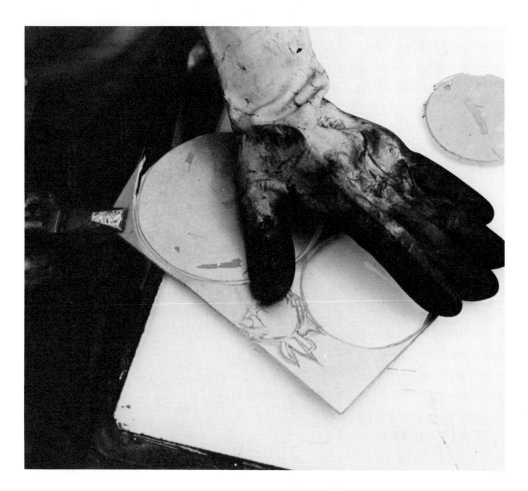

Figure 18. Pliers are used to separate the plates. Note the gloves worn to protect the hands from the sharp edges of the plate.

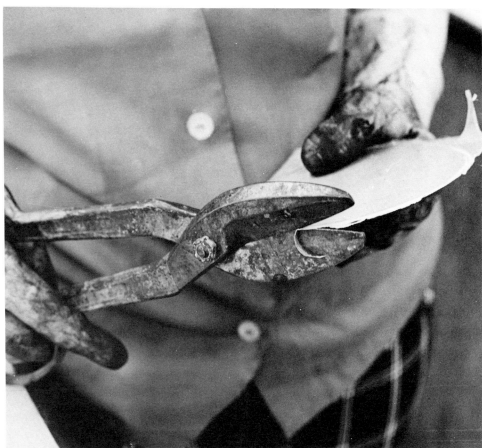

Figure 19. Cut the thin sharp edges of the plate with tin shears.

Bend the part of the plate you wish to separate with pliers, moving it up and down until it comes off (see Figure 18). If some parts of the plate separate but other parts don't, stop out the edges of the separated areas so that they won't bite further, and replace the plate in the acid.

After you've separated all parts of the plate surrounding the shape that you're biting, you must remove the sharp edges. Still wearing gloves, begin by trimming the thin excess plate with tin shears (see Figure 19). Then bevel the plate with a coarse bastard file. Remove *all* the sharp edges before beveling with finer files.

Remove the contact paper. It should come off easily, but if it doesn't, pour on alcohol to soften the glue in the areas that stick. When the contact paper is removed, the plate is ready for further biting or printing.

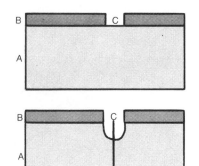

Figure 20. Top, copper plate (A) before biting, coated with ground (B) leaving exposed metal (C). Bottom, same plate (A) after biting. The acid bites the exposed metal (C) straight down.

BITING A COPPER PLATE WITH DUTCH MORDANT

When you use Dutch mordant to bite a copper plate, the result is a very accurate bite because, unlike nitric acid baths, Dutch mordant bites straight down (see Figure 20). Dutch mordant doesn't bubble, and it bites more slowly than nitric acid. The lines don't widen from the action of this acid, as they do from the action of nitric acid (see Figure 4). Finally, the bitten areas of the copper plate appear darker than the plate while the plate is in the acid in contrast to zinc, which appears lighter when bitten.

Materials and Equipment
copper plate
acid tray filled with Dutch mordant
tray of water or running water
drypoint needle
rosin stopout and brushes
rubber gloves (optional)

Process. Lift your copper plate from underneath or by the edges and place it in the Dutch mordant. Wash your fingers with cold water.

After 30 minutes remove your plate from the Dutch mordant and wash the plate and your hands in cold water. Take your drypoint needle and gently feel the depth of the bite by inserting the needle into the depressions created by the acid. If you would like the bite to be deeper, put the plate back into the acid for 10 minutes. Then take the plate out again, rinse it off, and test for depth with the drypoint needle. Do this every 10 minutes until you're satisfied with the bite.

Since Dutch mordant doesn't bubble, you can't observe foul biting easily. Close inspection, however, may show you the little points of dark in the ground which indicate foul biting. If so, remove the plate, wash it in cold water, blot it dry with a paper towel, and apply stopout to the questionable areas. When the stopout is tacky, replace the plate in the acid until it's finished biting.

DISPOSING OF USED ACID

The action of the acid on metal removes particles of metal from the plate. The metal then becomes part of the acid bath. The more the acid bath is used, the less effective the acid becomes. You can test the strength of any nitric acid bath by dropping a tiny pinch of bicarbonate of soda into a cupful of the acid. If there's a violent bubbling action, the acid bath is still usable. If there's a gentle fizzing, discard the acid bath. You can tell when Dutch mordant shouldn't be used any more because the solution turns milky. Nitric acid used to bite copper turns dense blue when it becomes useless; nitric acid used to bite steel turns completely brown when it's time to throw it out.

Materials and Equipment
used acid
running water
bicarbonate of soda
small glass or plastic jar with a plastic, acid-proof cover

Process. For used nitric acid, the first step is to neutralize the acid bath by pouring in bicarbonate of soda until the fizzing action stops, rendering the acid harmless. Then turn on the cold water tap and *slowly* pour the neutralized acid down the drain. This won't harm the pipes or the sewer system. However, if you have a septic tank or cesspool, pour the neutralized acid outside on the ground where you don't expect anything to grow.

Before neutralizing and disposing of Dutch mordant, pour about 2 oz. of the used mordant into a small plastic or glass bottle with a plastic acid-proof cover. You'll use this later when you add it to freshly made, unused Dutch mordant. Add bicarbonate of soda to the rest of the Dutch mordant to be on the safe side and then pour it slowly down the sink while running cold water.

Cleanup

1. Put away your acid to avoid evaporation. If you're leaving the acid in the tray, be sure to cover the tray. If you're putting the acid back into its bottle, place the acid bottle in the sink, and turn on the cold water tap. Turn on the extractor fan, place a funnel in the bottle, and pour the acid from the tray into the storage bottle. Be sure to seal the bottle, rinse the tray and funnel with cold water, and put all materials away.

2. Throw all rags, newspaper, and paper towels soaked with grounds and solvents into a metal garbage can with a metal cover. You can keep the waste can in the studio overnight, but it's wiser to remove all combustible materials from the studio every night.

ACID BATH CHART

BATH	GROUNDS TO BE BITTEN
Weak nitric bath for zinc 9 parts water 1 part nitric acid, 　　ACS commercial grade	aquatints hard ground—fine lines and crosshatching white ground
Medium nitric bath for zinc 6 parts water 1 part nitric acid	coarse-grain aquatint lift ground soft ground
Strong nitric bath for zinc 4 parts water 1 part nitric acid	hard ground or asphaltum—embossing, open biting, and viscosity methods
Strong nitric bath for copper 4 parts water 1 part nitric acid	asphaltum—deep biting on copper
Nitric bath for steel 12 parts water 1 part nitric acid	all grounds on steel
Dutch mordant 2 oz. potassium chlorate crystals 88 oz. warm water 10 oz. hydrochloric acid 2 oz. old Dutch mordant or a copper penny	all grounds on copper

WHAT WENT WRONG AND WHY

Problem	Cause	Solution
The lines I drew on a hard ground didn't bite evenly. The fine, widely spaced lines are very shallow, while the wider lines or lines drawn close together are quite deep.	The bubbling action of the acid will heat the acid in an area where there's a lot of exposed metal such as an area with wide lines or with lines drawn close together. On that same plate, a single line drawn in a large area of ground will bubble very slowly, and the acid will generate very little heat. Warm acid bites more quickly than cold acid, so the wide lines or lines drawn close together will end up deeper than a single line if they're all bitten for the same amount of time.	To increase the depth of bite in the fine lines without biting the rest of the plate, remove the plate from the acid when the coarse lines are bitten to your satisfaction. Wash the plate in cold water, and pat the surface dry with a paper towel. Stop out the lines that are already as deep as you want them to be. Wait for the stopout to become tacky, and replace the plate in the acid until the fine lines are deep enough.
The acid is biting well, but there are bits of material floating in the acid. They cling to the soft ground, causing spots on the textured areas to remain unbitten.	White ground or lift ground will sometimes leave particles of ground in the acid.	Since the acid is biting well, you should strain it. Arrange several layers of cheesecloth in a funnel, and place the funnel in the acid bottle. Pour the acid back into the bottle through the layers of cheesecloth which will act as a strainer.
After I used some acid to bite plates, I stored it for a while. Now that acid seems stronger than it was when I originally made it.	Some of the water in the acid bath must have evaporated, causing the acid to bite more quickly.	Add water to dilute the acid. Next time, be sure the plastic cap is screwed on tight before you store the bottle.
The acid bath seems to be biting very slowly. I would like to add more pure acid to make the bath stronger.	Either the acid is too weak for the kind of biting you're doing or it has been used too long. Particles of metal are absorbed into the acid with each biting—eventually the acid can't absorb any more metal and therefore it will no longer bite. If you add pure acid to dead acid, the dead acid will absorb the pure acid quickly without improving the strength of the acid.	Make a new acid bath. If your old acid is really dead, throw it out. If, on the other hand, it's merely weak, use it as a weak acid bath.
The nitric acid crystalized on a very cold day.	The crystalization was caused by a combination of the large amount of metal in the acid and the cold weather.	Throw the crystals down the sink while running cold water.
When I beveled the plate that was cut out in the acid, I had a difficult time getting a smooth edge.	The acid bites very irregularly.	Place the plate face down on the table, and bevel the back and sides of the plate until there are no sharp edges. Then turn the plate over, and bevel the top surface.

PART THREE
Printing Techniques

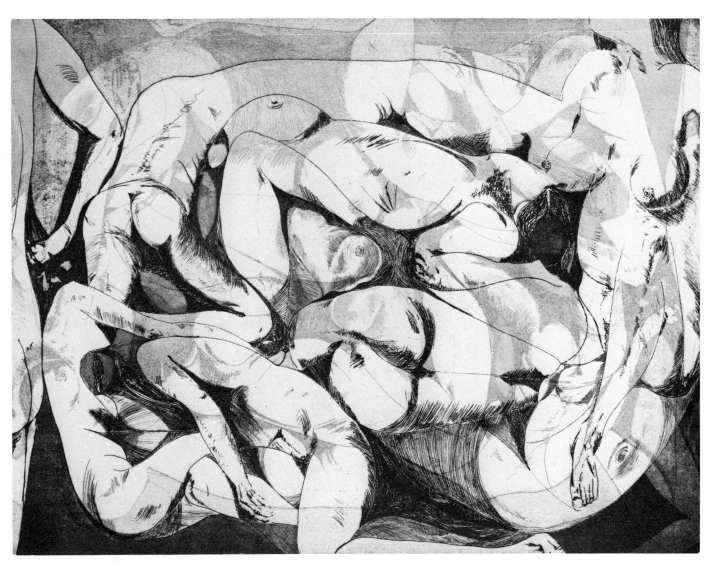

Juxtaposed *by Don Aronson. Intaglio, 18″ x 24″. Hard and soft grounds.*

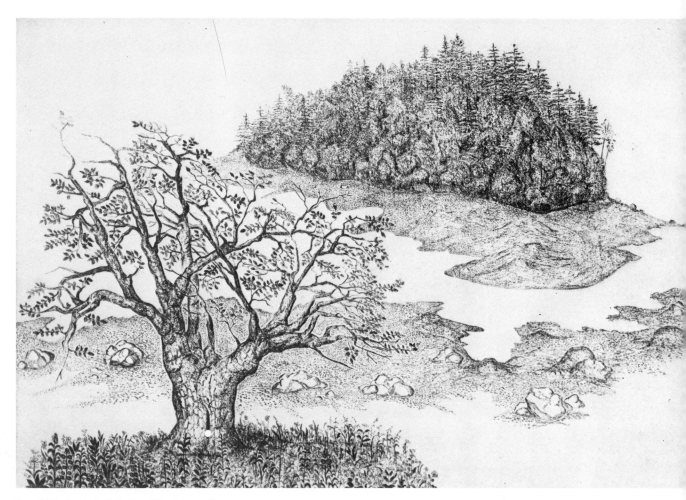

Low Tide *by Aida Whedon. Hard ground.*

One Moment *by Jackie Friedman.*
Figure printed with the viscosity method
at the same time as the rectangular plate.

Seed Pushing *(below) by Krishna Reddy.*
Intaglio and engraving.
Viscosity and aquatint print.

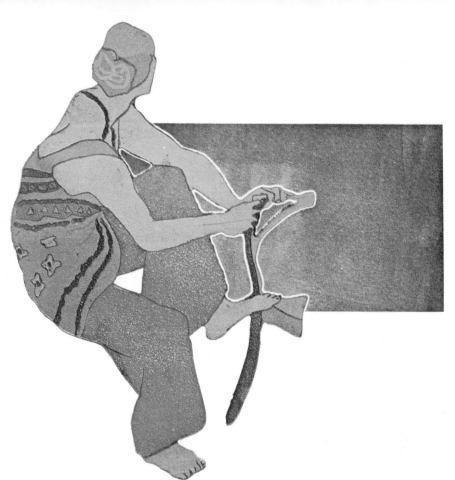

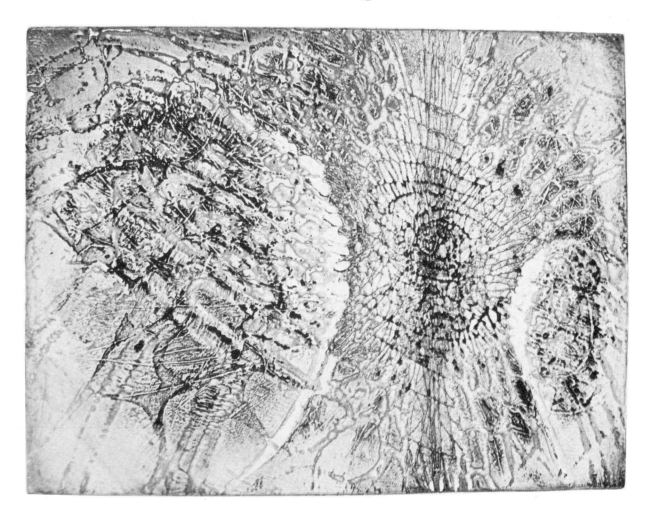

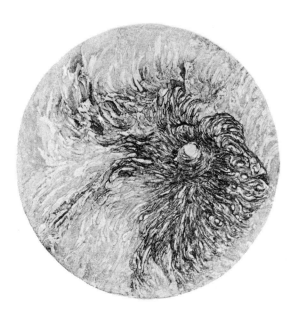

Sea Anemone *by Helen Quat.*
Intaglio, 16" diameter.
Viscosity print with aquatint.

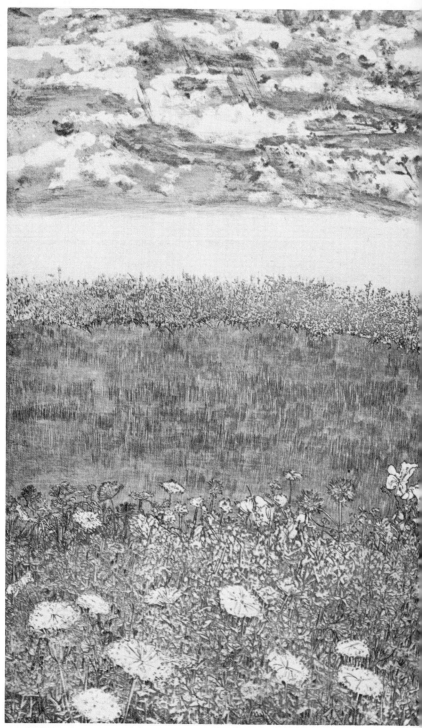

Between the Earth and Sky *by Ruth Leaf. Double intaglio with two plates, each 30" x 20*

Enclosures and Apertures #2 *(top right) by Lois Polansky. Intaglio, 19½" x 27½".*
Three plates, the largest (the wall fragment) printed with the viscosity method.

Anemone *(right) by Elaine Orens. Double intaglio with one plate, 18" x 26".*
Indian yellow printed first, then black.

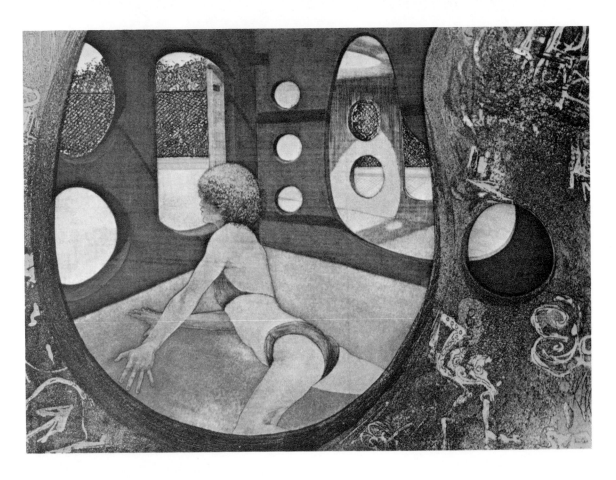

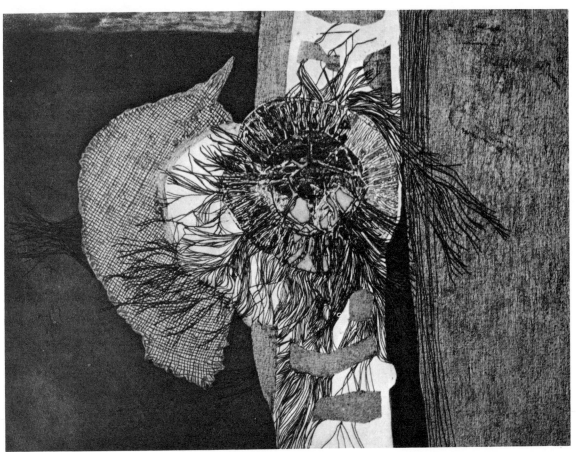

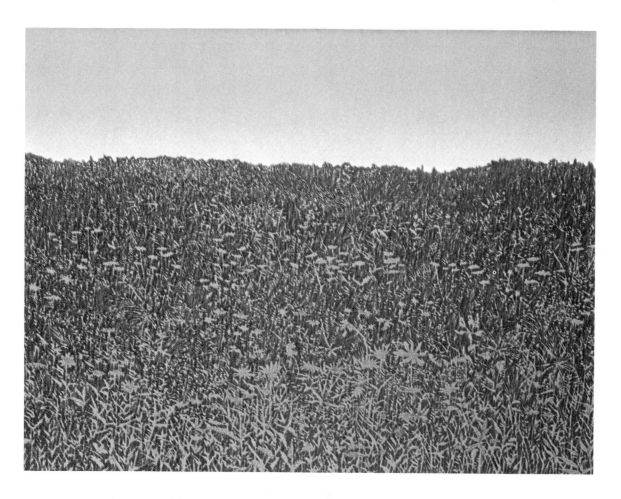

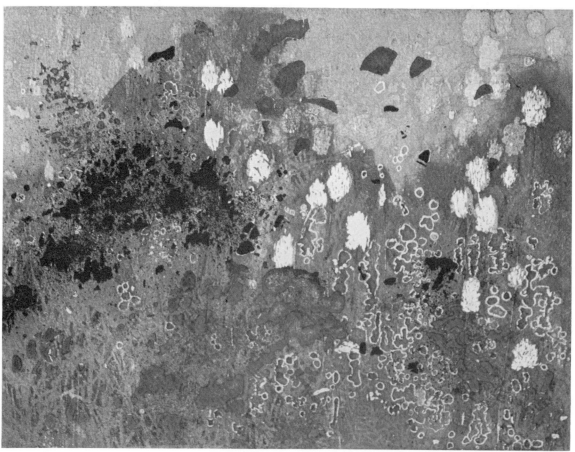

Field and Sky *(left) by Ruth Leaf.*
Intaglio, 18" x 24". Printed
first in relief with two surface
colors on the roller, and then
reprinted in intaglio. (Reproduced
in color on inside front cover.)

Moon Walk *(right) by Selene Yarnell.*
Multi-plate collagraph, 17" x 17".

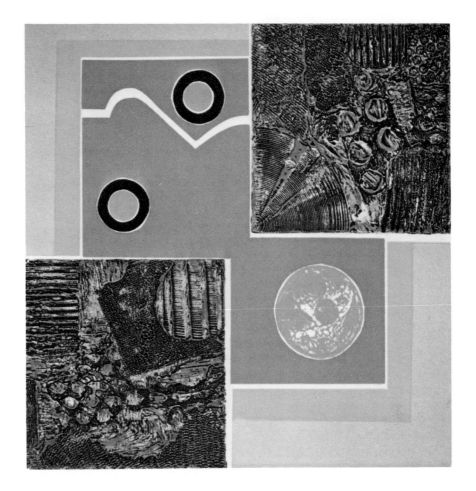

Wild Flowers *(left) by Joan Johns.*
Intaglio, 18" x 24". Two plates,
one inked in green and cobalt blue,
and the other with flowers inked
in red and yellow. (Reproduced in
color on inside front cover.)

Conception *(right) by Anna London.*
Intaglio, 24" x 24". Five
plates printed in three stages
with a combination of surface rolls
and intaglio colors. (Reproduced
in color on back cover.)

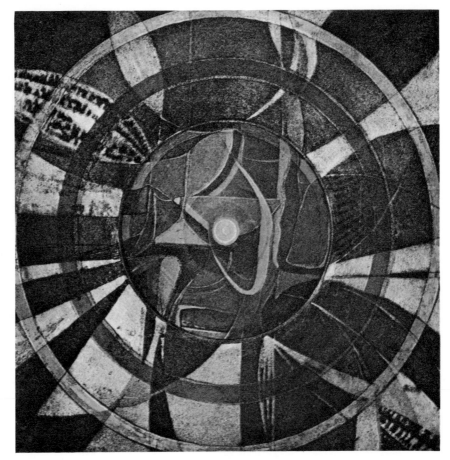

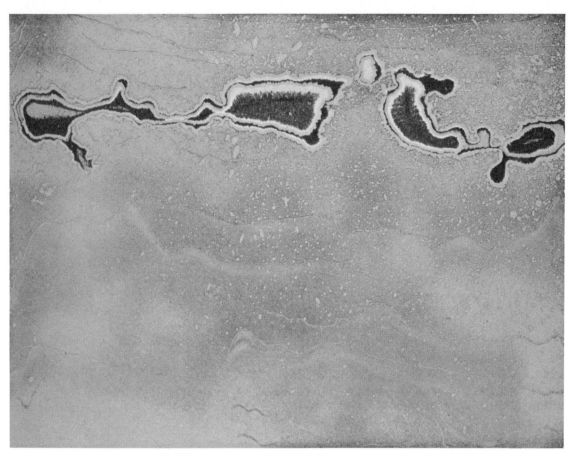

Cloudburst *by Ellen Zeifer. Intaglio, 18" x 24". Viscosity print made with yellow intaglio, blue hard (oily) roll, and red soft (dry) roll.*

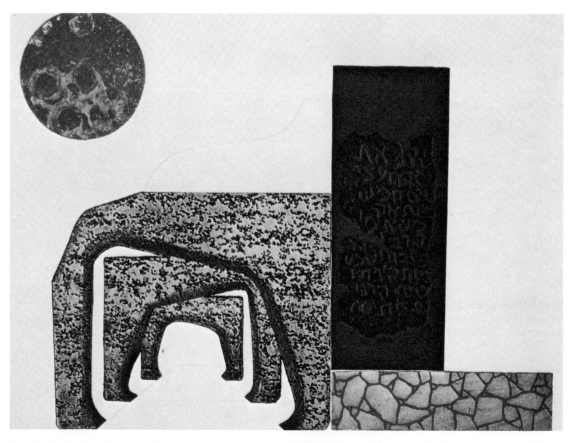

The Shrine *by Rina Rothholz. Tuilegraph. Separate pieces of tile in white relief and inked in black, orange, and blue, printed in two groups.*

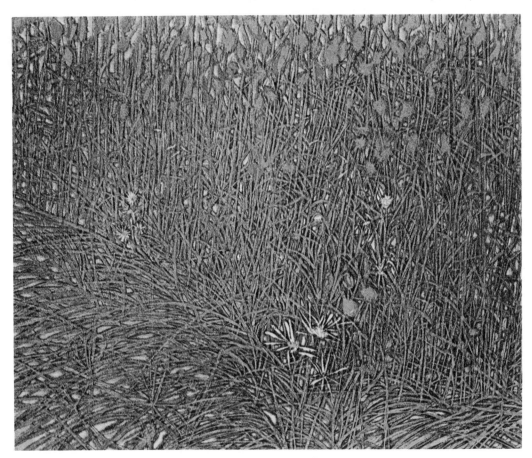

Salt Marsh *by Ruth Leaf. Intaglio, 15" x 18". Viscosity print with aquatint.*

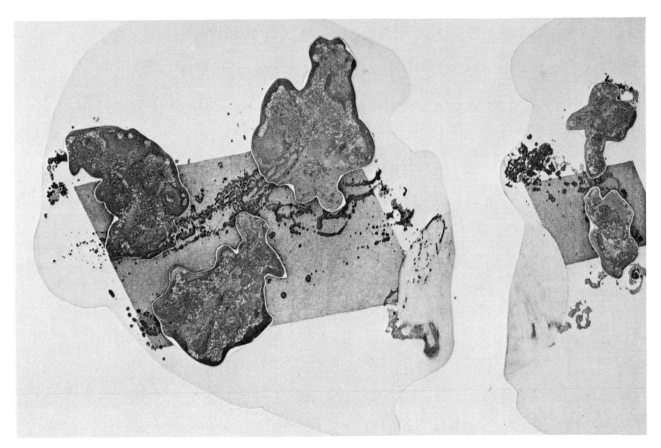

Quamasia *by Barbara Press. Five smaller plates placed inside two larger green plates and printed with the viscosity method.*

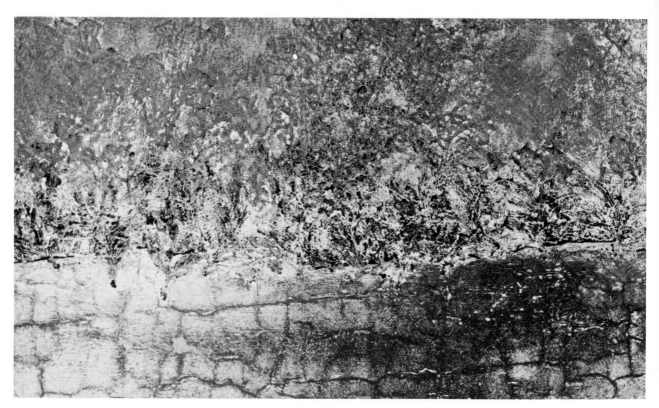

Garden Wall *by Florence Levine. Collagraph, 10¾" x 18½". Plate made of flower-shaped tarlatan and insulation paper glued to cardboard. (Reproduced in color on inside back cover.)*

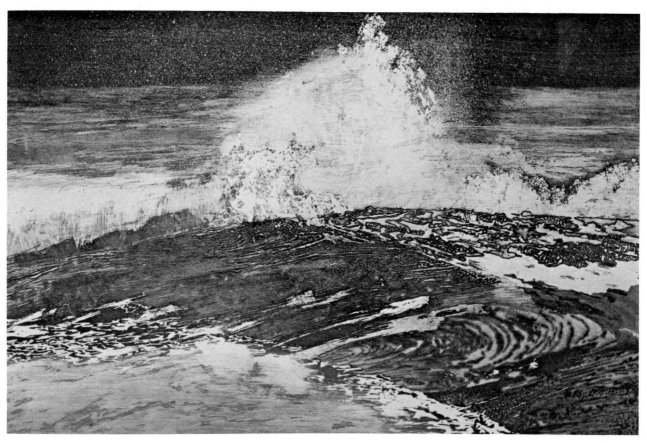

Restless Tide *by Shirley Roman. Intaglio, 18" x 28". Plate made combining soft ground, asphaltum, lift ground, and white ground. (Reproduced in color on inside back cover.)*

THIRTEEN

Basic Printing

An intaglio print is the impression on paper of a bitten plate that has been inked, wiped clean, and rolled through a press under heavy pressure with a piece of damp paper laid on its surface. The pressure of the press forces the damp paper, backed by soft felt blankets, into the lines or grooves of the plate. (See Chapter 3 for information on papers and how to dampen them.) The paper molds itself to the shape of the plate and picks up the ink deposited in the bitten areas. When the ink and paper dry, they become bonded together permanently; a well-cared-for print will last for hundreds of years.

SETTING THE PRESSURE

To obtain a good print, the pressure of the press must be evenly distributed over the entire plate. You should use three wool felt blankets to act as a cushion between the steel roller and the surface of the plate. They serve also to push the paper into the lines and grooves of the plate. For more information on blankets, see Chapter 4.

Materials and Equipment
press
two 1/16″ wool felt printing blankets
one 1/8″ pure wool felt printing pusher blanket
zinc, copper, or steel plate with well-beveled edges
blotters
water
sponge

Process. Place the plate to be printed between the roller and the bed of the press (see Figure 1). You should be able to move the press bed with the plate on it freely beneath the roller. Slide the plate under the press roller from side to side, making sure that both sides of the roller are at an equal distance from the bed of the press.

Lift off the plate and roll or pull the bed out to its full length on one side of the press. Place the two 1/16″ blankets on the bed, and then lay the 1/8″ blanket on top of them. Please note that it's easier to engage the blankets in the press if you don't line them up precisely on top of one another (see Figure 2). To engage the blankets with a press that has a rack-driven bed, turn the handle of the press until the blankets are under the roller. With a friction-driven press, you must push the end of the bed with one hand and turn the handle of the press with the other to get the blankets under the roller. After you do this, place the free ends of the blanket over the roller to clear the bed for the plate and the paper (see Figure 3).

Place your uninked plate face up in the center of the bed of the press. To test the evenness of the pressure, take a used blotter, dampen it by patting both sides with a clean wet sponge, and place it over the uninked plate. Pull the blankets down on top of the plate and blotter—to be sure there are no wrinkles in the blanket, pull each one taut.

Roll the plate and the blotter through the press. You should feel a slight resistance when the roller mounts the plate, but if the pressure is set correctly, it shouldn't be hard to turn the handle of the press. Remember, too much pressure is as undesirable as not enough pressure.

When you finish rolling the plate through the press, pick up the blankets and get them out of the way by placing them up over the roller again. Remove the blotter and look carefully at the impression of the plate embossed on it. The plate mark (the edges of the plate) should be equally embossed on all four sides; the lines and grooves on the plate should also be visible.

If the embossing on the blotter is uneven, then the pressure of the roller is lighter on one side. Tighten the screw on the side where the pressure is lighter. If the embossing is very deep and the blotter is shiny on one side, there's too much pressure—loosen the screw on that side. Turn the handle of the screw clockwise to tighten the pressure and counter-clockwise to loosen it. If your press has screws with micrometer heads, you should follow the same process for setting pressure with one difference—you can start with both sides of the roller at an equal distance from the bed. When you have set the pressure correctly, make sure that both micrometers read the same.

When you've finished your adjustments, make another test run with the blotter. Repeat the whole process as many times as necessary until the blotter shows all the lines and grooves of the uninked plate. You may have to take a new blotter after you've rolled it through the press several times if it becomes difficult to judge the depth of the embossing. You'll see the result of care taken in these preparatory steps of the printing process in the higher quality of the finished print.

PREPARING TARLATAN

Tarlatan as purchased contains a lot of starch and is too stiff to use on the plate. You must remove some of the starch to soften the tarlatan before you use it.

Materials and Equipment
1½ to 3 yds. tarlatan
garden or plastic gloves

Process. When you use the tarlatan, it should be shaped like a pad that fits comfortably in the palm of your hand (see Figure 4). You should prepare three balls of tarlatan at a time. If you have a large hand, cut three lengths of tarlatan 1 yd. each; if you have a small hand, cut the tarlatan into ½ yd. lengths.

Put on plastic or garden gloves if your hands are sensitive. Hold the tarlatan in both fists and scrub it vigorously against itself to remove some of the starch, just as if you were scrubbing an article of clothing to remove dirt, until the whole piece of the tarlatan is softened.

Shake the excess starch out of the tarlatan, and repeat the process with the other two pieces. Then crumple all three pieces of tarlatan into a ball that fits comfortably in the palm of your hand. Make the bottom of the ball flat and smooth.

HEATING AND INKING THE PLATE

The reason some printmakers heat their plate before inking is that a warm plate will permit the heavy intaglio ink to flow more easily into the lines and grooves than a cold plate will. Although it's not absolutely necessary to heat your plate, remember that it is necessary to add raw (not boiled) linseed oil to the ink to make it the proper consistency for printing.

Materials and Equipment
zinc, copper, or steel plate
black intaglio ink
raw linseed oil
dauber or small pieces of tarlatan
pieces of cut cardboard
hot plate, heated
palette knife
¼" plate glass or marble slab
newspaper

Process. Spread out some newspaper, and place a glass or marble slab and your plate next to each other on top of them. Remember that your inking area should be next to the hot plate (see Chapter 5).

Put some ink on the marble slab or glass, pick some of it up with your palette knife, and let it drop back to the glass. The ink should run off the knife very slowly in an unbroken stream. If it remains on the knife in a solid mass, add a few drops of raw linseed oil to the ink. Mix the ink and oil thoroughly with the palette knife with a grinding movement, and then test it again. Keep adding more raw linseed oil until the ink drops slowly and evenly from the knife to the slab.

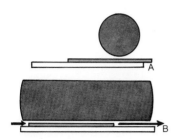

Figure 1. To be sure the roller is parallel to the bed, place the plate between the roller and the bed (A), and move it from one side to the other (B).

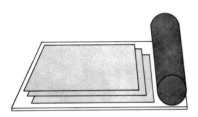

Figure 2. To engage blankets under the roller, stagger them as shown.

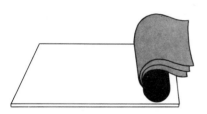

Figure 3. Blankets thrown over the roller to clear the bed of the press.

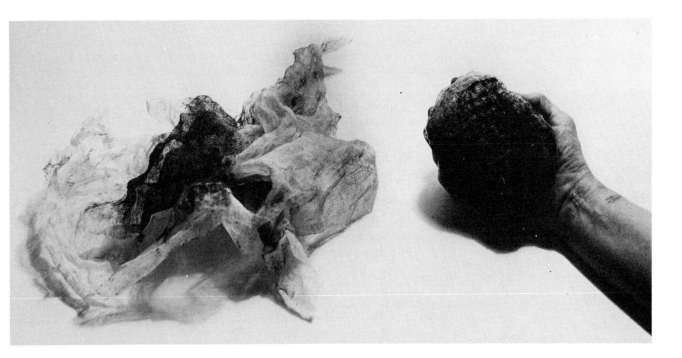

Figure 4. Piece of tarlatan, left, shaped into a flat pad held comfortably in the hand, right.

When the ink is ready, place your plate on the hot plate until its surface is warm to the touch—then remove the plate and put it back on the newspapers.

Put a blob of ink on the plate with the palette knife or a piece of cut cardboard. If you use the knife, take care not to scratch the plate. Whichever you use, the next step is to take one end of a piece of cardboard and push the ink back and forth across the entire plate. Push in all directions until the plate is covered with an excessive amount of ink. If the plate has cooled, place it on the hot plate again—during the inking process, the plate should always be warm. The exceptions to this rule are plates bitten with a very shallow or fine texture, such as a very fine aquatint or silk on a soft ground. These plates will produce a richer print if, after you apply ink to the warm plate, you let the plate cool before wiping with tarlatan. The cool plate will retain more ink than a warm one during the wiping process and you run less danger of wiping off too much ink.

After you have spread the ink on the plate with the cardboard, use the dauber or a piece of rolled-up tarlatan to rub it with a circular motion into the lines and grooves of the plate. There should be no uninked plate showing—if the plate does show through, zinc and steel will look silvery, while copper will appear golden-red.

When the plate is completely covered with ink, take a clean piece of cut cardboard and carefully scrape the surface of the plate to remove the excess ink. Put the excess ink back onto the glass or marble slab which was used for mixing ink—this ink can be used again and shouldn't be wasted. Continue to remove the ink until you've taken off as much as possible.

WIPING THE PLATE

When you use tarlatan, you'll wipe the surface of the plate without taking the ink out of the lines and grooves.

Materials and Equipment
inked plate
3 softened tarlatans
clean lint-free cloth
newspaper
gloves
hot plate
tableau paper or an old telephone book

Process. After you finish spreading ink on your plate, change the newspaper underneath—keep the area where you wipe as clean as possible. Then begin your first wipe. If you plan to use gloves to keep your hand clean—you don't have to do this—then put them on now. Also, if your plate has become cold and you want it warm for wiping, put it back on the hot plate. When your plate is warm, pick a tarlatan. You can save tarlatan from one printing session to another if it's not stiff with dry ink—the best tarlatan for the first wipe is one that has been used before and already contains some ink.

With the tarlatan in the palm of your hand, rub the surface of the plate in a circular motion. Press down onto the plate to push the ink into the lines. When the bottom of the tarlatan becomes saturated with ink, open the piece up and fold it again into a pad. The part you wipe with should be somewhat dry and able to pick up ink.

When the ink on the surface of the plate is evenly distributed, turn the plate over on the newspaper so that the inked surface lies face down. Wipe the back of the plate with a clean cloth—not the used tarlatan—until it's free of ink. Then remove the dirty newspaper and place the plate, inked side up, on a clean piece of newspaper.

For your second wipe, take a fairly clean piece of tarlatan and again wipe the plate with a circular motion, going first clockwise and then counter-clockwise all over the plate. Be sure to wipe every inch of the plate or the print will appear spotty or dirty. Apply less pressure for this second wipe than you did for the first wipe. As the bottom of the pad of tarlatan becomes saturated with ink, refold it as you did before.

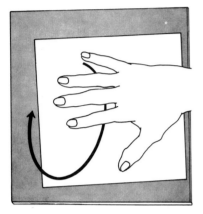

Figure 5. Tableau paper placed on the plate and moved in circular motion with gentle pressure.

At this point in the wiping process, you should paper-wipe your plate if you want very little plate tone. This step isn't always necessary when printing with black ink, but it's very helpful in color printing since color inks are harder to wipe. To paper-wipe your plate, place a piece of tableau paper (domestic woodcut paper) on the plate. Put your palm flat on top of the paper, press down slightly, and rotate your palm and the piece of paper gently over the whole plate (see Figure 5). When the paper is full of ink, turn it over and use the other side. If you have large tableau paper, fold it into a pad. With your thumb under one corner and your four fingers on top, rotate the pad as usual. If you have no tableau paper, you can use leaves from an old telephone book, one page at a time, in the manner described above.

Please note that you shouldn't use a paper-wipe on a plate that has been wiped cold. You wipe a plate cold—without warming it on the hot plate—in order to leave some plate tone on the surface, while the paper-wipe removes all plate tone. One process would cancel out the other; the result would be a very poor print.

When you do the third and final tarlatan wipe, use a clean or almost clean piece of tarlatan. Wipe the plate gently in a circular motion—if you apply too much pressure, you'll wipe some of the ink out of the grooves and back onto the surface of the plate.

Take a clean, lint-free cloth, and wipe the four edges of your plate (see Figure 6). Be careful not to wipe beyond the bevel onto the surface of your plate. If you do, you'll remove the plate tone and the resulting print will be spotty. The plate can be printed at this point; for very delicate, lightly bitten tones, you might go on and hand-wipe the plate's surface.

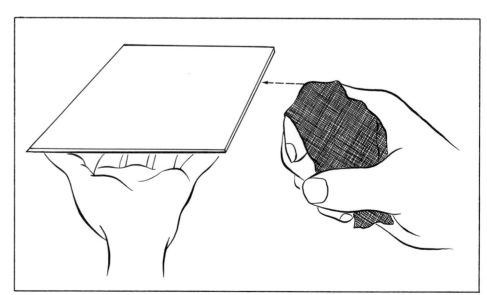

Figure 6. The beveled edges of the plate being wiped with a clean cloth.

HAND-WIPING THE PLATE

Sometimes it's inadvisable to use the paper-wipe (if you want a light, even plate tone on the surface—usually with an aquatint or engraving), or it's difficult to remove the halos or fuzzy tones around the lines (see Figure 7) even if you use the tarlatan diligently. Also, it isn't possible to get all the tone off an aquatint with tarlatan alone. In these cases a hand-wipe is used on the plate after the third tarlatan wipe.

Materials and Equipment
inked plate that has been wiped with tarlatan
talcum powder
clean cloth

Process. Place the plate on a flat surface. Gently pass the heel of your palm over the entire plate (see Figure 8)—start the sweeping motion off the plate to one side and end *off* the other side of the plate. If you stop moving on the plate, you'll leave a mark. While you're hand-wiping, you should hear a light and dry sound: if you hear a squeak, you're applying too much pressure.

After the first sweeping motion, put some talc on your palm; then wipe your hand on a clean cloth to remove the ink and the talc. Turn the plate and repeat the first sweeping motion. Do this at least three times (see Figure 8). After each wipe, remove the ink on your palm with talc, and clean the talc off with a cloth. Try not to get talc on the plate because the result will be a spotty print.

BLOTTING THE PAPER

The paper for printing should be damp and feel cold to the touch. You'll have to take it out of the water tray, and after you blot it, you should *not* be able to see water glisten on its surface. If you have previously dampened your paper according to the directions in Chapter 3, you may or may not have to blot your paper. If you soaked every piece of paper, you must blot each sheet before you use it; if you soaked every other piece, your paper is ready for printing without blotting.

Materials and Equipment
damp paper (see Chapter 3)
cardboard clips
blotters
rolling pin
paper towels

Process. Lift the paper out of the water tray with the cardboard clips (see Figure 9), let as much water as possible drip off into the tray, and place the paper between two blotters. Roll the rolling pin gently over the top blotter to remove the excess water. Don't use too much pressure or you'll wrinkle the paper. When you're finished with the rolling pin, the paper is ready for printing. Leave it between the blotters until your plate is on the bed of the press.

At that point if you can see water glistening on the paper, fold a clean paper towel and *gently* brush the surface of the paper so that the towel can absorb the excess water. You may have to do this even if you soaked every other piece of paper when you dampened the paper previously.

PULLING A PROOF

After you're finished inking and wiping your plate and preparing the paper, you're ready to print—the ink and the shape of the grooves in the plate will be transferred to the damp printing paper.

Materials and Equipment
inked plate
damp paper
cardboard clips
press set up for printing
clean cloth or paper towels
varnolene
hot plate

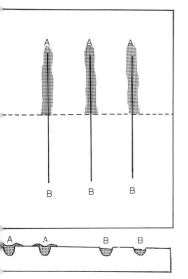

Figure 7. Diagramatic plate from above, top, and cross section, bottom. Halos of ink surround the intaglio lines (A), while the surface is clean (B) after hand-wiping.

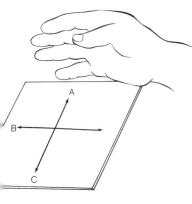

Figure 8. When hand-wiping your plate, the first sweeping motion should be from (A) to (C), the second from (B) to (D), the third from (C) to (A), the fourth from (D) to (B), and so on.

Process. To begin, rub the bed of the press with a drop of varnolene on a clean cloth or a paper towel to be sure that it's clean. Let the bed dry completely before printing.

If you want to, you can place the plate on the hot plate. Don't touch the inked surface, and heat the plate until it's warm to the touch. Try not to overheat—if you can't hold the plate comfortably in your bare hands, then it's too hot. The ink on a plate that is too hot will harden, causing the damp paper and blankets to shrink on contact, stick to the plate, and ruin the print.

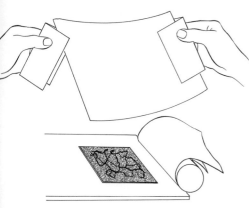

Place the plate, warm or cold, on the bed of the press with the inked surface up. If you didn't use gloves when you wiped the plate and your hands are full of ink, use cardboard clips to remove the paper from the blotters. Holding the paper on opposite sides with the clips, place it over the inked plate (see Figure 9). Be careful not to move the paper once it rests over the plate—you'll smudge the ink in the margins of your print. Now, one by one, pull the blankets down over the paper and plate. Pull each blanket taut to be sure that there are no wrinkles.

Now roll the bed through the press. You're printing!

Figure 9. Damp paper held on both sides with cardboard clips being placed over the inked plate.

After you've rolled the bed through the press, pull up the blankets, and place them out of the way over the roller. Pick up the edges of the print with the cardboard clips, and gently lift both sides simultaneously off the plate slowly until the print is free of the plate. Lay the print face up on a flat, clean surface. Never pull a print off the plate quickly—the paper may tear or wrinkle and ruin the print.

Remove the plate from the bed of the press, and clean the bed with a cloth and a few drops of varnolene. Leave the press bed dry—if you print a plate on a bed that's wet with varnolene, the varnolene will show in the margin of the print.

To print again, you must ink the plate in the manner described above. After you print for a while, the printing process should become automatic. Finally, don't clean the plate between inkings if you're using only one ink over and over again. The second print is usually richer than the first, and subsequent prints have the same richness as the second.

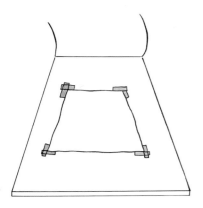

Figure 10. The four corners of the paper outlined in masking tape to register the paper on the bed of the press.

CENTERING AND REGISTERING

When you print an edition, you must center the plate within the paper and register the paper.

Materials and Equipment
press set up for printing
dry sheet of paper, the same size as the edition paper
masking tape

Process. First make sure the press bed is clean and dry. Then place the dry sheet of paper in the center of the bed. To register the paper, outline its four corners with tape (see Figure 10).

Remove the paper. The rectangle described by the tape will allow you to center your plate (see Figure 11). Leave the tape on the press throughout the printing session and remove it only when you're finished.

MAKING A COUNTERPROOF

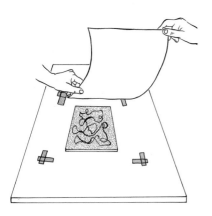

Figure 11. The plate centered within the taped rectangle.

After you've taken a first proof, you may want to make a counterproof, the reversed image of the original proof (see Figure 12). The image on the plate and the counterproof will be exactly the same. The counterproof isn't as dark as the original print, and it may lose some of the detail; but it lends valuable assistance when you need to do a lot more work on the plate. You must print a counterproof *immediately* after you pull a proof, while the ink is still wet.

Materials and Equipment
wet proof immediately after printing
a piece of chipboard or cardboard the same size as the proof paper
damp proof paper the same size as the original proof
press set up for printing

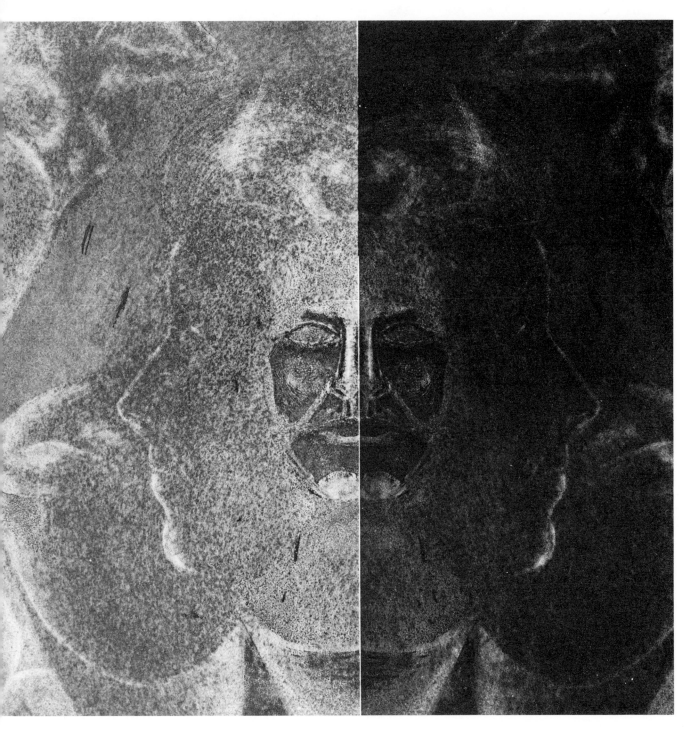

Figure 12. The proof, right, is a mirror image of the counterproof, left, and the plate. Note that the counterproof is lighter than the print from which it was taken.

Process. Place the wet proof, image up, on the bed of the press, and cover it with the dampened proof paper. Next, position the cardboard or chipboard over the two pieces of paper. Make sure the chipboard covers the paper completely so the pressure will be the same as it would be if you were printing a plate.

Pull the blankets down over the print, paper and chipboard, and roll the bed through the press. Pick the blankets up, and lay them over the roller. Remove the chipboard, and separate the two proof papers. The image on the counterproof will be exactly the same as the image on the plate; therefore the counterproof can be used as a reference when adding to or making changes on the plate.

DRYING PRINTS

If a print doesn't dry properly, it will wrinkle.

Materials and Equipment
blotters
tissue paper or newsprint
glassene (optional)
weight—piece of plate glass or heavy wooden board the size of the blotters
table

Process. After you pull your first print, place a blotter on a table or flat surface reserved for drying prints. If your hands are full of ink, use the cardboard clips and place the print, ink side up, on that blotter.

Place a piece of clean tissue paper or newsprint over the print, covering the image completely. Make sure that the tissue or newsprint is lying flat—smooth it out if necessary. Place a second blotter over the print and tissue paper or newsprint. The tissue paper or newsprint prevents the offsetting of ink onto the blotter. Thus while the tissue or newsprint gets dirty, the more expensive blotter remains clean and reusable. Please note that if your ink is very thick and sticky, it's a good idea to place a piece of glassene over the print, instead of tissue paper or newsprint. The ink won't stick to glassene, while it may stick to tissue paper or newsprint.

After you print again, lay the new print over the top blotter. Put a tissue on top of this print and another blotter on top of the tissue, and so on. At the end of the printing day, place a large weight of heavy glass or wood on top of the prints and blotters. Leave the pile alone for a day or two.

After a few days remove the prints from the blotters. These will now be damp, having absorbed the moisture from the damp printing paper. Place the prints between dry blotters. As you remove the blotters, tissues, and prints, stack them carefully in separate piles—if there isn't enough table surface, use the floor. You can use the blotters and tissues again when they dry if they aren't dirty or wrinkled. Handle the prints carefully in order not to scratch or rub the surface. The surface ink on the print may be dry, but it sometimes takes a year for the ink underneath to dry completely. In any case, you should never touch the surface of a print.

After all the prints, tissues, and blotters have been stacked, place a clean, dry blotter on a table. Put a dry print on top of the blotter, another blotter on top of that print, another print on top of the blotter and so on, until all the prints are sandwiched between blotters. Tissues aren't necessary this time—the ink on the print should be dry enough so it won't offset onto the clean blotter.

After four days to a week, depending on the moisture in the air, the prints should be dry and ready to be signed, (see Chapter 23, page 219). The print is dry if it doesn't curl or buckle after being removed from the blotters.

CLEANUP

1. Scrub your plates with varnolene and a brush such as a toothbrush or any natural bristle brush. Push the varnolene into all the lines and crevices of the plate that might retain ink. *Never leave a plate with ink in the lines overnight*. After scrubbing, wipe the plate with a few drops of kerosene on a clean rag, and then put the plate into a plastic bag for short-term storage. If you're going to store a plate for any length of time, coat it with a mixture of Vaseline and varnolene and then put the plate into a plastic bag.

The Vaseline is cut with varnolene to make a rather liquid paste—brush it onto the plate with a 2″ wide soft-hair brush. This is especially important for a steel plate, since steel corrodes very quickly when exposed to the moisture in the air. Don't wrap any plate in newspaper, even for overnight storage, as the acid in newspaper ink will corrode a plate in a few hours if the weather is damp.

2. Wipe the bed of the press with a few drops of kerosene on a clean cloth.

3. Remove the blankets from the press by rolling the bed out until the blankets are no longer engaged and then lifting them off. The blankets will be moist from the damp printing paper; if you left them in the press overnight, they would cause the bed and the roller to rust. Also, the blankets would be flattened by the roller if they were left under pressure. So hang them on a line by clipping the ends with clothespins or metal clips and letting them hang free. *Never* throw blankets over a thin line, especially when they're wet—the mark of the line will become embossed into the blanket.

4. Turn off the hot plate. When it's cold, wipe it with a few drops of varnolene on a cloth to remove any ink on the surface.

5. Throw away any piece of tarlatan that is stiff with ink. Hang reusable tarlatans—tarlatan with holes not completely clogged with ink—on a bar at the end of the press or on lines used solely for this purpose so air can circulate through the holes. Never bunch tarlatans together in an enclosed space—this could cause a fire because of the heat generated by the oil in the ink.

6. Scrape up intaglio inks with a palette knife, and put them back into their containers for reuse.

7. Scrape the glass or marble slab clean with a razor blade, and then wipe it with a cloth dampened with varnolene. To remove the film left by the varnolene, pour a few drops of denatured alcohol or water on the glass or marble slab, and wipe with a clean cloth. Take care to clean the slab after every printing—dried ink is extremely difficult to remove.

8. Empty the water tray. The water, usually full of sizing and other debris from the paper, can't be used again. Pour the water into a pail if there's no sink nearby. Move the tray so one corner hangs over the edge of the table, and tilt the opposite corner slightly. Holding the pail in one hand, pour the water carefully into it. This isn't as easy as it sounds—you could end up with water on the floor or in your shoes. When the trays are empty, wipe them with a sponge and turn them upside down so they'll be clean the next time they're used.

9. If you used a dauber, place it in a plastic bag, and close the bag to keep the dauber clean. A dried dauber with bits of dust or metal can damage a plate beyond repair.

10. Throw away any rags, newspapers, or pieces of cardboard containing solvents or ink. Don't leave dirty or inflammable materials in the workshop overnight.

WHAT WENT WRONG AND WHY

Problem	Cause	Solution
There are white areas in the lines of my print.	1. You didn't ink the lines sufficiently.	1. Use more ink and pressure when you spread the ink onto the plate with the dauber.
	2. There wasn't enough pressure in the press.	2. Use a damp blotter over the paper when printing.
	3. The lines are extremely deep.	3. With your finger rub a little raw linseed oil into the deep lines before inking the plate.
The plate tone is scratchy in the print.	You didn't soften the tarlatan enough.	Soften the tarlatan more by removing more of the starch.
There are dark halos around the lines on the plate's surface after I finish wiping.	You didn't do the third wipe long enough or gently enough.	If you haven't hand-wiped the plate, do so.
The ink was sticky, and the plate was extremely hard to wipe.	There isn't enough raw linseed oil in the ink.	Add a few drops of raw linseed oil to the ink and mix thoroughly. Warm the plate during the inking and wiping processes.
The black intaglio ink appears gray in the print.	There's too much linseed oil in the ink.	Add stiffer ink to the oily ink until the mixture runs off the palette knife very slowly. Then ink the plate again.
There is ink around the plate mark in the print even though I wiped the edges.	The pressure of the press caused ink on the back of the plate to be squeezed out.	Check the back of your plate before printing to make sure it's clean. Change the newspaper you work on when it gets dirty.
The paper I printed on is cut at the plate mark.	1. The edges weren't beveled or weren't beveled enough.	1. Bevel the edges if you haven't done so, or bevel them more.
	2. The acid bit the edges and sharpened them.	2. Bevel the edges again.
	3. The pressure is too great on the press.	3. Loosen the pressure. Check the blankets to be sure that they weren't cut also. A cut in any blanket will show on the print—you can't use a blanket that is cut for edition printing, although you can still use it for experimental printing or proofing.

Problem	Cause	Solution
There are splotchy, light areas on the print.	The paper wasn't dampened evenly.	Soak the paper longer, and dry it more carefully.
Small white spots appear on the print after it has been drying between blotters.	When the paper was drying between the blotters, foreign bits of material or bits of the blotter adhered to the paper.	Change your blotters. Also check the paper carefully before printing and gently brush over the surface of the paper with a clean, damp paper towel to pick up any foreign matter, just in case.
Pressed fold marks on the blanket appear on the print.	You didn't pull the blankets taut before printing.	Dampen the marks on the blanket with water, and run the blanket through the press several times under normal pressure—this will sometimes remove the marks. If the fibers of the blankets are actually broken, however, the blankets are ruined. Use them only with highly embossed plates or collagraphs.
There are strangely shaped marks on the print.	If a highly embossed plate was printed with these blankets before you pulled your proof, that plate left an impression on the blankets. That impression printed onto your proof.	Change the blankets. Use old blankets for highly embossed plates.
The print appears very shiny.	Too much pressure.	Loosen the pressure on the press.
The ink is oozing out of the wide, deep lines.	The ink was too oily to be used with deep lines.	Add stiff ink to the oily ink. Then, using a soft tarlatan, wipe the areas with deep lines very thoroughly.
There are scratch marks on the plate that weren't there before printing.	Your dauber—or whatever you used for working the ink into the plate—contains dried ink or has pieces of metal embedded in it.	Throw the dauber or cardboard away, and burnish the scratches on the plate with machine oil and a burnisher.

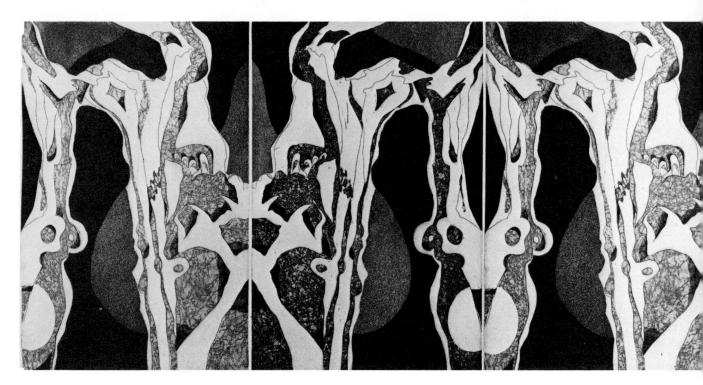

Triptych *by Joan Miller. Intaglio, 18″ x 36″. Hard and soft grounds.*

FOURTEEN

Double Intaglio Printing

This chapter deals with the technique of registering two plates, one after the other, to make one print, and with the procedure for printing a double intaglio. A double intaglio is made by printing one intaglio color over another, producing a three-color print. You can do this with two plates inked in different colors, or with a single plate printed, cleaned, inked, and then printed again on the same paper. Take a look at the color section to see what a double intaglio looks like.

Because the double intaglio process and double registration involve a rather complicated series of steps, don't attempt them until you're completely familiar with and have mastered the contents of the following chapters: Chapter 7, *Hard Ground*; Chapter 8, *Soft Ground*; Chapter 9, *Aquatint*; Chapter 12, *Acids*; and Chapter 13, *Basic Printing*.

If you're going to use two plates, then any combination of grounds on either plate—hard ground, soft ground, aquatint, white ground, or sugar lift—works very well as you can see in Figures 1 and 2. Please note, though, that if you're only going to use one plate, then a very densely bitten plate or a plate bitten with line only isn't suitable for double intaglio.

PLATE REGISTRATION FOR TWO PLATES

If you're going to use two plates for a double intaglio, then they should be *exactly* the same size. You'll need a mat to register one plate over the other so that the second plate can be etched in proper relationship to the first.

Materials and Equipment
bitten and beveled plate
plate, beveled but unbitten, *exactly* the same size as the first
X-acto knife or single-edged razor blade
straight edge—a metal or a bar of metal
matboard 12″ larger in length than the plates

Process. Trace the outline of one plate on the matboard, leaving a 6″ border at the top and bottom. Then cut the shape of the plate out of the matboard with the X-acto knife or the single-edged razor blade. Make sure that the corners are square.

Laying the mat on a flat surface, put the plate into the cut-out hole. The plate should slip in easily—if it doesn't and the fit is too tight, then enlarge the opening by cutting two inside edges of the mat slightly larger.

REGISTERING A BITTEN IMAGE ON A SECOND PLATE

In order to bite the second, unbitten, zinc plate in relation to the first, you must take a proof from the first, already bitten, plate. Then you have to transfer—counterproof—the image on the proof to the surface of the unbitten plate.

Materials and Equipment
bitten plate inked with black intaglio ink and wiped
unbitten plate, beveled and scrubbed, the same size as the first
press set up for printing
mat cut for plate registration
damp proof paper as large as the mat

Process. First, place the mat on the bed of the press. Pull the blankets down over the mat, and turn the handle of the press until the roller rests on the edge of the mat, catching the mat between the blankets under the roller and the bed.

Lift up the blankets, lay them over the roller, and place the bitten, inked plate into the hole in the mat (see Figure 3). Push the plate firmly into place so at least two adjacent

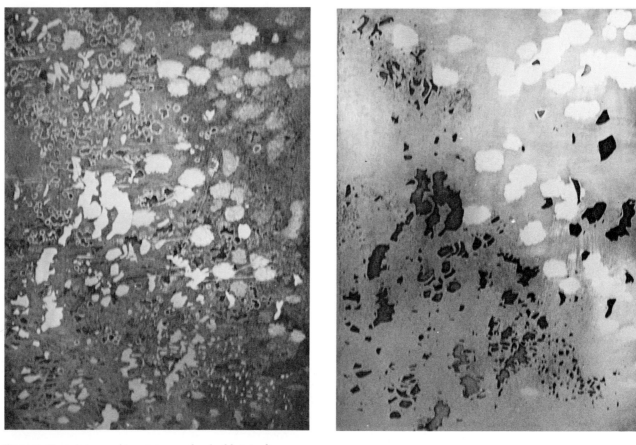

Figure 1. Two plates used to print one color double intaglio.

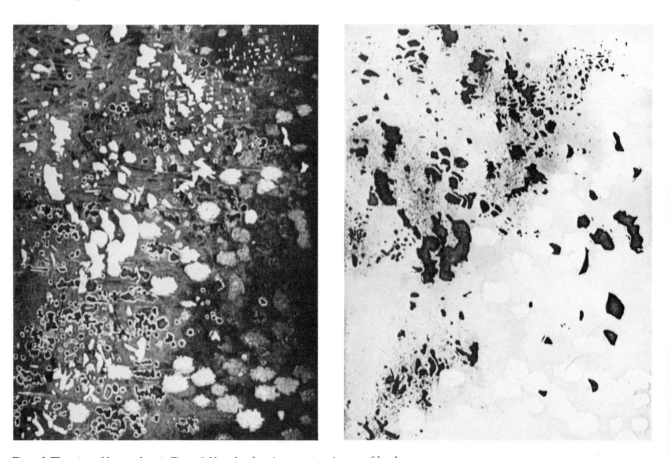

Figure 2. The prints of the two plates in Figure 1. Note that the prints are mirror images of the plates.

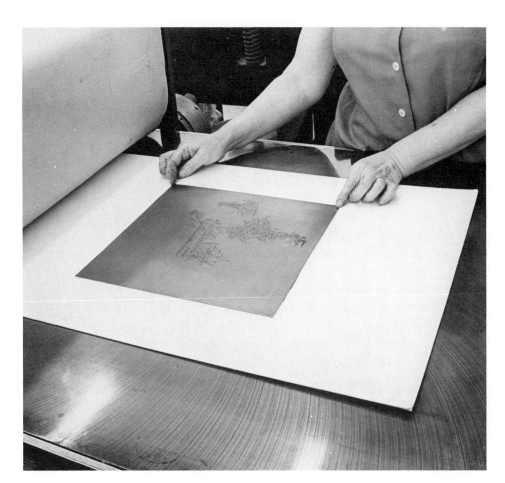

Figure 3. The inked plate placed into the hole cut out of the mat. Note the mat is caught under the roller so that it can't move.

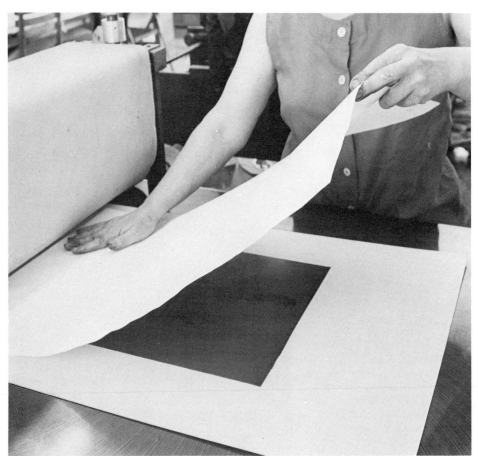

Figure 4. Damp paper is placed over the mat and the inked plate.

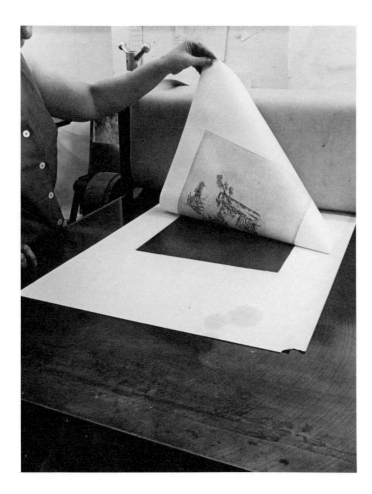

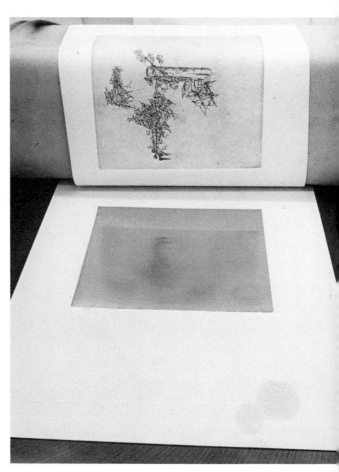

Figure 5 (above). After you run the plate through the press, lift off the paper. Note that the mat and the paper are held in place under the roller, while the plate in the mat is accessible.

Figure 6 (above right). The clean plate in the mat under the proof taken of the first plate.

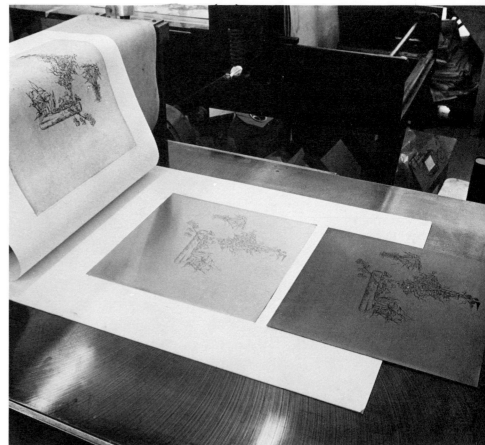

Figure 7 (right). From left to right: the proof draped over the blankets, the second plate in the hole in the mat with a counterproof printed on its surface, and the first intaglio plate. The images on both plates are the same.

sides of the plate are in complete contact with the mat. Remember which two sides these are, and place the damp printing paper over the plate and mat (see Figure 4).

Pull the blankets down over the mat, plate, and paper, and run the plate through the press. Stop turning the handle of the press, however, before the roller rolls off the edge of the mat—leave the mat and paper caught under the roller so they can't move. Place the blankets up over the roller and then lay the paper over them. You should be able to lift the plate out of the opening in the mat (see Figure 5).

Remove the inked plate and place the clean, beveled plate in exactly the same position (see Figure 6)—the same two adjacent sides of the plate should touch the mat.

Lower the proof onto the clean plate, place the blankets over the paper and plate, and roll the bed through the press until the paper, plate, and mat are free of the roller.

Lift up the blankets and the proof and place them over the roller. The clean plate should have a clear counterproof printed on it (see Figure 7)—i.e., the image on the proof should be transferred to the clean plate. Remove the plate from the bed without touching its inky surface.

AQUATINTING THE COUNTERPROOF

You can lay an aquatint directly over the inked counterproof on the plate. Using the image on the plate as your guide, you can bite the aquatint wherever you want tone in the finished print. In other words, the first plate printed for a double intaglio will supply the lines and image; this second plate will add background tone. Please note that this method is one of many possible ways to do a double intaglio print. The next section in this chapter, *Retaining the Image*, is another method. You can't use both methods on one plate!

Materials and Equipment
plate with counterproof
rosin bag
hot plate
1 pointed sable and 1 oxhair brush
rosin stopout
tray with weak nitric acid bath for a zinc plate or Dutch mordant for copper

Process. Shake the rosin onto the plate over the inked image, heat the plate, melt the rosin, and cool the plate on the bed of the press as described in Chapter 9. Then, using the stopout and a suitable brush, stop out all areas that are to remain white including the edges of your plate. Make sure that none of the stopout runs over the edges onto the surface of the plate. Although you don't usually stop out the edges of an aquatinted plate, you must when you do a double intaglio print to insure that the plate retains its original size for proper registration of both plates.

Bite the plate according to the instructions in Chapters 9 and 12.

Please note that the two plates will be printed one over the other. You must consider, therefore, the depth of the bite in relation to how the plates will look when they are printed together. All is not lost, however, if you do overbite or underbite the plate—you can always scrape an overbitten plate back to the desired tone, and you can bite an underbitten plate once more. Keep this in mind when you pull the first proof.

RETAINING THE IMAGE

Another possibility for your second plate of a double intaglio is to use a lift ground to retain the image of the counterproof. To fix the image of the first plate on the second for this purpose, you have to place the second plate with the counterproof in the acid for a little while. Although the intaglio ink of the counterproof is not a ground, it will protect the surface of the plate in acid for a very short time. Thus, when you remove the plate from acid and wipe off the ink, you'll be able to see a faint image that you can use as a guide for applying the lift ground.

Materials and Equipment
plate with counterproof
tray with a weak nitric acid bath
tray with cold water

newspapers
varnolene
paper towels

Process. Place the plate with the counterproof made of intaglio ink into the acid. The plate will start to bite immediately. As soon as the surface becomes discolored—in a minute or less—remove the plate from the acid, and place it in the tray of cold water.

Remove the plate from the water, and lay it on newspaper. Pour varnolene over the plate, and scrub with paper towels to remove the loosened ink and the varnolene.

The plate should now have a shiny and clearly visible image against a background of discolored plate. (The print may have a slight tone where the plate was exposed to the acid. You can easily remove this tone with fine steel wool after the lift ground is bitten.) You can apply the sugar lift ground in the usual manner according to the directions in Chapter 10. Thus the image on this second plate will relate to and register with that on the first plate.

INKING THE PLATE(S)

When you print a double intaglio, you must consider not only the two basic colors with which you ink your plates, but also the third color that will result when the two combine. See the pigment chart in Chapter 6 for information on what colors lend themselves to double intaglio printing.

Before deciding which inks would be esthetically pleasing for the plate or plates you're using, however, try your skills in the following procedure. If you use Indian yellow on one plate, cobalt blue on the other, and you wipe the plates as directed, you'll end up with a print that is blue on top, green in the middle, and yellow on the bottom.

Materials and Equipment
1 sheet dry printing paper and masking tape for registration
press set up for printing
1 or 2 zinc plates
4 clean, prepared tarlatans
tableau paper or a telephone book
2 color intaglio inks, such as Indian yellow and cobalt blue
linseed oil
2 palette knives
hot plate
2 sheets of ¼″ plate glass, one for each color
10 pieces of cut cardboard
newspaper
lint-free cloths

Process. Before inking your plate or plates, register the paper on the bed of the press (see Chaper 13, *Centering and Registering*, page 142, and Figures 10 and 11).

When you're set up for registration, remove some Indian yellow intaglio ink from the jar with a palette knife, and place it on one of the glass plates. If the pigment and oil have separated, remove all the ink from the jar and mix it thoroughly. The ink should run off the knife quickly onto the slab. If it doesn't, add some raw linseed oil, and mix the ink once again.

Put the plate to be inked in yellow on the hot plate. Let it get warm to the touch but not too hot to handle. Then remove the plate, and put it on newspaper in order to apply the ink. With a clean piece of cut cardboard, put some ink on the plate's surface. Pull and push the ink around the plate until it covers the surface completely and all the lines appear to have ink in them—add more ink if necessary. If the plate is deeply bitten, twist a small piece of tarlatan into the shape of a dauber and use it to force the ink into the lines (see Chapter 17, Figure 4).

Remove the excess ink with a piece of clean cut cardboard by scraping the cardboard gently across the plate. Deposit the excess ink on the glass plate. Please note that yellows or colors mixed with yellow will turn gray-green when rubbed across a zinc plate. Don't mix this gray-green color with the color remaining on the glass. Instead, put it into a clean jar, and use it another time when you want gray-green ink.

For your first tarlatan wipe, take a clean tarlatan shaped into a pad and wipe the plate in a circular motion. Press down as you wipe to push the ink into the lines. Be sure to wipe every part of the plate. Please note that when you print in color, you should use a fresh tarlatan for each color. You can use the same tarlatan, however, to wipe one color until it's too full of ink to be effective.

When the ink is evenly distributed over the entire plate, use a second, clean pad of tarlatan to wipe more ink off the surface of the plate. This time wipe in a gentle circular motion over the entire plate. If the plate cools at any time, warm it again on the hot plate—wiping a color intaglio ink is easier when the plate is warm.

Next, use tableau paper to pick up excess ink on the surface of the plate. See Chapter 13, page 140, for directions. When you're finished, wipe the plate gently again with the cleaner of the two tarlatans to restore some of the plate tone that was removed by the tableau paper.

Because the tableau paper removes *all* of the surface color on the plate, i.e., the plate tone, you can use it to remove color from a specific area. The top part of your first double intaglio is going to be blue, but if you print blue over yellow, the result will be green. Therefore you must wipe the yellow off the plate as much as possible where you want the blue to predominate—in this case, at the top.

After you wipe the top of the plate gently with the tableau paper, wipe the edges of the plate with a lint-free cloth. Your first plate is now ready to be printed. If you're using two plates, put the first one aside and ink the second. This time, for your last step use the tableau paper to wipe the blue off the bottom of the plate in order to allow the yellow of the first plate to show clearly in the print.

If you're using one plate for both printings, you must print once, ink the plate again with the second color, and then print again. Please note that if the second color ink is darker than the first (as it will be if you print cobalt blue after Indian yellow), you don't have to clean the plate before inking a second time. It's a good idea to try both ways—with and without washing the first color ink off. If your second color is lighter than your first, however, you must clean the plate with varnolene after you print the first time. Then wipe the plate with a clean cloth or with paper towels and alcohol. When it's dry, you can ink it again.

PRINTING A DOUBLE INTAGLIO

Don't heat the plate(s) immediately before you print a double intaglio. A warm plate would cause the paper to shrink, making registration of the second plate impossible.

Materials and Equipment
1 or 2 inked intaglio plates
press set up for printing
masking tape
pre-dampened printing paper or paper soaking in a tray of water (see Chapter 2)
blotters for drying paper and 1 dampened to keep the print from drying
rolling pin (optional)
newspaper
varnolene
clean cloths
paper towels
alcohol

Process of Printing a Double Intaglio. Blot your paper with a rolling pin, and wipe its surface with a paper towel if necessary (see Chapter 13, page 141). If you didn't register the paper before you inked your plate(s) according to instructions in Chapter 13, then do so now. Using the paper registration marks as a guide, place the plate on the bed of the press leaving a 6″ margin between the bottom of the plate and the end of the paper. Position the damp paper on top of the plate within the four taped corners as marked (see Figure 8). Pull the blankets down over the paper and the plate, and roll the plate through the press until you no longer feel the pressure of the plate. You should be able to feel the pressure lessen as the plate leaves the roller. Stop turning the handle just after this happens.

Lift up first the blankets and the printing paper, and place them over the roller. The 6″

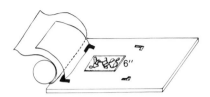

Figure 8. The paper is placed inside the taped registration mark; the plate is positioned within those marks, leaving a 6" margin between the bottom of the plate and tape marks for the edge of the paper.

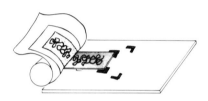

Figure 9. Use masking tape to mark two corners and one side of the plate for registration before you remove the first intaglio plate from the press. Note that the blankets and paper are caught under the roller.

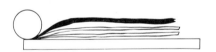

Figure 10. Place a damp blotter and the blankets over the printing paper to keep it damp while you ink and wipe the second plate.

margin of paper that you left between the bottom of the plate and the end of the paper will cause the paper to be caught under the roller. *Don't remove the plate from the bed of the press—it must be registered before you remove it.*

Mark the two corners of the plate at the end farthest from the roller with masking tape (see Figure 9). Make sure the tape is very close to the plate and also put one piece of tape along one side of the plate. The tape will act as a guide for registration of the second plate of the double intaglio.

Remove the first plate. If you're printing the double intaglio with only one plate, then wipe the bed of the press with a dry clean cloth. Lay the printing paper—with one end still caught between the roller and blankets and the bed of the press—down on the bed of the press. Then put a damp blotter, larger than the paper, on top and lay the blankets down over both the paper and the blotter. This will prevent your paper from drying while you ink the plate a second time (see Figure 10).

Ink and wipe the plate for the second time. If you're using the Indian yellow and cobalt blue inks, remember to wipe the blue completely off the bottom of the plate so the yellow can predominate there over the print. When you're finished, pick up the blankets and lay them over the roller. Remove the damp blotter, pick up the printing paper, and rest it over the blankets.

Whether you're printing one plate twice or two different plates, place the second intaglio plate within the taped corners made around the first plate before you removed it. Be sure to put the plate in the register marks correctly and not upside down. Remember, the print is a mirror image of the plate.

Pull the paper down over the plate, and test the four corners with your fingertips or nails to be sure that the plate fits perfectly under the plate mark on the paper. All four beveled edges of the plate should correspond with the embossed plate mark on the back of the print. If they don't, then shift the plate carefully until they meet. To check registration when the paper is over the plate, you can also apply pressure with your fingers on the paper in an area where light and dark inks are next to each other, lift up the paper, and look at the print to see if the two images are meeting correctly.

After you have determined that your registration is correct, pick up the printing paper again and place it back over the blankets. Remove the registration tape around the plate, being very careful not to shift the plate. If you don't remove the tape before printing, your print will contain embossed tape marks. (Another way of registering two plates of the same size is to trace the outline of one of the plates on newsprint, and then trace the outline of the paper you're going to use in relation to the outline of the plate. Place the newsprint under a thin—1/16" to ⅛"—piece of plastic on the press bed and use the outlines as a guide to place your plates and paper.)

Put the paper and blankets down over the plates and roll the bed through the press until both the plate *and* the paper are free of the rollers. Then lift up the blankets, and remove the paper gently with cardboard clips. If you used Indian yellow on one plate and cobalt blue on the other, then your print should be blue on the top, green in the center, and yellow on the bottom. Once you've seen how wiping affects the plate and print, try any combination of colors and wiping.

CLEANUP

For cleanup after printing, see Chapter 13.

WHAT WENT WRONG AND WHY

Problem	Cause	Solution
The paper slipped out of the press before I printed the second plate.	1. You didn't leave a 6″ margin of paper between the bottom of the first plate and the end of the paper. 2. You turned the roller too far from the plate after the first printing so there wasn't enough paper for the rollers to hold.	Remove the print from the press. Turn the press until the roller clears the registration marks made for the paper. Place the second plate into the registration marks made for the first plate, and then use the paper registration marks to position the paper. Match the plate edge with the plate mark on the printing paper as you would under normal conditions (see above). When you've finished registering the paper and plate, press down firmly on them with one hand at one end. Slip your other hand under the other end of the print—fold the print over if necessary—and carefully remove the registration tape. Lay the print down flat, and replace the blankets carefully without moving the plate or paper. Then pull the plate through the press.
After I registered the print and the second plate with my fingertips, the registration was fine, but the margin of the paper had spots of ink on it.	The shifting of the paper necessary for this kind of registration will leave ink on the margin.	Place the paper in a tray of cold water while the ink is still wet. Use a clean piece of silk (any clean texture usually used for soft ground will do), and gently rub the area of the margin that has ink on it. Then remove the paper from the water, and blot with a paper towel to absorb the excess water. If you used a blotter, the fresh ink would offset onto the blotter, and you wouldn't be able to use that blotter to blot clean paper. Please note than if you inadvertently destroy the surface of the paper while you're rubbing ink off the margin, the print can't be used.
Instead of the texture normally seen on the first part of a double intaglio, there's a bubbled texture.	1. Bubbles can be caused by shifting the paper when it's put down on the plate. 2. If the plate is warped, it may move under the paper during printing. 3. Bubbles can also occur if the intaglio ink is extremely oily.	1. Position the paper carefully into the registration marks on one end of the bed. Holding that end down firmly in place with one hand, put the other end of the paper in place with the other hand. 2. If the plate is warped, try to straighten it out. Put a blotter on the bed of the press, and place the cleaned plate face down on the blotter. Then put wax paper or newsprint over the plate to protect the blankets. Pull the blankets down, and roll the plate through the press. 3. Add a pinch of magnesium carbonate to the intaglio ink to stiffen it.
The second time I printed a double intaglio with cobalt blue and Indian yellow, the yellow in the print was much greener than the yellow in the first print.	Yellow ink interacts with a zinc plate. There is an even greater interaction if there's a trace of solvent on the plate. This would occur if you used varnolene to remove the yellow ink after the first printing, and didn't clean all the solvent off the plate before you printed again.	After cleaning the plate with varnolene and removing all the ink and solvent with paper towels or a cloth, pour a small amount of denatured alcohol on the plate, and wipe it off with a clean dry cloth. Alcohol cuts grease, such as the oil in the ink and varnolene, and evaporates very quickly. When you ink the plate with Indian yellow a second time after cleaning your plate with alcohol, the plate will be dry and the yellow should be purer.

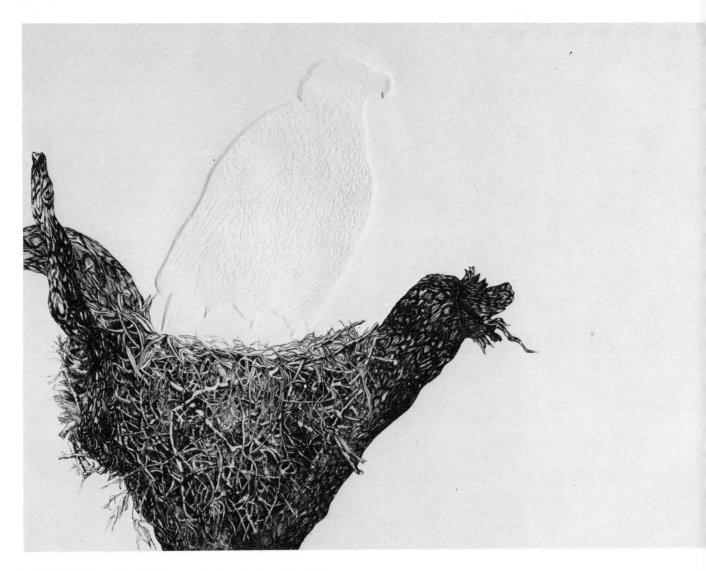

Pieta *by Stelly Sterling. Hard ground and embossing, 18" x 28".*

FIFTEEN

Color Printing and Embossing

This chapter describes a variety of ways to add surface color to intaglio prints, including rolling a surface color onto a deeply bitten plate with an uninked intaglio—relief printing—and applying surface colors over stencils. In addition, printing a plate with no ink at all—embossing—is covered; this is a method not precisely included under the heading of surface color, but related to it by technique.

PREPARING A PLATE FOR RELIEF PRINTING

A relief print is one that uses the surface rather than the grooves of the plate for printing (see Figure 1). The area not to be printed must be bitten down so the roller carrying the ink will come into contact with the surface of the plate only (see Figure 2). Because of the especially deep biting, the same plate can be rolled through the press without any inking at all—surface or intaglio—to produce a deeply embossed print (see Figure 3).

Materials and Equipment
zinc plate, beveled and cleaned (see Chapter 7)
asphaltum and rosin stopouts or special stopout and brush
strong nitric acid bath
grease pencil
hot plate, heated
clean cloth
denatured alcohol
varnolene

Process. You may begin by drawing your image on the clean plate with a grease pencil which can be removed with a clean cloth to change the image or with asphaltum stopout where the entire plate must be cleaned if you want to remove part of the drawing. If you use the grease pencil, go over the lines with a brush coated with asphaltum stopout before continuing.

When you finish drawing with asphaltum, heat the plate on the hot plate until the asphaltum stops smoking—this means that the varnolene in the asphaltum has vaporized. Then place the plate on a cold surface such as the press bed to cool.

When the plate is cool, the asphaltum should be dry and hard to the touch. Reinforce it by applying rosin stopout over the asphaltum. Please note that you could use special stopout instead of asphaltum—if you do, then you don't have to coat special stopout with rosin stopout. When the plate is put into a strong nitric acid bath, the two stopouts, one over the other, are stronger than either alone (as is special stopout)—when you put the plate into the strong acid there will be less chance of false biting.

Place the plate in a strong nitric acid bath without waiting for the rosin stopout to dry. (You *do* have to wait for the special stopout to dry.) Because of the strength of the acid, you must watch the plate closely for false biting, undercutting, or overheating. If you're biting large open areas in this strong acid, the acid may become hot, and there's a danger that the hot acid will lift off the stopout. If bubbles appear where they aren't wanted (false biting) or if the plate seems to be fuming, remove the plate from the acid by tilting the tray so there's no acid on the end that you'll be touching. Pick the plate up at the end carefully—it may be very hot—and rinse it immediately in cold water.

Dry the plate with a paper towel. If you removed it because you thought it might have overheated, make sure that no stopout lifted off. Repair the damage, if any, and replace the plate in the acid. If you removed the plate because unwanted bubbles appeared, check for false biting or undercutting. Undercutting occurs when the edges of the stopout are worn away because the acid bites underneath them. Stop out all sus-

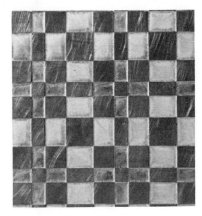

Figure 1. The lighter portions of the design bitten into this part of a zinc plate, made by Barbara Levine, are 1/32" beneath the surface of the plate.

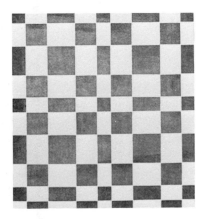

Figure 2. Detail of the print of the plate in Figure 1 rolled with a dark surface ink. The white areas are those that were deeply bitten. Note that because of the application of a surface ink, the embossing quality appears to be lost.

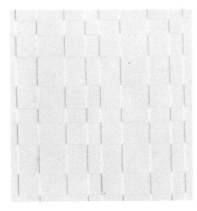

Figure 3. Detail of the embossed proof of the plate in Figure 1. Because no ink was used, you can see the depth of the bitten areas of the plate.

picious areas and paint the edges of any undercut with more stopout (see Figure 4) before putting the plate back into acid.

To make a relief or embossed print, the acid must bite the plate halfway down to the bottom. You'll be able to see the depth easily after it has bitten sufficiently. Then remove the plate, and place it in cold water.

Dry the plate and remove the stopout by pouring on alcohol and varnolene at the same time. Soak the combined stopouts in both solvents for a few minutes before you try to remove them by scrubbing with a brush. Then wipe the plate with a paper towel. When the plate is clean and dry, it's ready to be printed.

INKING A RELIEF PRINT

Here you'll roll ink with a hard roller (see Chapter 1, page 15) onto the surface of a deeply bitten plate. The print will be a relief print, as there will be no ink in the in taglio section (the deeply bitten areas).

Materials and Equipment
press set up for printing
hard roller, preferably larger than your plate
¼" plate glass, large enough for the roller
flat surface or another piece of ¼" plate glass larger than the plate
vegetable shortening
palette knife
surface inks
raw linseed oil
paper

Process. Choose the color of your surface ink, remove some of it from the can with a palette knife, and place the ink in one corner of the plate glass. The amount of ink will depend on the size of the plate and how many prints you're going to make.

If the ink has a tendency to dry quickly and form little hard pellets or cling to the rollers, remove any dried pieces and mix in a small amount of vegetable shortening thoroughly—1 part vegetable shortening to 10 parts ink. Commercial offset printing inks have drying elements added to them very often, and they tend to dry very quickly. Imported inks, on the other hand, are usually made with less dryers and can be used without the vegetable shortening.

If your ink is very tacky or stiff and difficult to mix with a palette knife, add a few drops of raw linseed oil. Use the palette knife to distribute the oil evenly into the ink.

When you're satisfied with the consistency of the ink, smear a thin film of it across the glass plate with the palette knife (see Figure 5). If you want to roll more than one color onto the plate at the same time, smear thin, short lengths of different colors in a line, leaving an inch or two between them. This way, when the roller is moved a little to the right or left each time you roll, the colors can combine. Proceed as usual—this is called a rainbow roll.

Roll the hard roller through the ink to the end of the slab and back, picking it up at the end of each up-and-back motion. This will cause the roller to spin slightly, so that when you replace it back down on the glass again, it will be in a different position than it was the first time. Don't roll back and forth without picking up the roller—this doesn't help to spread the ink. You'll notice that the ink picked up on the first roll will be deposited back onto the glass if you have spun the roller and changed its position (see Figure 6).

Continue to roll, picking the roller up at the end of each motion until the roller is covered completely with a thin smooth layer of ink. The glass plate will also have a thin layer of ink over its surface (see Figure 7). Check both roller and glass plate to be sure that there are no bits of debris or dried ink on either. If there are, you must remove them with a paper towel or a clean cloth. Then roll again until the ink is smooth on both the glass and the roller.

Place the plate on a flat surface such as another piece of glass. Roll across the surface of the plate with the inked roller. Apply some pressure so the ink coats the surface, but not so much pressure that the roller dips into the deeply bitten areas. This may take

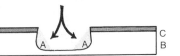

Figure 4. Paint the sides of the bitten areas (A) of the plate (B) with stopout to keep the acid from biting underneath the ground (C).

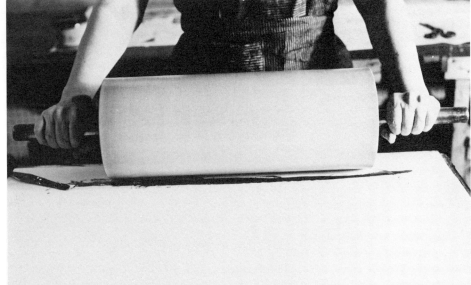

Figure 5. A narrow strip of ink spread across the glass in front of the roller.

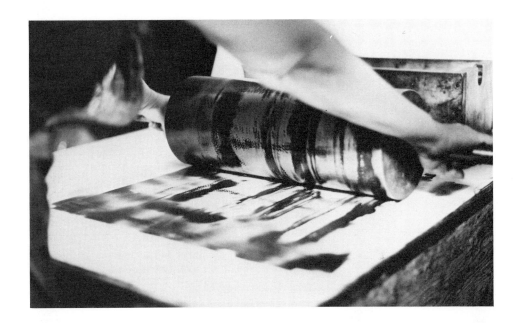

Figure 6. Spin the roller at the end of each roll so the ink will be deposited in different areas of the glass and roller.

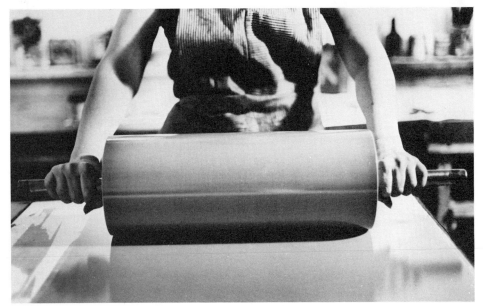

Figure 7. Both glass and roller covered with even layers of ink.

some practice. If you're dissatisfied with the look of the plate, clean it with varnolene and a paper towel, make sure that the plate is completely clean and dry, and try again When the plate is properly rolled with ink, it's ready to be printed.

Please note that if the width of your plate is more than 3 times the diameter of the roller or if your plate is longer than your roller, you may have trouble rolling an even, smooth layer of ink on your plate. You may end up with lines in the ink giving a plaid effect. It's better to use an adequately sized roller if possible.

PRINTING A RELIEF PRINT OR EMBOSSING

A deeply bitten plate printed with the surface inked will make a relief print. The same plate printed without ink will result in an embossed print. You can register the paper and print relief prints and embossings the same way you would print a single intaglio print (see Chapter 13). Just remember that once the paper is lying on top of the plate, *don't move the paper or the plate*—the ink may smudge and you'll get a poor print.

CUTTING A STENCIL

Stencils are useful if you want to roll a color onto *certain areas* of the plate, rather than onto the entire plate. To prepare the stencil for cutting, you must print the plate's image on the stencil paper as a guide for cutting the stencil. Do this by printing first a proof and then a counterproof onto the stencil paper (see Chapter 14, pages 149 and 153). When you have your counterproof on stencil paper, allow the ink to dry overnight before cutting out the stencil.

Materials and Equipment
matknife or single-edged razor blade
stencil paper with *dry* counterproof printed on it
very fine sandpaper

Process. Lay the stencil paper on newspaper, and using a matknife or a single-edged razor, cut away those areas on the stencil where you want to roll color onto the plate. Cut the stencil a little larger than the actual shape desired to compensate for the thickness of the stencil paper, which will keep the roller away from the plate.

If the cut edges of the stencil are not smooth, sand them gently with very fine sandpaper.

USING A STENCIL

When you use a stencil to roll surface color onto an inked intaglio plate, the ink will be deposited on the plate only where you cut openings in the stencil. You'll need a medium or soft roller (see Chapter 1, page 15) to do this.

Materials and Equipment
plate inked with black or color intaglio ink
surface ink
cut stencil
two ¼″ pieces of plate glass, larger than the inked plate
palette knife
medium or soft roller, larger than the hole(s) cut in the stencil
masking tape
vegetable shortening

Process. Place the plate on one of the sheets of plate glass. Then position the cut stencil over the plate, making sure that the holes in the stencil correspond to the areas on the plate where the surface color is to be rolled. Fasten the stencil to the glass plate with masking tape to keep it from moving.

Ink the roller—follow the same procedure (described on page 161) as you did when you prepared to ink a relief print. After the ink is evenly distributed over the roller and the glass slab, roll it once over the openings cut in the stencil. Don't push the roller back and forth over the plate since the roller will pick up intaglio ink after one roll. Rolling that roller over the plate more than once would cause that intaglio ink to be redeposited on the surface of the plate, thereby muddying the surface ink.

If you're using a small roller, you may have to reink the roller for each opening in the stencil. If so, wipe the roller each time with a clean cloth and varnolene to remove any intaglio ink picked up in a previous roll, and make sure that the roller is dry before you use it again.

After the inking is completed, lift the stencil carefully to avoid smudging the ink, and print the plate (see Chapter 13).

CLEANUP

See Chapters 12 and 13 for cleanup instructions for acids and printing. In addition, clean and store the roller in the manner described in Chapter 1.

WHAT WENT WRONG AND WHY

Problem	Cause	Solution
The ink in my surface roll contains little bubbles.	The surface ink has too much linseed oil in it.	Add fresh ink from the can to the oily ink you've been using. Be sure to mix it in thoroughly with a palette knife.
The border of the print has ink around it.	You moved the paper after it came in contact with the plate.	Be sure that you hold one end of the paper down *securely* on the bed of the press while you're positioning the other end. Once the paper is in contact with the plate, don't move it.
No matter how carefully I roll the plate, the ink gets into the lower, bitten areas.	1. The roller is too soft.	1. Use a harder roller, one that has a durometer of 60 (see Chapter 1, page 15).
	2. You didn't bite the plate deeply enough.	2. You'll have to stop out the top surfaces of the plate again and replace it in the acid. This way the areas where the surface ink isn't wanted will become deep enough to avoid contact with the roller.

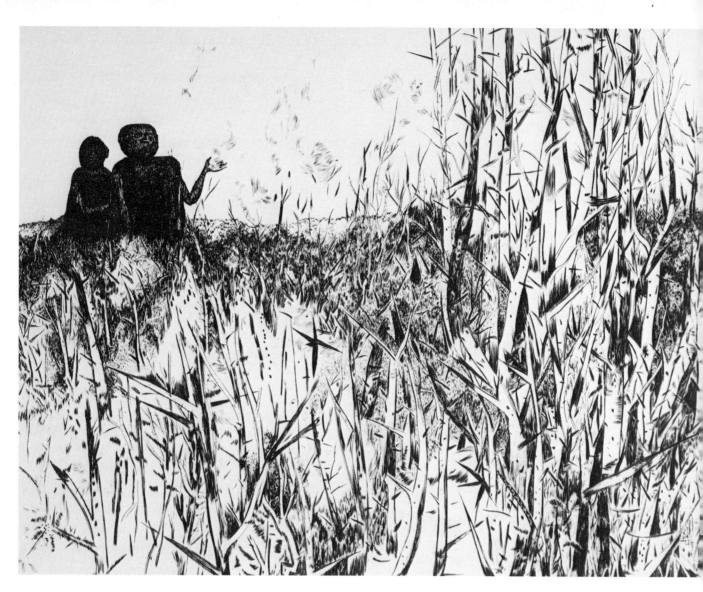

Brambles, Second State *by Gerson Leiber. Engraving, 18″ x 24″.*

SIXTEEN

Viscosity Method

The viscosity method of printing will enable you to produce a print that has three colors while you roll your plate through the press only one time. What makes this possible is the fact that inks of varying viscosities, i.e., rates of flow controlled by different amounts of oil, have the power to repel or combine with one another. In addition, hard and soft rollers are used to deposit ink on different levels of the plate. The visosity method was first utilized on a large scale in Atelier 17 in Paris, a printmaking workshop founded by Stanley William Hayter.

UNDERLYING PRINCIPLE

The principle of the method can be demonstrated by putting a spot of light (runny) oil on a piece of paper and then trying to draw a pen line through it. The pen line will appear clearly on either side of the oil spot but not on top of it.

The viscosity of ink is the condition of having a high resistance to flow—a viscous ink is thick. If you add raw linseed oil to ink, the ink will become oiler (looser)—the oil will lower the viscosity of the ink and make it flow faster or more easily. An ink of higher viscoslity with no linseed oil added—a drier (tackier) ink—rolled over the lower viscosity ink—an oily ink—will attract a thin film of oily ink to the roller, leaving the rest of the first color layer intact. In other words, the high viscosity ink is comparable to the pen of the preceding paragraph, and when it's rolled over the low viscosity (oily) ink, it will appear on either side of the low viscosity ink but not on top.

THE BASIC PROCEDURE

For the viscosity method to work well, you must bite your plate to three levels. Then you'll ink the intaglio section with intaglio ink (high viscosity) and wipe it clean with tarlatan and paper. The intaglio ink will remain only in the deepest level of the plate, leaving the two upper levels receptive to surface inks. Next you'll roll a hard roller charged with surface ink of low viscosity—i.e., with raw linseed oil added to it—over the plate. This roller will deposit the oily ink on the *top* surface of the plate *only*. Then you'll take a soft roller charged with an ink of higher viscosity—dry, with no oil added—and roll it over the plate. As this roller picks up a thin film of oily ink from the top surface, it will deposit the dry ink on the second surface (just as the pen line appeared on either side of the drop of oil above). The colors on each level will appear on the plate pure, i.e., unmixed.

Once you understand the method just described, you can try many variations. One possibility is to use the soft roller charged with an ink of high viscosity (dry) over the plate first. The dry ink on this roller will cover the two upper levels of the plate. Then roll a hard roller charged with an oily ink over the top surface of the plate. The dry ink already on the top surface will accept the oily ink on the hard roller. Thus the top surface color will be a mixture of the two colors used, while the color on the lower level will be the unmixed dry ink.

You'll have to choose colors for this method by trial and error—the possible color combinations are unlimited. Intaglio and surface colors can be any shade which you desire. It would be wise, however, to limit your first experiments to a black or blue intaglio ink and two inks of primary colors for the surface. Within these three color combinations there are six possible variations, depending on which color is used for the intaglio.

This chapter will deal with a simple demonstration of the viscosity method, including biting a small test plate to three levels, preparing the intaglio ink and the two surface inks for rolling, and preparing the plate for printing with those inks. *It would not be a good idea to attempt this until you're familiar with the methods described in all of the previous chapters.*

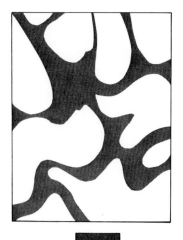

Figure 1. The stopouts (A) cover half the plate. This plate may be put into a strong nitric acid bath.

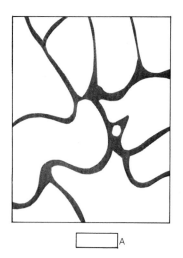

Figure 2. Here the exposed plate (A) is larger than the amount of stopout applied. This plate should be bitten in a medium nitric acid bath.

BITING THE PLATE TO THREE LEVELS

In Chapter 15, pages 159–160, I described how to bite the plate to two levels for relief printing. You'll use the same technique—with asphaltum and rosin stopouts or special stopout to bite your plate to three levels for the viscosity method. You can use any size plate as long as the rollers are big enough to cover the length and width of the plate in one roll without offsetting. See Chapter 1 for more information on rollers.

Materials and Equipment
zinc plate, beveled and clean (see Chapter 7)
bastard file
powdered cleanser
sponge
asphaltum and rosin stopouts or special stopout and brushes
hot plate, heated
strong, medium, and weak nitric acid baths
varnolene
alcohol
paper towels
scrub brush
spatula
work gloves

Process. Begin by drawing on the surface of the plate with asphaltum stopout and a brush. The area under the drawing will become the top surface level of the finished plate and will be rolled with a hard roller and the oily ink.

Put the plate on the heated hot plate and leave it there until the varnolene in the asphaltum stops smoking, as described in Chapter 7 for hard ground. When it does stop smoking, take the plate off the heat. Put it on the bed of the press to cool, and place it back on your working surface.

Using a brush, paint over the asphaltum with rosin stopout. The combined stopouts will protect the plate from the acid better than either one by itself. Now the plate is ready for the first biting. (You could also use special stopout—see Chapter 6, page 58 instead of the asphaltum and rosin stopouts. The plate would be ready for biting as soon as the special stopout was dry.)

If the asphaltum covers a large portion of the plate, leaving less than half the plate exposed to acid, put the plate into a strong acid bath (see Figure 1). If the asphaltum coating is less extensive and there is a large area of unprotected plate to be bitten—more than half the plate—place the plate in a medium acid bath (see Figure 2). In either case the unprotected areas of the plate will begin to bite immediately. Use a feather to wipe away the bubbles. If you're open-biting your plate—this occurs when a large area of the plate is exposed to strong acid—the plate may start fuming. See Chapter 12, page 117, for information on what to do should this occur. And if it does happen, put the plate in a medium bath when you continue biting.

Check the plate often for false biting or undercutting (see Chapter 15, Figure 4). Paint any necessary areas with rosin stopout, replace the plate in the acid, and allow the plate to bite until you can see a very definite level. Then remove the plate from the acid. Blot it dry with paper towels, *but don't remove the stopouts.*

Now it's time to apply another coat of rosin stopout (or special stopout) on top of the previous one to produce the second level. The area coated now will be the level inked with the soft roller and dry surface ink, while the area of the plate that remains exposed will become the third level or the intaglio (see Figure 3). So brush on your stopout, replace the plate in the same acid, and bite the plate for the second time. Allow the plate to remain in the acid until another very definite level can be seen, and then remove the plate. Rinse it off and blot it dry. At this point you can either clean and print the plate or—without removing the stopout—apply an aquatint to the third (still exposed) level with spray enamel (see Chapter 9) or with rosin as described below.

To add an aquatint to the intaglio (third) level of your plate with rosin, dry the plate thoroughly with a paper towel after removing it from the water, and shake rosin over the exposed areas. Then, heat the plate on the hot plate until the grains of rosin melt.

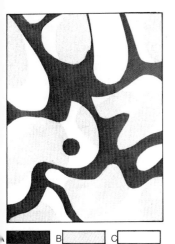

Figure 3. The first level stopped out (A) remains on the plate. The rosin stopout (B) is applied to produce the second level. The uncovered plate (C) will bite down to another level and become the intaglio.

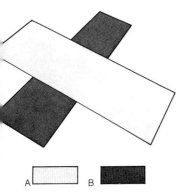

Figure 4. The first color rolled on (A) is an oily ink of low viscosity. The second color (B)—a dry ink of high viscosity—is rolled over the first. The second color appears clearly on either side but not on top of the first color.

(See Chapter 9 for detailed information.) When that happens, remove the plate from the hot plate and cool the plate on the bed of the press.

Now place your plate in a weak nitric acid bath for 5 minutes, removing the bubbles with a feather. If the texture of the aquatint seems to be disappearing, remove the plate immediately. Otherwise, after 5 minutes, take the plate out of the acid, rinse it in cold water, and pat the surface dry with a paper towel. You've finished biting your plate now—place it on newspaper, pour on varnolene and alcohol, allow the solvents to remain on the plate for a few minutes, and scrub with a scrub brush to loosen the stopout. Remove the stopouts and solvents with a cloth or paper towels. When the plate is clean and dry on both sides, it's ready to be inked for printing.

PREPARING THE SURFACE INKS

You'll need to prepare two surface inks for your plate, one for the top level with raw linseed oil added to make its viscosity lower than the dry ink for the second level.

Materials and Equipment
2 surface inks
2 palette knives
2 small rubber rollers (see Chapter 1, Figure 5)
raw linseed oil
two ¼" glass plates larger than the plate to be printed
vegetable shortening
magnesium carbonate

Process. Place a small amount of each of the two inks on separate glass plates. Choose the color that will be rolled on the top level of the plate. For about 1 tbsp. of ink add 10 drops of raw linseed oil, and mix the ink and the oil very thoroughly with the palette knife until the ink is of an even consistency. The oil should be completely mixed into the color. You'll use the second color as it comes out of the can unless it's so thick it doesn't spread onto the roller, in which case you'll have to add a small amount of vegetable shortening, ⅛ tsp. per tablespoonful of color, to *both* inks. Sometimes the ink as it comes out of the can is very oily. You can make it stiffer by adding 1 tsp. of magnesium carbonate for every tablespoon of ink.

Dip one of the small rollers into the oily ink. Roll the roller back and forth, picking it up at the end of each roll and spinning it, until both the glass and the roller are covered with a smooth layer of ink. Then roll a swatch of this ink onto a clean part of the glass. Be sure that the ink rolled is evenly applied.

Dip the second roller into the second surface ink. Roll the roller back and forth as you did before to get even layers of ink on the roller and slab. Then roll this roller with the dry ink across the first swatch of oily ink. The second color shouldn't be visible over the first color on the glass, although you should be able to see it clearly on either side (see Figure 4). Also there should be a very thin layer of the oily color coating the dry ink on the second roller. If this doesn't work, and the colors mix on the glass, add more linseed oil to the first color. Clean both rollers and dry them thoroughly before repeating the testing process. Please note that if the small rollers you're using are neophrene or rubber, you can clean them with varnolene, as it dries more quickly than kerosene and won't harm these rollers. If the rollers are gelatin, however—or if you don't know what they are—use kerosene. Continue testing until the second color rolls over the first without mixing. When the inks roll properly, the plate is ready to be inked.

PRINTING TWO SURFACE COLORS

Here you'll roll the hard and soft rollers coated with the two inks you just prepared onto a plate already inked with an intaglio ink. You *must* know Chapter 13—*Basic Printing*—backwards and forwards—before you attempt this.

Materials and Equipment
plate bitten in three levels and inked with black intaglio ink
hard and soft rollers with stands (see Chapter 1)
2 surface inks on two ¼" thick pieces of plate glass large enough to accommodate the rollers
2 palette knives
one ¼" thick plate glass, larger than the zinc plate

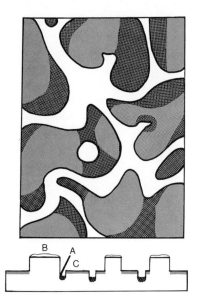

Figure 5. After the intaglio ink (A) has been applied and wiped, a hard roller with an oily ink (B) is rolled over the surface of the plate. Then, a soft roller charged with a dry high viscosity ink (C) (no oil added) is rolled over the surface and down into the second level. See the color section for prints using this method.

Process. Pick up some of the low viscosity (oily) ink on a palette knife and spread it along the bottom of one sheet of ¼″ thick plate glass (see Chapter 15, Figure 5). Roll the hard roller through the strip of ink as you did the roller in Chapter 15, Figure 6, until the layer of ink on the glass and the roller are of an even consistency (see Chapter 15, Figure 7). Then put this roller on its stand or in its box until the second roller is charged with ink.

Repeat the process with the soft roller and the high viscosity ink—when you roll this dry ink out on the glass, it should have a matte finish.

Now place the inked intaglio plate on a clean ¼″ thick plate glass slab larger than the plate. Roll the hard roller over the plate without applying any pressure. The pressure of the roller is sufficient to charge the surface of the plate. If the amount of ink on the plate doesn't seem thick enough, recharge the roller and roll again. Please remember that once you start rolling the roller across the plate, you can't stop until the roller rolls off the plate. If you stop the roller on the plate, you'll create a line which will show on the print. When you're finished rolling, replace the roller in its stand. Its surface should have the impression of the surface of the plate, but no intaglio color on it.

Roll the soft roller over the plate, applying moderate, even, downward pressure. Then replace that roller in its stand. Its surface will be coated with a thin layer of the first surface color and, possibly, some intaglio color. Don't roll the soft roller over the plate more than once.

Wipe the edges of the plate with a clean cloth and your plate is ready. Print it according to the instructions in Chapter 13. The colors on the print should be clear, separate, and unmixed (see Figure 5). Before you can ink the plate again for another print, you must prepare the rollers and the glass plate for use (see below).

RETIRAGE

After you print, if your plate still has a lot of ink on it, try pulling another proof before you ink your plate again. This process, called retirage or maculature, will yield prints of very soft, muted—and many times beautiful—colors.

CARE OF THE PLATE, ROLLERS, AND INKS BETWEEN EACH INKING

You're going to have to clean the soft roller before each roll, and you'll have to keep the inks in good condition.

Materials and Equipment
kerosene
4 or more lint-free cloths
paper towels
single-edged razor blades

Process. You can reink the plate with black (or any dark) intaglio ink without cleaning it between prints. If, however, you use a light color intaglio ink, you'll have to clean the plate with varnolene and dry it thoroughly before inking it again.

The hard roller doesn't have to be cleaned between each inking, since no other ink touches its surface. After several rolls, however, you'll find bits of fuzz or lint on the roller. You should clean it then with kerosene and a lint-free cloth—pour enough kerosene onto the cloth to make the cloth wet, wipe the roller until no ink is left on the surface, and dry it thoroughly with a clean cloth.

The soft roller, which picks up a thin layer of the oily ink, must be cleaned between each roll the same way you clean the hard roller.

You don't have to clean off the glass plates on which you rolled the inks until they no longer look smooth or until you can see bits of dust of fuzz imbedded in them. When this happens, scrape the rolled ink off the glass plate with a single-edged razor blade until the glass is clean. Dispose of the scraped ink immediately. Then pick up some of the unused ink at the edge of the glass, and spread it along the bottom of the glass for rerolling. Please note that before every roll with a clean roller, you should place ink at the base of the glass, even if there's ink left there from the previous roll. If you just cleaned the glass with a razor, add extra ink.

Since the preparation for printing plates in the viscosity method is extensive, you should try to allot yourself enough time to print as many prints as possible. The time needed for preparing inks for this kind of printing is the same for one print as for ten.

CLEANUP

1. See Chapter 7 for cleanup concerning plates and equipment after using grounds; Chapter 12 for cleanup concerning acids; Chapter 13 for cleanup after printing.

2. Don't replace surface inks removed from their original containers back into those containers. You can keep them for a few days tightly wrapped in wax paper or tinfoil. If you have a freezer, you can freeze color inks for an unlimited amount of time—they'll be perfect when defrosted.

3. Pay special attention to the rollers—they become unusable if they're pitted or covered with dry ink. Clean plastic and gelatin rollers thoroughly with kerosene, until no color shows on a clean cloth as you wipe their surfaces. Leave a thin layer of kerosene on the roller—it will help to keep the surface pliable. Wash rubber or neoprene rollers with varnolene. Some manufacturers suggest using alcohol after the varnolene.

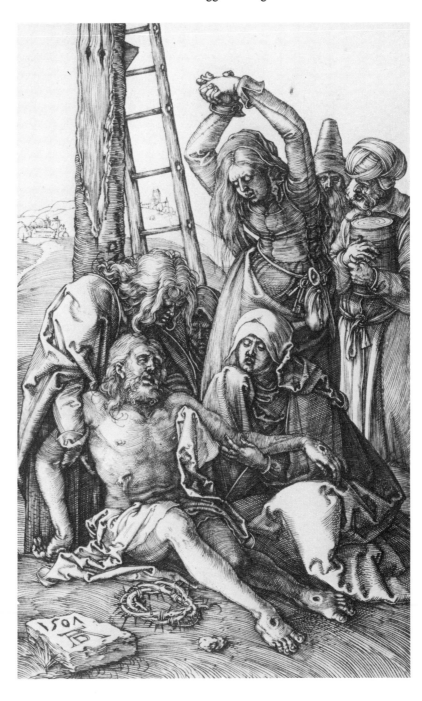

The Descent from the Cross
*by Albrecht Dürer (1471-1528).
Engraving. Courtesy Metropolitan
Museum of Art, New York City,
Fletcher Fund.*

WHAT WENT WRONG AND WHY

Problem	Cause	Solution
After I printed two or three prints that were fine, the color on the soft roller began to mix with the top surface color.	Commercial inks have dryers in them. After a while the inks begin to dry and the viscosities change.	Add a few drops of oil of cloves or a small, equal amount of vegetable fat to both inks to retard drying.
When I print a plate which I had no difficulty printing previously, I find I can't get the viscosity to work.	On a very dry day or when using an air conditioner, ink has a tendency to dry very quickly. A plate which printed well on a rainy day may not print well at all on a very dry day.	If turning the air conditioner off or adding retarding agents such as oil of cloves or vegetable fat doesn't help, wait for a better day to print.
More ink rolls on one side of the plate than on the other.	You'll notice that if you're left-handed, the layer of ink rolled will be heavier on the left side; and if you're right-handed, the right side will have more ink.	When you're rolling, consciously bear down more on the side that previously had less ink.
Little pieces of ink appear on the glass and the roller, and I have difficulty removing them.	The top surface of the ink in the can tends to dry after the can has been opened.	To prevent this from happening, after removing some ink from the can, smooth the surface of the ink left inside with a palette knife. Place a piece of plastic wrap over the surface of the ink, and smooth out all the air bubbles before closing the can. If you already have dry ink on the surface, try to remove as much of it as possible before putting on a plastic wrap. As a last resort, if some of the ink is good but it's impossible to remove the dried particles, remove all the ink from the can. Place the ink in the center of a double layer of cheesecloth. Pick up the four corners of the cheesecloth, making a bag with the ink in the center. Use a palette knife to push the ink out of the bag. You'll lose a lot of ink, but whatever is strained through the cheesecloth will be usable.

Problem	Cause	Solution
There's an area on the surface of my plate that the hard roller never touches.	If the surface underneath the plate is uneven the hard roller will pick up the highest spots only.	The best solution, of course, would be to find a flat surface for the plate to rest on while you're rolling. If this isn't possible, place one or two pieces of newspaper underneath the plate in the area that isn't picking up the ink to compensate for the unevenness of the surface.
There's a line of ink right across my print.	When you roll a hard roller with oily ink, a line is formed when you pick the roller up off the glass.	Don't remove the roller abruptly, but roll it off the glass slowly. A good analogy is that you want to work the way an airplane leaves the ground—in a slow upward climb—rather than the way a helicopter takes off—straight up.
In some areas of the plate the ink relationships are fine, but in other places the colors are mixing.	You haven't mixed the linseed oil thoroughly into the ink.	Mix the ink thoroughly with a palette knife. Before rolling out the color again, clean up all the ink rolled out on the glass for the previous inking.
Sometimes the surface ink rolls on well; at other times, very little ink appears on the surface of the plate.	You may be leaving too much intaglio ink on the surface of the plate. The plate oil in the intaglio ink makes that ink very oily. As a result, it will accept only a thin film of ink from the oily roller, leaving most of the ink on the roller.	Paper-wipe your plate to remove all the plate tone from the surface.

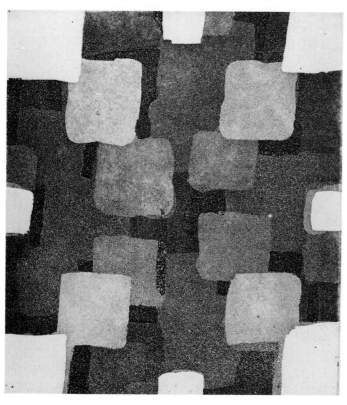

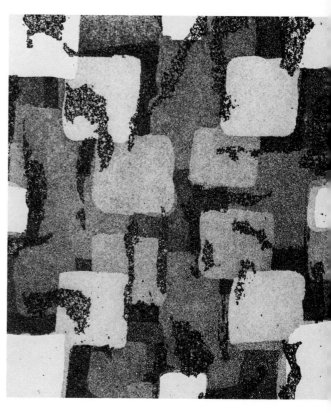

Figure 1. There are five different grays plus white in this proof. The plate was immersed in a weak nitric acid bath five times. The bite was timed for 2, 4, 8, 16, and 32 minutes to create the progression of tones.

Figure 2. In this proof of the same plate used in Figure 1, the darkest tone is the coarse aquatint applied over the fine aquatint—there are now seven variations of tones ranging from white to black.

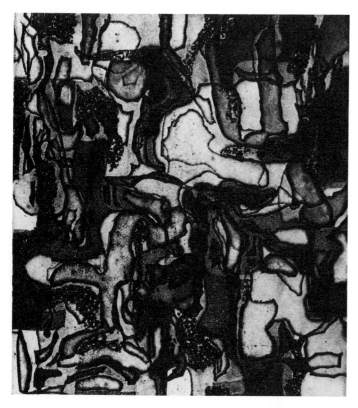

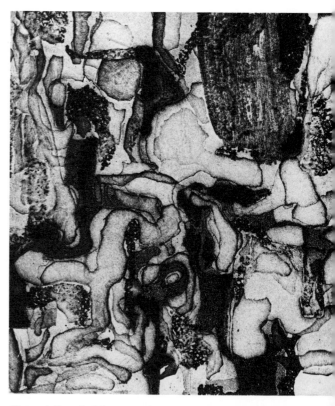

Figure 3. Proof of the same plate used in Figures 1 and 2—the plate is now bitten into three levels. Compare this proof with the one in Figure 2—you'll notice where the aquatint on the surface of the plate has been bitten away.

Figure 4. Proof of the same plate used in Figures 1, 2, and 3, taken after the plate was scraped and polished with a scraper and a flexible shaft.

SEVENTEEN
Viscosity and Aquatint

Once you've mastered the viscosity method (Chapter 16), you may want to try a further elaboration of it—making and printing a plate in which viscosity printing is combined with aquatint. In this method, the rolled-on surface inks with their different oil consistencies are broken into the dots of an aquatint on the plate. The finished plate resembles a pointillist painting. This difficult technique was discovered by Krishna Reddy, a printmaker (see page 129). Don't try this method until you're confident that you're completely familiar with the materials in the earlier chapter of this book, especially Chapter 16.

THE BASIC PROCEDURE

Try a test plate with a simple geometric design first so you learn the possibilities of color variations. Once you understand the procedure you can use any design for this method that is compatible with the principles of viscosity printing.

This chapter will deal with biting the plate with aquatint in different levels, using a flexible shaft tool, and printing the plate. First you'll apply a fine-grain aquatint to the plate. Then you'll bite the plate in acid five times, stopping out more and more of the design after each biting. After proofing the plate at this stage in black intaglio ink, you'll apply a coarse-grain aquatint and bite that. After you proof the resulting plate in black intaglio ink to see the variation of gray tones, you'll ink the plate with an intaglio color, and roll on two surface colors with rollers of different durometers charged with inks of varying viscosities. This rolled color will be deposited on the plate in dots because of the aquatint—you'll be able to see this both on the plate and in the print. Then you'll rebite the plate, scrape and polish it, and print it with three surface inks plus the intaglio ink.

PREPARING THE PLATE

Before you bite your plate, you must prepare it by applying an aquatint (see Chapter 9) and drawing a geometric design over the melted rosin.

Materials and Equipment
cooled zinc plate with fine-grain aquatint applied
lithographic pencil or crayon
rosin stopout and brushes
weak nitric acid bath
water tray or running water
alcohol
paper towels
press set up for printing
varnolene

Process. Take the lithographic crayon and draw a geometric image over the melted rosin on the plate. The lithographic crayon serves to delineate the design throughout the whole biting process and to prevent the stopout you'll brush on from spreading.

Stop out those areas of the plate that are to remain white, and place the plate in the weak acid bath for 2 minutes. Feather the plate often to remove the bubbles (see Chapter 12). When the 2 minutes are up, remove the plate, and place it in cold water. Pat it dry very gently with a paper towel and stop out the second area. Then place the plate in the acid for 4 minutes. Continue to feather the plate.

After 4 minutes, remove the plate from the acid again, place it in cold water, pat it dry again, and stop out the third area. Put the plate back in the acid for 8 minutes. Feather the plate again. Then after 8 minutes remove the plate from the acid, repeat the same process and stop out the fourth area. Place the plate in the acid for 16 minutes. Feather the plate.

After 16 minutes, take the plate out of the acid, follow the same process, and stop out the fifth area. Then place the plate in the acid for 32 minutes, feathering the plate often. After 32 minutes, remove the plate, put it in cold water, and dry it. The plate will now have been in the acid for a total of 62 minutes.

Place the plate on a bed of newspaper, and remove the stopouts and aquatint with a scrub brush and alcohol. Clean and dry the plate with paper towels.

Bevel the plate at this point and proof it with black ink to see if there are five distinct grays (see Figure 1). Also, the proof will help you to decide where you would like to apply a deep black (compare Figures 1 and 2). After you print the plate, clean it with varnolene.

REBITING WITH COARSE-GRAIN AQUATINT

The plate now has five grays, ranging from light to dark. To make a deeper tone, you have to apply a rough-grain aquatint (see Chapter 9).

Materials and Equipment
plate previously bitten five times with a fine-grain aquatint with coarse-grain aquatint
   now applied
lithographic pencil or crayon
rosin stopout and brushes
nitric acid bath
water tray or running water
alcohol
varnolene
press set up for printing
paper towels

Process. Use the lithographic crayon or pencil to draw the outlines of the shapes to be bitten over the coarse-grain aquatint—these shapes will bite deeper and print darker than any other areas on the plate.

Brush stopout over the areas of the plate that you don't want to expose to the acid. (You can also stop out these areas before you apply the coarse-grain aquatint (see Chapter 9, page 95).

Place the plate in the acid for 30 minutes, feathering often. Then remove the plate from the acid, and place it in cold water. Pat it dry with a paper towel, and remove the aquatint and stopout by scrubbing the plate with alcohol and a brush. Wipe everything off with a cloth or with paper towels. Now print the plate in black intaglio ink (see Figure 2) or with two surface colors and one intaglio ink (see below).

PROOFING THE AQUATINTED PLATE

To do this, you'll use two surface colors and one intaglio color. This is the same printing process as described on pages 167–168 of the preceding chapter—you'll ink and wipe the plate with your intaglio ink, roll on an oily ink with a hard roller, then roll on a dry ink with a soft roller. Your plate will have been bitten with aquatint into seven levels ranging from an unbitten surface to a very deep intaglio. The intaglio ink will be dense where the plate was deeply bitten and will be wiped away from the top surfaces. The hard roller with oily ink will deposit color on the unbitten areas and on the dots left by the rosin over the surface of the plate. The soft roller, with the stiff, dry ink will hit the space left between the top surface and the intaglio. Both rolled surface colors will break up into little dots.

You'll need the same material and equipment, and you'll follow the same procedure you did for preparing your surface inks and for printing the viscosity method in Chapter 16. The proof you pull after printing your inked plate should appear to have more than the three colors actually used because of the way in which the color is distributed on the plate. For example, suppose you use a blue intaglio, an oily (low viscosity) yellow rolled with the hard roller, and a dry (high viscosity) red rolled with the soft roller. You'll end up with areas of pure yellow, of yellow and red combined (orange), of pure red, of red and blue combined (purple) where the soft roller gets down close to the blue intaglio, and of pure blue in the deepest intaglio. If you don't get this range of color, the aquatint on your plate isn't bitten deeply enough, has overbitten, or else the rolled inks weren't prepared at the proper viscosity.

You can check on the cause of the difficulty by proofing the plate in a black intaglio ink if you haven't already done so. That proof should show *clearly* a darker gray for each time the plate was put into the acid. The white dots caused by the rosin melted onto the plate should be clearly visible over the whole plate except, of course, in the area that was stopped out before the plate was put into the acid. (This area appears white in the print.)

If the black intaglio proof seems to be right, then the difficulty lies with the viscosity of the inks or with the pressure you applied while you were rolling. Test your surface inks again. When you're rolling colors onto the plate, be sure to allow the hard roller to pass over the plate without exerting any downward pressure. Apply only light pressure when you roll with the soft roller. You should then get a print with the proper variation of color.

REBITING THE PLATE

To add more depth and excitement to your prints, you can rebite the plate so the aquatint will appear only at the top levels of the plate. The rest of the plate will be bitten to a second and a third level (see Figure 3).

Materials and Equipment
plate bitten in levels with both fine and coarse-grain aquatint
asphaltum and rosin stopouts or special stopout and brushes
lint-free cloth
paper towels
strong nitric acid bath
varnolene
alcohol
scrub brush
press set up for printing
black ink intaglio
tray of water or running water
heat lamp
newspaper

Process. Brush asphaltum stopout or special stopout over those areas of the plate that are to remain unbitten (those to remain aquatinted). Then place the plate under the heat lamp until the stopout is dry (see Chapter 7, Figure 9). If you used asphaltum stopout, then when it's dry, brush rosin stopout over it. If you used special stopout, it's not necessary to cover it for reinforcement.

Place the plate in a strong acid bath, and leave it there until you can see a definite level. Refer to Chapter 12 for more detailed information on biting plates in acid. When you see the level, remove the plate from the acid, place it under running water or in a tray of water, and pat it dry with a paper towel.

You'll notice that the aquatint that was bitten lightly in the earlier process has disappeared completely where the plate has been exposed to the acid, while there's still some aquatint texture left in the areas where the aquatint was bitten deeply. Brush rosin stopout or special stopout over the parts of the plate where you would like a second middle level. Then replace the plate in the strong acid until a third distinct level can be seen. When this happens, remove the plate, and place it in cold water or under cold running water. Pat it dry with a paper towel, place it on a bed of newspaper, and pour alcohol and varnolene over it. Allow the solvents to stand for a minute, and then scrub with a brush. Clean the plate of the excess stopouts and solvents with a lint-free cloth.

Pull a proof or two in either black intaglio ink or in color inks before you continue to work on the plate. You'll be able to compare this print(s) with the previous prints of this aquatinted plate. The proofs may help you decide where the plate should be scraped or polished (see below).

SCRAPING AND POLISHING

In Chapter 16 the plate was bitten into three levels and printed with an intaglio ink and two surface colors. By using a scraper and the flexible shaft tool to polish, scrape, and burnish the plate—as described here—the surface of the plate will be altered so that there will be many levels rather than three distinct levels. This produces an even richer interplay of color.

Materials and Equipment
plate with aquatint bitten in levels rebitten into three more levels
scraper
flexible shaft machine tool with carbide burrs and polishing equipment (see Chapter 2)
light machine oil or 3 & 1 Oil
burnisher
safety glasses
press set up for printing

Process. Using the scraper, remove the sharp edges made by the acid when it bit the plate to the second and third levels (see Figure 4). Apply some light machine oil to the area which is being scraped. Instead of following the scraping directions in Chapter 7, you should use a great deal of pressure when you scrape here—try to remove a sizable piece of metal with each pass of the scraper.

When you finish scraping, put on safety glasses. Pick up the flexible shaft, insert a carbide burr in the chuck or collet, and go over the areas you have scraped with the scraper. Then replace the burr in the flexible shaft tool with a polishing disc. Polish some—but not all—of the areas of the plate so that you can see a difference when the plate is proofed. With experience you'll be able to judge more easily what areas should be polished.

Next, burnish some of the areas of the plate, using light machine oil in these areas (see Chapter 7, page 77 for instructions). When you're done, take a proof of the plate and compare it to the proof you took before you began scraping (Figure 3 vs. Figure 4). You can continue to scrape, burnish, and proof the plate until the proof is pleasing to you. Then print the plate in color.

PRINTING WITH THREE SURFACE COLORS

After you ink the plate with an intaglio color, you'll use soft, medium, and hard rollers on the plate, each charged with a color of different viscosity. The first time you do this, try a light color intaglio—for example, yellow or orange. Or try making the intaglio transparent by the addition of a transparent base.

Materials and Equipment
aquatinted plate bitten in three levels, scraped, and polished
press set up for printing
3 surface color inks
transparent base
soft, medium, and hard rollers with stands
3 small rubber rollers
palette knives
magnesium carbonate
raw linseed oil
5 sheets of ¼" thick plate glass
kerosene
lint-free cloths

Process. To begin, place some of the light color intaglio ink on one ¼" plate glass. Add the transparent base in a ratio of 1 part transparent base to 3 parts ink on the glass. Mix thoroughly with a palette knife until the ink is the consistency of heavy sweet cream. If the ink becomes very sticky, add a few drops of raw linseed oil. Then ink the plate with the intaglio ink (see Chapter 13 if necessary), and put the plate aside until you're ready to roll on surface color.

Place approximately 1 tbsp. each of the three different color surface inks on three different pieces of ¼" plate glass. Add 15 drops of raw linseed oil to the ink that will be used with the hard roller and mix them in thoroughly with a palette knife. Then add 5 drops of raw linseed oil to the ink that will be used with the medium roller and mix them in thoroughly. You'll use the third color as it comes from the can.

Use the three small rubber rollers to test the viscosity of the surface colors just as you did for two colors in Chapter 16 (see page 167). Roll out the low viscosity ink—the one with 15 drops of oil added—with the first roller on a glass slab. Charge the second roller with ink of higher viscosity—with 5 drops of oil added—and roll it over the first color. The roller will deposit ink on both sides of the first roller, but not on top of it because the oilier ink will reject the drier ink. Then roll the third roller, charged with high viscosity ink—with no oil added—over the other two colors. This roller will deposit ink on the slab next to the other two colors—there should be three distinct colors visible on the glass—but not on top of each other (see Figure 5).

Where the three rollers intersect, the first surface color which was applied—the ink of lowest viscosity—should remain as a pale version of the color which was originally rolled, before the other two colors were rolled over it. That is because the stiffer (drier) inks on the other two rollers peeled a little ink off the first color each time they passed over it. The two rollers going over the first color should not, however, have *added* any color to the color on the glass. Thus, if the first color was yellow, the second blue, and the third red, the yellow should not have any blue or red mixed with it—instead, it should be a pale, clear yellow.

If the second color did mix with the first, then add a few more drops of raw linseed oil to the first color ink on the glass. If the third color mixed with the second, add magnesium carbonate to the third ink to make it thicker (of higher viscosity). In either case, clean the rollers and test the ink again before proceeding. When all three colors are clearly visible on the glass, the relationship of the viscosities of the ink are correct.

When the relationship of the viscosities of the inks is correct and can be seen on the plate glass, charge the large rollers with ink. Use the hard roller with the ink containing 15 drops, or more, of raw linseed oil, the medium roller with the ink containing 5 drops of raw linseed oil, and the soft roller with the stiffest ink with no oil added and possibly with some magnesium carbonate mixed in. Replace each roller in its stand after it has been charged with the ink.

Place the inked intaglio plate on a piece of ¼″ plate glass. Guide the hard roller over the plate without any downward pressure, and then replace the roller on its stand. *Never leave a roller lying with its surface touching anything.* Next, roll the medium roller over the plate, applying a very light downward pressure. Replace the roller in its stand, and roll the soft roller over the plate with a firm—but not heavy—downward pressure. Again, replace the roller on its stand.

At this point, you should clean the rollers with lint-free cloths and kerosene. If you don't clean the roller until after you print, it might not be dry enough—traces of kerosene might remain—to roll out the ink for the next print.

If you want to, you could print the plate now. The print would have four distinct colors, although the surface color would be very pale, since the medium and soft rollers each picked up a thin film of surface color when they were rolled across the plate. You may want this pale effect, but if you'd rather reinforce the surface color or apply another color altogether, use the contact inking process (see below).

CONTACT INKING

Instead of using another roller to apply another color, with contact inking you'll place the plate inked with intaglio ink and rolled with three surface colors color-side down on a flat, inked surface.

Materials and Equipment
plate inked with 1 intaglio color and 3 surface colors
fresh surface color
raw linseed oil
small gelatin roller
palette knife
sheet of ¼″ plate glass, larger than the plate

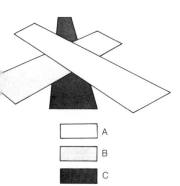

Figure 5. The first (oily) color (A) is rolled onto the plate glass. The second color with less oil added (B) is rolled over the first. The third color with no oil added (C) is rolled over the first and second colors. Each color is distinct and clear. Where they intersect, only a pale version of the first oily color (A) appears.

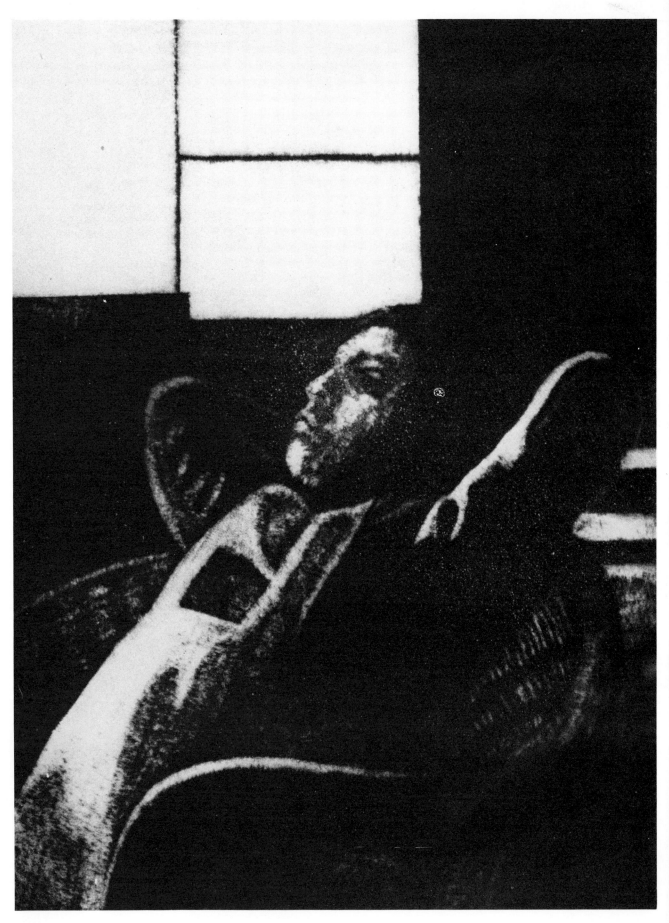

Child in a Wicker Chair *by Nat Cole. Aquatint, 24″ x 18″.*

Process. Place some fresh surface color on the glass with a palette knife. Add 20 drops of raw linseed oil to the ink and mix it in thoroughly. The ink should be quite oily, but not too oily to roll. If the roller skids rather than rolls, the ink is too oily—add more fresh ink to make it less so.

Roll the ink onto the glass with the gelatin roller, covering a portion of the glass which is larger than the plate. The rolled-out ink should be evenly distributed, having no thick or thin areas of ink. Place the plate with its inked side down in the middle of the ink on the glass. With the palms of both hands facing down, slap the back of the plate once. The top surface of the plate will come in contact with the ink rolled out on the glass. (The plate will pick up ink only where it touches the glass). Then placing the second and third fingers of each hand on opposite sides of the plate, carefully pick the plate up straight off the glass (see Figure 6). *Be very careful not to slide the plate on the glass!* Turn the plate over—it should have a reinforcement of new color on its top level only. Now print the plate.

The print of this plate will appear to have more than three levels. If the image isn't esthetically satisfying to you, you can scrape or polish it further. It's also helpful to try different combinations of color to see how the different colors add to the possibilities of the plate. Remember, however, that each time you use a new ink, you'll have to test the relationship of the viscosities of all the inks to each other.

CLEANUP

Refer to Chapters 7, 12, and 13 for cleanup procedures.

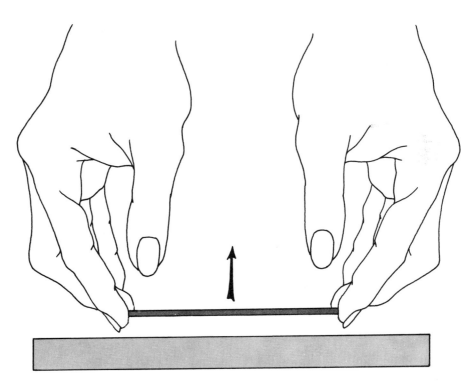

Figure 6. Lift the plate straight up to avoid smudging the contact ink.

Problem	Cause	Solution
The plate is warped.	Putting an aquatint on the surface of a large plate with a small hot plate does tend to warp the plate.	Use a large hot plate that heats evenly to avoid warping the plate. You may have to wait longer for the aquatint to melt, but it's worth it. If a large hot plate isn't available and the plate warps, place the plate in a tray of very hot water. After the plate becomes hot, place it *quickly* face down on the bed of the press between two blotters larger than the plate. Run it through the press. (You must, of course, use blankets.) Don't use excess pressure. Repeat this process several times if necessary.
The hard roller doesn't touch every part of the surface of the plate.	1. The plate is warped.	1. Try to flatten your warped plate (see above).
	2. The surface under the plate when you roll isn't perfectly flat.	2. Place several pieces of newspaper under the area of the plate where the roller isn't touching before you roll.
	3. The roller you're using has an uneven surface.	2. Change rollers.
The only areas where the plate breaks into points of color are the areas on the plate where the second (coarse) aquatint was applied.	You might not have bitten the plate deeply enough.	Check your acid. A plate with aquatint applied should begin to bubble immediately when placed in the acid. If it doesn't, make a fresh weak nitric acid bath.

PART FOUR
Other Mediums and Methods

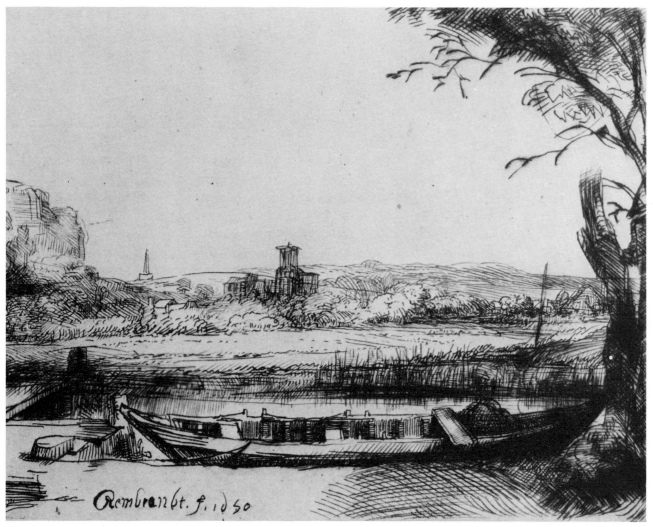

Canal with Large Boat and Bridge *by Rembrandt (1606-1669). Drypoint. Courtesy Metropolitan Museum of Art, New York City, Gift of Mrs. Ernest A. Fairchild.*

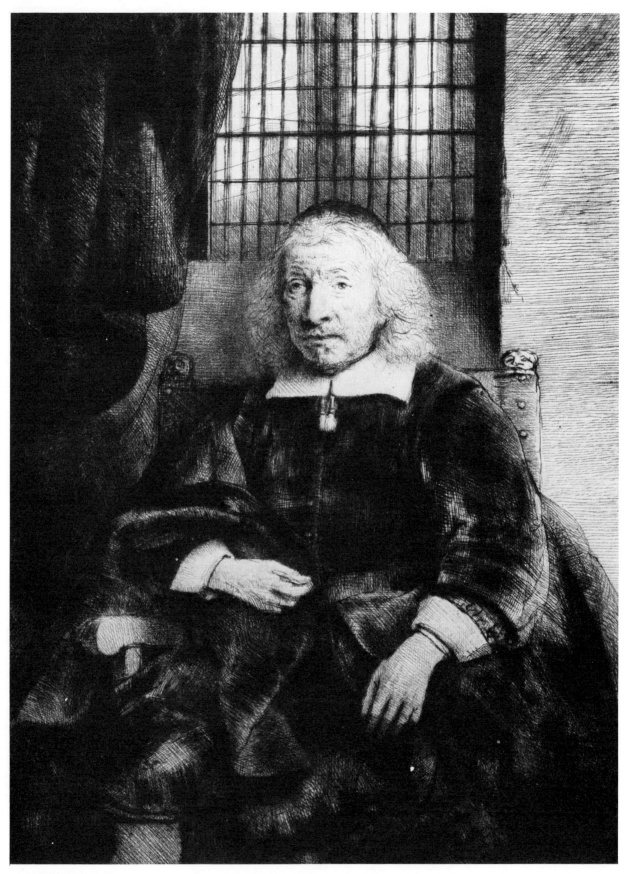

Jacob Haaring *(The "Old Haaring") by Rembrandt (1606-1669). Drypoint. Courtesy Metropolitan Museum of Art, New York City, The H.O. Havemeyer Collection.*

EIGHTEEN
Drypoint

When you cut lines directly into the plate with a carbide steel point or a diamond point, the finished plate is called a drypoint. The drypoint needle doesn't remove metal as the burin does in engraving (see Chapter 19); rather, it displaces the metal to one or both sides of the line, forming a burr (see Figure 1). The burr retains the ink, as the line itself is very shallow. The velvety dark lines created by the burrs that hold the ink give the drypoint its characteristic look. When the burr is worn down by the pressure of printing (this happens very quickly if you use a copper plate), the line will print lightly and the image loses its vitality. You must take a great deal of care, therefore, to preserve the integrity of the burr. If you want to print a large edition, your copper plate must be commercially steel-faced. Don't use zinc for a drypoint—it would wear down much too fast.

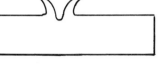

Figure 1. The burr on a drypoint catches the ink underneath the curls of metal that are displaced by the needle.

DRAWING ON THE PLATE

You'll use a lithographic crayon to put your drawing directly on the plate as a guide for the drypoint needle. Before you begin, you must bevel your plate—see Chapter 7 for directions.

Materials and Equipment
copper or steel plate with beveled edges
lithographic crayon
cloth

Process. Draw directly on the plate with the lithographic crayon. You can remove areas of the drawing if necessary simply by rubbing them off the plate with a cloth. When you're satisfied with the crayon drawing, you can use the drypoint needle.

USING A DRYPOINT NEEDLE

The drypoint needle, when used correctly, will raise a burr on the plate. Use a test plate for your first drypoint so you'll feel free about experimenting with different types of lines.

Materials and Equipment
drypoint needle, with a carbide steel or diamond point
copper or steel plate
black intaglio ink
linseed oil
scraper
burnisher

Process. If you're using a steel drypoint needle, be sure that the point is sharp and round. See Chapter 2, page 23, for directions for sharpening a drypoint needle.

Hold your needle firmly, just as you would hold a pencil (see Figure 2). Draw your first line with the needle held perpendicular to the plate. This will give you a line with a burr on both sides of it (see Figure 3). Next, draw a line with the drypoint needle tilted toward the plate, forming an angle of 60° with the plate (see Figure 3). This will give you a burr on only one side of the line. If you hold the needle closer to the plate at a smaller angle than 60°, the burr raised will be extremely fragile and will disappear in the first printing.

Experiment with lines and curves on the test plate until you feel that you have control of the needle. You'll notice that the more firmly you hold the needle, the more control you have. Rub oily black intaglio ink gently into the plate so that you can see your progress. You'll have to examine the line on the plate itself rather than proofing the

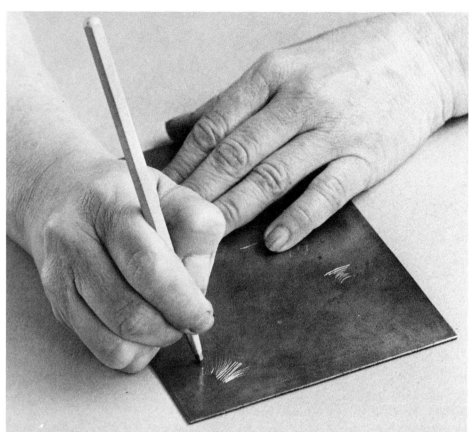

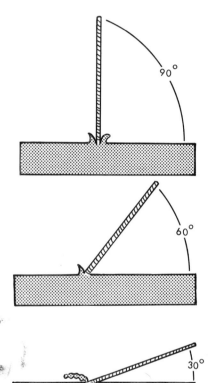

Figure 3. From top to bottom: a drypoint needle held straight up—the line produced by the burr will print in a lovely, rich black when printed with black intaglio ink; the drypoint needle held at an angle of 60° from the plate—the line produced by this burr will only be half as dark; the needle held at an angle of 30° from the plate—the line produced will most likely disappear fast during the inking process.

plate—drypoints aren't trial proofed since each time the plate is printed, a little of the burr is lost.

Because the drypoint is so fragile, there's no difficulty in removing unwanted burrs or lines. Scrape out any unwanted burrs the same way you would scrape out unwanted lines in an etched plate (see Chapter 7, page 74). You'll find that the burr offers little resistance to the scraper. To remove the line after the burr has been removed, burnish it according to the directions in Chapter 7, page 77.

Before you begin work on a final plate, you should print your test plate.

PRINTING A DRYPOINT

The drypoint needs special care when it's printed in order to avoid—as much as possible—crushing the burr. For general information on printing, see Chapter 13.

Materials and Equipment
edition paper—Italia or Dutch paper—either presoaked or soaking in a tray of water
blotters, rolling pin, and paper towels to blot the paper (see Chapter 13)
cardboard clips
black intaglio ink
¼″ thick plate glass or marble slab
raw linseed oil
tarlatan
talcum powder
press set up for printing
garden gloves
palette knife
hot plate

Process. Prepare your black intaglio ink on the slab by adding raw linseed oil until the ink runs off the palette knife to the slab in a slow, *continuous* stream. Ink used for printing a drypoint should be oilier than ink used for an etching.

Your tarlatan for drypoint printing should be especially soft, with most of the starch

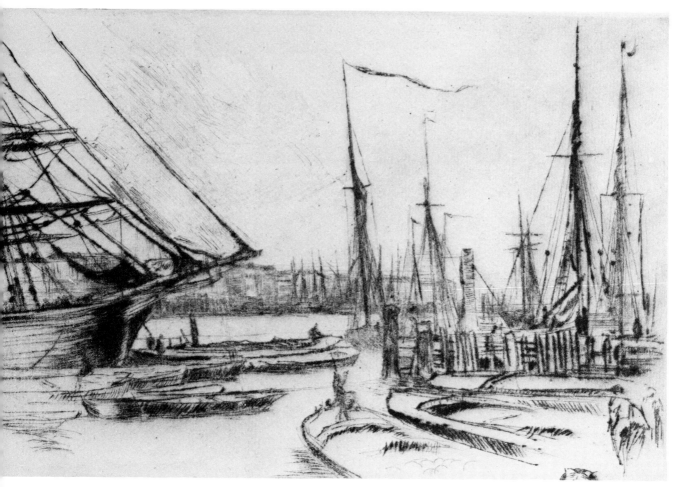

Sketch from Billingsgate *by James A. McNeill Whistler (1834-1903). Drypoint. Courtesy Met-*
ropolitan Museum of Art, New York City, Harris Brisbane Dick Fund.

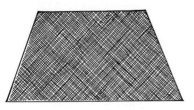

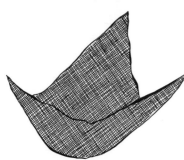

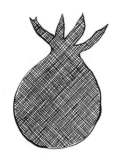

Figure 4. To make a dauber, take a 3″ square of tarlatan, top, gather the ends, center, and twist them together, bottom.

removed (see Chapter 13, page 138). After you prepare your tarlatan, cut a 3″ square out of it and make a small dauber. Just take the four corners of the 3″ square and twist them together (see Figure 4).

Next, place your plate on the hot plate until it's warm to the touch but not too hot—if it's too hot to touch, then it's too hot. Dip the dauber into the intaglio ink and transfer some of the ink from the slab to the plate. With a gentle rocking motion and a light downward pressure, cover the whole plate with the ink.

For fear of damaging the burr, you can't remove the excess ink with a cardboard as you would if you were inking an etching. Therefore, the next step is to use the softened tarlatan to wipe the plate with a gentle, circular motion over the entire surface. Avoid rubbing the plate vigorously as this, too, could damage the burr. When the ink is evenly distributed over the plate with the tarlatan, you should hand-wipe the surface (see Chapter 13, page 141).

Blot your paper if necessary (see Chapter 13, page 141), and make sure that the pressure on the press is slightly looser than it would be if you were printing an etching. Your blankets should be clean and fluffy—if possible, use new blankets, since they're best for printing a drypoint.

When you're ready, place the plate on the bed of the press. Using cardboard clips, place the dampened paper on top of the inked plate. Then pull the blankets taut, and roll the plate through the press.

Please note that when you're printing a drypoint, you should allow yourself enough time to print as many prints as you'll want for the edition. If you have to clean your plate to store it between printings, the repeated scrubbing will weaken the burr.

CLEANUP

The cleanup process is basically the same as cleaning up after printing an etching. See Chapter 13 for information on what to do with the press blankets, hot plate, intaglio ink, glass or marble slab, and water tray. The differences in the cleanup process are listed below.

1. Only clean and store your plate if you absolutely must. Pour varnolene on the surface, and gently wipe the ink and solvent off with a cloth. Repeat this process as many times as is necessary until all the ink has been removed. As you work, remember that the burr on the drypoint plate is fragile—don't scrub it.

2. Throw away the tarlatan dauber.

WHAT WENT WRONG AND WHY

Problem	Cause	Solution
It's difficult to draw with the steel drypoint needle—it resists going in some directions.	If your drypoint needle isn't completely round, the needle will pull in one direction.	Polish the needle until it's perfectly round—see Chapter 2 for directions.
After I pull two or three prints, some lines begin to disappear, although the rest of the plate is intact.	Lines drawn with the needle held at an angle of less than 60° from the plate will disappear immediately.	Add additional lines with the needle either next to the lines that aren't printing or in the same grooves. Unfortunately, however, you lose some of the freshness of the drypoint when you reinforce lines.
When I wipe the drypoint, the tarlatan gets caught in the burr.	Either your tarlatan isn't folded into a flat pad on the bottom, or you're exerting too much downward pressure when you wipe.	Open the tarlatan out flat. Tuck the ends in so that the part of the tarlatan that will touch the plate is shaped like a perfectly flat pad. Wipe the plate very gently in a circular motion. If the tarlatan still gets caught in the burr, then hand-wipe the plate.

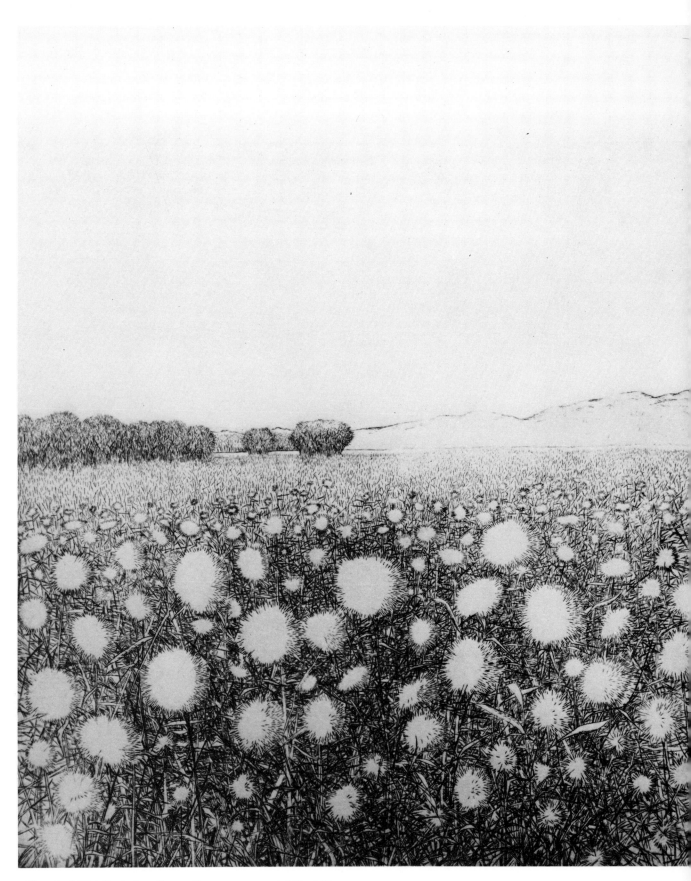

Adirondack Field *by Robert Kuzyn. Engraving on steel, 20″ x 20″*

NINETEEN

Engraving

Engraving is one of the earliest means of expression known to man, dating from the time when magic images were carved into the walls of prehistoric caves. The use of an engraved metal plate for the purpose of making a print, however, was not developed until the fifteenth century in Europe. This method consists of incising lines directly into a plate with a tool called a burin. The engraved line that results swells and tapers as the burin enters and then leaves the plate, giving the printed line its singular appearance. Many artists combine engraving with etching because this process requires so much time and skill. Copper is the metal most frequently used, although steel is sometimes substituted.

DRAWING ON THE PLATE

You must draw an image onto the plate to act as a guide for the engraved lines. Don't go to the trouble of doing this until you feel confident when you use the burin (see below).

Materials and Equipment
grease pencil or lithographic crayon
copper plate
Dutch mordant in tray
lint-free cloth or paper towels
varnolene
pad of newspaper

Process. To begin, draw on the shiny surface of the copper plate with a lithographic crayon or grease pencil. Use the lint-free cloth to erase any areas of the drawing that need changing.

When your drawing is complete, immerse the plate in the Dutch mordant for a few minutes—until its surface becomes discolored. Then remove the plate from the acid, rinse it immediately in cold water, and let the water drain off. It's not necessary to dry the plate.

Place the plate on a pad of newspaper, and pour a small amount of varnolene on its surface. Remove the lines made by the grease pencil and the varnolene by wiping with a cloth or paper towels. The lines or areas of the plate on which you drew with the grease pencil were acid-resistant and, as you can see, were not affected by the acid. You now have a shiny image of your drawing on a plate that has been dulled or discolored by acid. If you don't want to have a drawing on the plate as a guide, immerse the plate in acid to remove the high polish on the surface—the glare of the polished copper is hard on your eyes.

ENGRAVING WITH A BURIN

You'll use a burin to incise the engraved textures and lines into a copper plate. Until you master the technique, practice engraving on a small test plate. To engrave properly, the burin must be sharp and held correctly (for sharpening technique see Chapter 2). To hold the burin properly, lay your hand on the table with the palm up. Place the handle of the burin in the heel of your palm, with the bottom of the V of the shank facing up (see Figure 1). Your thumb and the third finger should hold the shank on either side while the forefinger rests near the point *as a guide only*—you don't push down on the point of the burin when you engrave. Pressure exerted by your forefinger will just impede the progress of the burin through the metal. Next, turn your hand over, and rest the burin on the table. You should be able to slide the burin back and forth easily with the bottom of the V of the shank touching the table. If your fingers

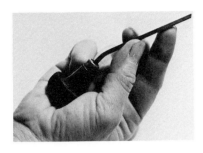

Figure 1. To hold the burin properly, tuck it into your hand so that the handle rests against your palm. Your thumb and third finger go on either side; your forefinger rests near the tip.

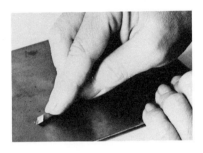

Figure 2. Engraving a line into the plate with the burin. The hand you're not using must always rest behind the burin. Notice the forefinger is guiding the burin, not pushing down.

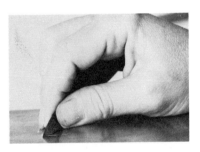

Figure 3. To remove the burr, place the scraper flat on one side and push it forward in the direction of the burin cut.

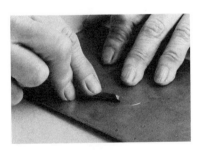

Figure 4. Making a circular cut—notice that my left hand turns the plate, while the other hand holding the burin doesn't turn at all.

are in the way, you aren't holding the burin correctly. Rearrange it in your palm until you're comfortable and can move the shank easily on the table.

Materials and Equipment
copper plate—small if this is your first time engraving, prepared with a drawing if not (see above)
sharpened burins Nos. 6 and 10
scraper
machine oil or 3 in 1 oil
tracing paper or translucent paper

Process. The position of your entire body plays a part in the engraving of a line. To be in the correct position, sit with your knees facing the direction in which you'll be cutting—if you're right-handed, your knees should be pointing toward your left and vice versa. The elbow of the hand holding the burin should rest comfortably on the table.

Holding the burin as described above, engage the point in your plate. If you're right-handed, you should hold the plate steady with your left hand, rest your right elbow lightly on the table, and push the burin forward with your palm (see Figure 2). The movement of your hand should start at your shoulder. If you keep your wrist relaxed, the burin should move forward without slipping. If the burin doesn't move easily, the angle of its entry into the plate is too steep—you must lower your wrist. If you're working on a test plate—and you should be if this is your first engraving—then just practice. If you've put a drawing on your plate, then follow the lines of the image.

After engraving a line, you'll notice a burr at the end of the cut. To avoid cutting your hands and the printing paper, you must remove this burr. Place the flat side of the scraper on the plate behind or on the engraved side of the burr (see Figure 3). Move the scraper without tilting it in the same direction as the burin cut and remove the burr. (If you were to scrape the burr from the uncut side, you would push it back into the line rather than remove it). Practice making parallel lines of about the same length until you have control of the burin—remove the burr after each line.

The next step is to learn how to make a circular line. To do this, place a thin pad of newspaper, smaller than the plate, under the test plate to reduce the friction between plate and table. The plate now turns easily. To make a circular line, engage the burin in the plate, and turn the plate slowly with your left hand (if you're right-handed) while pushing gently with the burin in your right hand. You turn the plate, not the burin, to make a curved line (see Figure 4).

For a dotted texture, engage the point of the No. 10 burin in the plate, turning the plate completely around while the burin is engaged. Then remove the burr with the scraper, checking the point of the burin to see that it remains sharp. Place one dot next to another until a texture results. Of course, you can control the tone of the texture by the placement of dots—if the dots are close together, the tone will appear darker when you print; as the distance between them increases, the tone will appear lighter.

You can get a texture with triangular cuts by pushing the burin into the plate at an obtuse angle and then pulling the burin back from the cut (see Figure 5). Again, remove the burr with a scraper, and repeat the process until you're satisfied with the texture created. The closer the triangular cuts, the darker the tone in the finished print (see Figure 6). For dark lines and textures, you'll see that burin cuts that are close to each other are preferable to very deep grooves that are difficult to print.

SCRAPING OUT AN ENGRAVED LINE

You can scrape out an engraved line the same way you would scrape out an etched line—see Chapter 7, page 74. Try to achieve the sloping depression shown in Figure 7 of that chapter, because if the depression is shallow, you can polish the plate (see Chapter 7, page 77) to remove the tone created by the scraper. If, however, the depression is deep, you'll have to straighten it out by an application of tape to the back of the plate (see below).

CORRECTING A DEPRESSION ON THE PLATE

If a deep depression is left in the plate after scraping, you'll have to level the hollowed area so it won't be visible in the print. This process is called repoussage. You can use

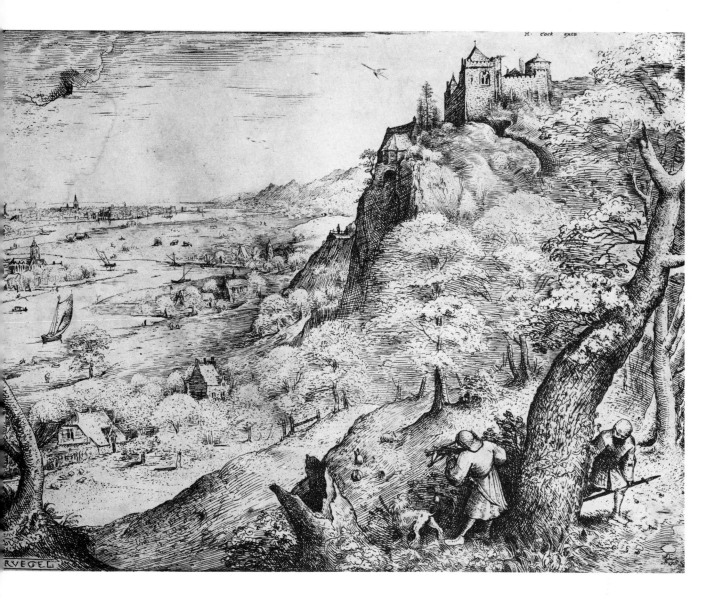

Hunting Wild Rabbits *by Pieter Brueghel the Elder (1525?-1569). Engraving, 8⁷/₁₆″ x 11⅜″. Courtesy Metropolitan Museum of Art, New York City, Harris Brisbane Dick Fund.*

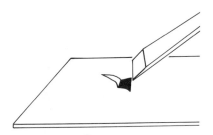

Figure 5. Pulling the burin back out of the cut to create a triangular dot.

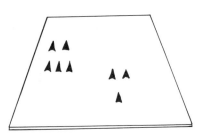

Figure 6. When the triangular cuts made by the burin are close together (left), the overall tone will appear darker in the print than when the cuts are farther apart (right).

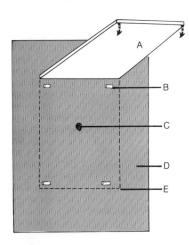

Figure 7. The back of the plate (A) placed down over the circles of tape (B) to cover the hole (C) in the blotter (D). The plate and platemark must be aligned.

outside calipers to accomplish this if you have them (see Chapter 2, page 28). If you don't have access to outside calipers, however, use the following method. Before you begin, bevel your plate if you haven't already done so.

Materials and Equipment
press set up for printing
engraved plate with a deep hollow depression caused by scraping
masking tape or another pressure-sensitive tape
blotter
black intaglio ink
varnolene
grease pencil
tarlatan
lint-free cloth or paper towels
single-edged razor blades
tissue paper large enough to cover the plate

Process. Ink the plate *only* in the area of the depression, and wipe that inked area with a tarlatan. Then put the plate on the bed of the press, and place the blotter on top. Pull the blankets down, and run the plate through the press.

Remove the blotter and the plate from the press—the blotter should have the impression of the plate embossed on it with the depressed area inked and visible. Next, remove the ink from the plate with varnolene and a lint-free cloth or paper towels, making sure that the plate is dry on both sides.

Using a single-edged razor blade, cut the shape of the depressed area out of the print on the blotter, and discard that piece of the blotter. Then place the frame-like blotter, print side down, on a flat surface. Cut four pieces of masking tape or another pressure-sensitive tape, and roll them into circles with the sticky side facing out. Put the tape on the back of the blotter inside the corners of the plate mark. The next step is to place the plate, printing surface facing up, on the back of the blotter, making sure the plate is aligned with the platemark on the blotter (see Figure 7). Press the plate down in the four corners so that the tape sticks to both the plate and the blotter. The hole in the print will be aligned with the depression on the front of the plate. Trace the outline of the hole on the back of the plate with a grease pencil. Then remove the blotter and tape from the plate.

Completely fill in the grease pencil outline on the back of the plate with fresh masking tape. If the depression on the front of the plate is very deep, place one piece of tape over another.

Put the plate, printing surface up, on the bed of the press, and cover it with tissue paper. Pull the blankets down, and run the plate through the press. The masking tape will push the hollow depression up so that the top surface of the plate will be level and ready to be polished (see Chapter 7, page 77).

PRINTING AN ENGRAVING

Before you print, make sure your plate is beveled (see Chapter 7). When you do print, use a stiffer, less oily ink than you would use for printing an etching. The engraved line is smoother than an etched line, and you can easily wipe an oily ink out of the grooves. The paper you use for engraving should be smooth, with sizing, rather than a handmade or unsized paper. See Chapter 13 for printing instructions.

CLEANUP

1. Place a piece of cork or an eraser on the ends of the burin and the scraper to protect the cutting edges.

2. Wipe the burnisher with a drop of 3-in-1 oil on a cloth.

3. Wipe the plate with kerosene to prevent corrosion, and put it into a plastic bag. If you printed the plate, remove the ink with varnolene before wiping with kerosene.

4. Sweep up the bits of metal caused by engraving and scraping from the work surface. These pieces of metal can cause damage if they come in contact with grounds or inks.

5. To prevent fire, throw out newspaper or cloths with oil or kerosene on them.

WHAT WENT WRONG AND WHY

Problem	Cause	Solution
The burin won't move through the copper unless I rock it from side to side.	1. You're exerting too much pressure on the point of the burin.	1. Don't press down with your forefinger. See that your wrist and elbow are down near the table.
	2. Your burin is dull.	2. Check to see if your burin is dull—if it is, then sharpen it according to directions given in Chapter 2.
The burin keeps slipping as I engrave a line.	You're holding the burin incorrectly.	If the bottom of the shank of the burin isn't held vertically in relation to the plate, you lose control. When the burin is engaged in the plate, be sure you're not leaning on it to the right or left.

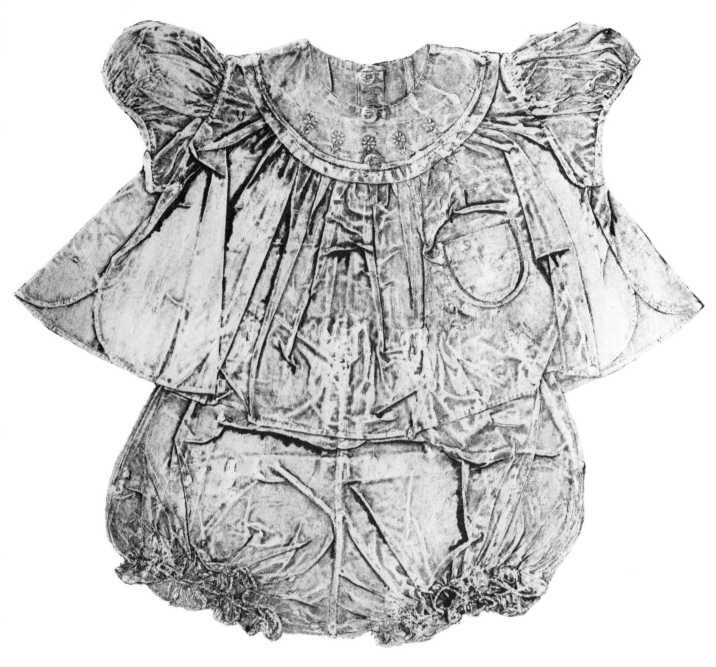

Yessir, that's my baby! *by Alyce King Vaccino. Collagraph.*

TWENTY
Collagraphs

The word "collagraph" is made up from a union of the words "collage" and "graphic"—a collagraph plate is made the same way a collage is made. and it's then printed. Collage, of course, is the medium in which papers. drawings. paintings. and other materials are glued together to make a single work of art. The collagraph plate can consist of cardboard, metal, or Masonite, and of materials and found objects that can be printed in relief or in intaglio on an etching press.

To make a collagraph, you can either glue all the objects to be used to a base of metal, cardboard, or Masonite, or you can ink them separately and assemble them for printing. Before you try an ambitious collagraph. familiarize yourself with the medium by making a test plate which will permit you some experimentation and freedom. After making and printing your test plate. you'll be better able to determine which methods to use when you want to arrive at a particular solution or to get a certain effect.

ASSEMBLING A ONE-PLATE COLLAGRAPH

Individual materials used for this method will all become part of a single collagraph plate. Please note that because the plate must dry after each application of glue or gesso, there are many waiting periods between stages—don't hurry these drying stages. It can take days or even weeks to assemble a plate—and if you let a completed plate rest for a month before you print, it becomes extremely sturdy.

Materials and Equipment (see Figures 1. 2. and 3)
chipboard, thin metal, or Masonite to use as a base plate
oaktag
fabrics
found objects
thin string
matknife or single-edged razor blades
scissors
tin shears for metal-based plate or hacksaw for Masonite-based plate
2" wide nylon, oxhair, or camel's hair brush
Elmer's glue
rectangular pieces of cut cardboards
pencil
container or jar wide enough for a 2" wide brush
straight pins
gesso or modeling paste
cold water
sandpaper, medium to fine
smooth block of wood. approximately 2" x 4" x 5"
¼" plate glass. larger than the plate

Process. If your base plate is made of chipboard. use a matknife or a single-edged razor blade to cut it to the size and shape that you desire. Keep in mind that the plate doesn't have to be square or rectangular—it can be round or free-form. Cut the shape with a beveled edge by tilting the razor blade or matknife at an angle instead of holding it straight up and down while you cut. If your base plate is made of Masonite. cut it with a hacksaw; if it's made of thin metal, cut it with tin shears. Cut the materials you want to use—fabric, string, oaktag, and so on, into various shapes. Then arrange all of them on your base plate until you're satisfied with the effect. The pieces of material can touch one another or even overlap. When you like the design. trace the position of all the shapes onto the plate with a pencil, and then remove the materials from the plate.

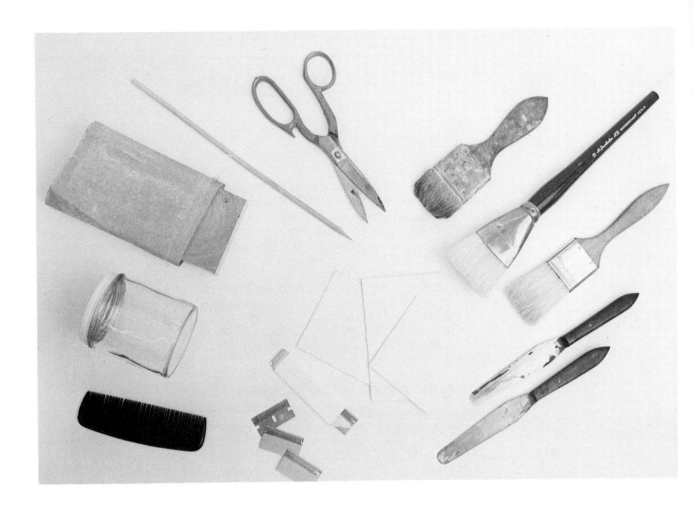

Figure 1 (above). Some of the tools you'll need when working with a collagraph (from the extreme left and moving clockwise): comb, jar with screw top, block of wood wrapped with sandpaper, stick to draw with, scissors, 3 brushes, 2 palette knives, 3 razor blades, razor blade holder, and 3 pieces of cut cardboard.

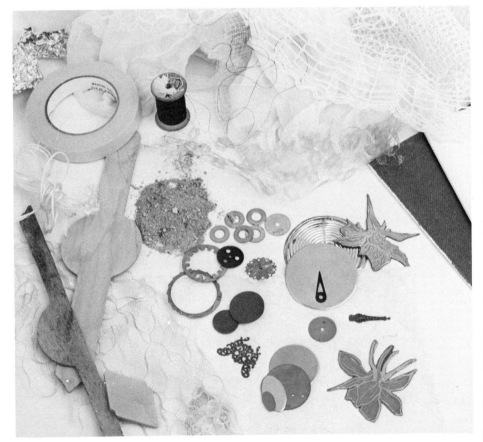

Figure 2 (right). Some materials that may be incorporated into a collagraph, top left to right: tin foil, tape, laces, thread, and textures. Bottom left to right: more textures, very thin pieces of wood, sand, washers, jewelry findings, gaskets, cut zinc plates, watch parts, Masonite, and oak tag.

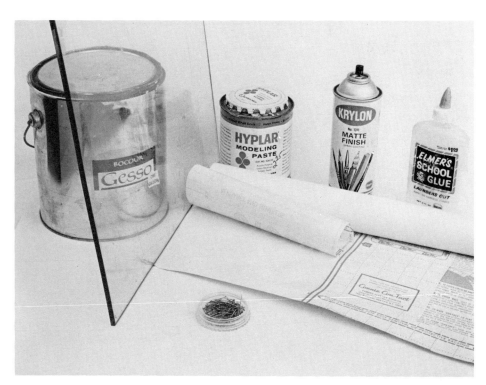

Figure 3. More materials you'll need to make collagraphs, from top left to right: gesso, plate glass, modeling paste, Krylon, and Elmer's glue. Underneath are contact paper and straight pins.

Either pour the Elmer's glue into a container large enough to hold the 2″ wide brush or squeeze the glue out of the container directly onto the plate and then spread it around with pieces of cut cardboards. Make sure that you cover the *whole* plate with a coat of Elmer's glue. The pencil drawing of the shapes will be visible through the glue (see Figure 4). While the glue is wet, place the first layer of materials on the plate. Using the 2″ brush, cover the material with another coat of Elmer's glue. Rinse the brush in cold water immediately after you use it—if the glue dries on the brush, you won't be able to remove it.

If the material you're gluing on won't stay down on a cardboard plate, push straight pins through the material into the plate to keep it down until it dries (from 15 minutes to 4 hours depending on the weather). If your base plate is metal or Masonite, you can't use straight pins, but you can put a piece of ¼″ glass, larger than the plate, over the material shapes to keep them down (see Figure 5).

Continue to glue on each layer of material, textures, found objects, or shapes of cut cardboard one at a time. Allow each layer to dry before you add another, until your design is completed. At this point, you can add texture with the glue alone. The container of Elmer's glue usually has a spout which allows a limited amount of glue to ooze out when you squeeze the container. By turning the container upside down over the plate and squeezing it, you can draw with the glue.

After the glue is dry—or, if you don't draw with the glue, when the last layer of material is dry—coat the plate with a thin coat of gesso or modeling paste using the 2″ wide soft brush. Don't add water to the gesso or modeling paste, and wash the brush in cold water immediately afterwards. Allow the gesso to dry, and then apply a second, *thin* coat of gesso or modeling paste (add water this time if necessary). This additional coat will fill in the areas around the pasted forms—these areas would otherwise collect large amounts of intaglio ink that would bleed (be pushed out of the crevices by the pressure of the press) when the plate was printed.

Allow the plate to dry *thoroughly* for a few days. Then sand the surface with medium to fine sandpaper. To facilitate the sanding, wrap the sandpaper around a small smooth block of wood (see Figure 1). When you're finished, run your hand over the plate. There shouldn't be any sharp edges or areas where the materials glued on aren't firmly attached.

If there are glued areas lifting, brush another coat of gesso over these sections. Insert straight pins or cover the surface with plate glass to hold all edges down. After the gesso has dried completely, wait a day or two. Then, if there are no unattached areas

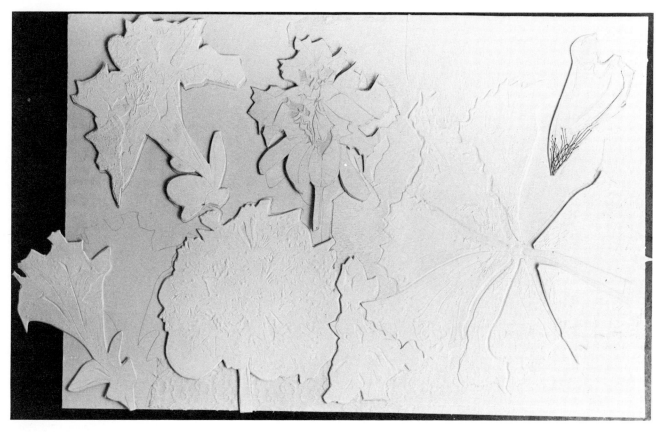

Figure 4. Here's a collagraph plate with a matte finish that has been coated with Elmer's glue. Notice that the pencil outline of the shaped pieces is still visible. The shapes will be glued down within the drawn outlines.

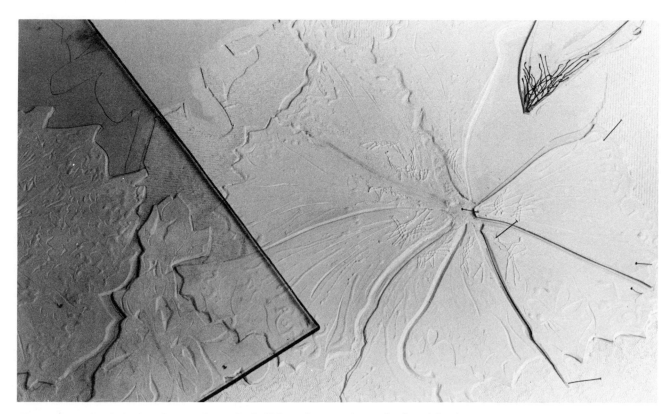

Figure 5. A piece of ¼'' plate glass may be used to hold down the pieces being glued until the glue is dry. Notice the straight pins to the right of the photograph pushed through the cardboard shapes to the cardboard base to hold the two surfaces together.

on the plate, apply a final coat of gesso over the entire surface, and sand the plate again until all of the rough areas are gone.

PROOFING THE UNINKED COLLAGRAPH

When the gesso or modeling paste is dry, and before you make the plate waterproof, you should run the plate through the press without ink. This uninked proof, or embossing, will give you an idea of what the proof will look like. Also, the pressure of the press will remove any air that may be trapped between the glued pieces—this will improve the lamination. You'll make this embossing with a blotter rather than with proof paper because the thickness of the blotter will allow the forms to show more readily.

Materials and Equipment
collagraph plate sanded smooth
press
old blankets
dry blotter, larger than the collagraph
foam rubber blanket

Process. Place the plate on the bed of the press (before you position the blankets in the press). Push the plate between the roller and the bed of the press—it should pass completely and freely under the roller. If it doesn't, turn the screws of the press counterclockwise to loosen them until the plate does pass easily between the bed and the roller.

Place the old felt blankets in the press, as described in Chapter 13. If your plate has both high and low levels, you can use either one or two old blankets alone to print, or combine them with one foam rubber blanket. If you're combining felt and foam blankets, place a damp blotter over the plate lying on the press, put the foam rubber blanket over the blotter, and pull the felt blankets (already caught under the roller) down taut over the foam blanket. Pull the plate through the press.

Caution: If there is any difficulty in turning the press, don't force it—turn the press back to release the plate. Loosen the screws until the plate passes through the press with a comfortable amount of pressure. This shouldn't happen if the plate passed easily under the roller before you positioned the blankets.

Look at the impression on the blotter. If you're not satisifed with the image, you can add more materials now, the same way you added them before—layer by layer. Then let the plate dry, and again apply two coats of gesso or modeling paste. This is also the time to check the plate for holes or crevices, where the intaglio ink might collect and smear the print. If there are holes, fill them with gesso or modeling paste, and let the plate dry.

FINISHING THE COLLAGRAPH PLATE

If the base of your plate is metal or Masonite, the back is waterproof and impervious to varnolene. If the plate is cardboard, however, you should either brush on gesso to coat the back and edges the same way you coated the front, or you can cover the back of the plate with contact paper. Before you ink your plate, you must also seal the front, back, and edges with Krylon spray. (You must seal any area of a metal-based or Masonite-based plate where gesso or modeling paste has been applied.)

Materials and Equipment
plate
gesso and brush
pencil
contact paper
Krylon spray
single-edged razor blade
scissors or matknife
press set up for printing

Process. If you're going to cover the back of the plate with contact paper, lay the plate on the contact paper without removing the backing which protects the glue. Trace the outline of the plate with a pencil, and cut the contact paper 1″ larger than the plate on all sides with a matknife or scissors. Then remove the protective paper from one edge of the contact paper. Place this edge on the back of the corresponding edge of the plate. Pull the paper backing off slowly from the contact paper while pushing the contact paper onto the back of the plate with your other hand (see Chapter 12, pages 118–121). See that the contact paper covers the back of the plate completely and smoothly. Then run the plate through the press to be sure that the contact paper adheres securely to the back. Trim the excess contact paper with the single-edged razor blade by running the blade all around the four edges of the plate.

If you're brushing on gesso to coat the back and sides, let the first coat dry before adding the second. When the gesso is dry or the contact paper is securely on, spray the front of the plate with Krylon acrylic spray. Make sure the plate is *completely* covered, as gesso and modeling paste are porous and will otherwise absorb the ink when you print. Spray the front of the plate twice, allowing the plate to dry between coats. If the back is covered with gesso or modeling paste, you must spray it, too, with two coats of Krylon spray. (The back doesn't have to be sprayed if it's metal, Masonite, or if it's covered with contact paper. Do be sure, however, to carefully spray the edges where the contact paper and the plate meet.)

Note that the plate is ready to be printed as soon as it's dry. However, the longer you wait, the sturdier the plate becomes. You can print your collagraph plate as you would an intaglio plate in black and white (see Chapter 13) or in color (see Chapters 14–16).

ASSEMBLING A MULTI-PLATE COLLAGRAPH

The first time you do this, it would be a good idea (again) to make a test plate with the materials listed below and to follow the procedure outlined here. After you do the test plate, creative possibilities should suggest themselves.

Materials and Equipment
matknife or single-edged razor blade
piece of cardboard smaller than 8″ x 10″
Krylon acrylic spray
sandpaper—medium and fine
one 8″ x 10″ flat sheet of aluminum, 1/32″ thick
small, etched intaglio plate, about 3″ x 4″, beveled and clean

Process. Cut a shape—any shape—out of the cardboard with the matknife or single-edged razor blade and use the sandpaper—first medium, then fine—to create a beveled edge on the cut cardboard shape. Next, spray the cut cardboard shape on *both* sides with Krylon acrylic spray. Allow that first coat to dry and spray again.

Place the plates—the cardboard shape, the etched intaglio plate, and the flat sheet of aluminum—one over the other to decide their relationship (which goes on top and where) for printing.

PRINTING THE MULTI-PLATE COLLAGRAPH

You'll ink and counterproof the separate plates assembled above on stencil paper to make a template, or guide, which will help you print your collagraph. Please note that you can use this process to print any combination of intaglio plates, cardboard, or found objects of different shapes and sizes.

Materials and Equipment
3 plates assembled above—the cardboard shape sprayed with Krylon front and back, the etched intaglio plate, and the flat sheet of aluminum
3 or 4 pieces of proof paper soaking in a tray of water
blotters for drying proof paper
4 damp blotters for printing
press set up for printing—set the pressure to accommodate the etched intaglio plate with old felt blankets
stencil paper, 12″ x 20″
clear mylar, 18″ x 24″
2 gelatin or soft rubber rollers
hard rubber roller
intaglio ink, any color
3 surface colors

PRINTING A MULTI-PLATE COLLAGRAPH

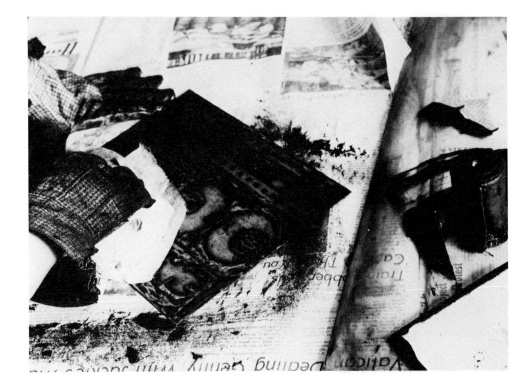

Intaglio Wipe. *After you apply the ink and remove the excess with cut cardboard (see the piece at the bottom right of the photograph), wipe your collagraph with tarlatan just as if it were a metal etching plate.*

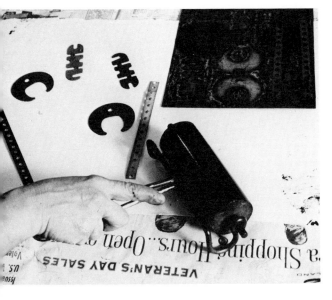

Surface Rolls. *On the left side of the photograph are pieces of the collagraph that were rolled with the black surface ink on the soft roller shown. These pieces will be placed on the collagraph plate prepared with black intaglio ink at top right.*

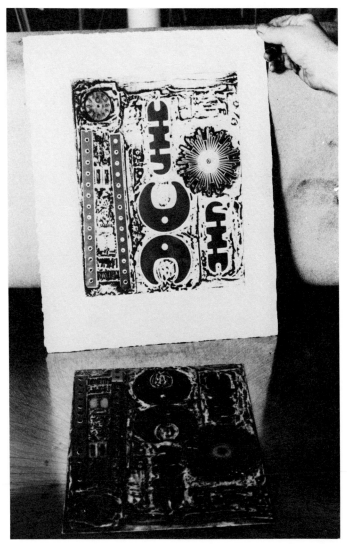

Finished Print. *Here's the collagraph print and plate. Note the difference between the black intaglio ink and surface ink.*

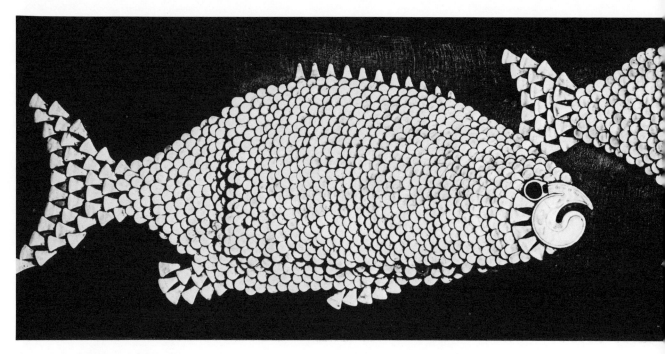

Plate of **The Twelfth Sign** *by Fiddy Hochman. Collagraph constructed of "pop-top" can tabs layered on a galvanized metal sheet with acrylic modeling paste.*

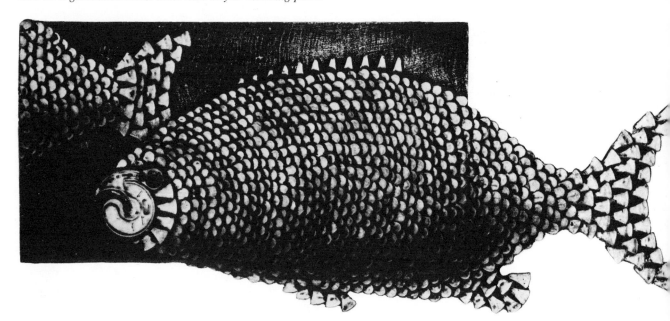

The Twelfth Sign *by Fiddy Hochman. Collagraph, approximately 14″ x 30″.*

Process. Ink the etched intaglio plate with intaglio ink as described in Chapter 13. Intaglio ink used for a collagraph should be a little oilier than the intaglio ink usually used on a metal plate. Then, using the hard roller, roll a surface color onto the intaglio plate. Next, using a gelatin or soft rubber roller, roll another surface ink on the aluminum plate. Roll the third surface color on the cardboard shape with the clean gelatin or rubber roller.

Dry one sheet of wet proof paper between blotters and place theestencil paper on the bed of the press set up for printing. Place the sheet of aluminum, inked side up, in the center of the stencil paper, leaving 5″ of the stencil paper free on two sides of the plate—the sides next to and farthest from the roller. Remove the proof paper from the blotters, and place it over the plate and the stencil paper. Place the four dampened blotters over the paper. Since the press is set to accommodate the thicker intaglio plate, the pressure isn't adequate for the thin aluminum plate without the pressure added by the damp (not wet) blotters.

Pull the blankets taut over the blotters, stencil paper, aluminum plate, and proof paper, and roll the plate through the press. *Don't roll past the blotters and paper*—leave them caught under the roller. Only the plate should pass completely under and be free of the roller.

Lift up the blankets, blotters, and proof paper, lay them over the press roller, and remove the aluminum plate. Then lower the proof paper back down over the stencil paper. Lower the four blotters and the blankets also, and roll the press back. You are transferring the image from the proof paper to the stencil paper. Be careful not to roll past the proof paper—it should remain caught under the roller.

Place the blankets over the roller, and remove the blotters. Then lift up the proof paper, and drape it over the blankets. You now have one color on the proof paper and a counterproof of that color on the stencil paper.

Place the cardboard shape charged with surface ink within the color printed on the stencil paper on the bed of the press. Remember that the print is a mirror image of the plate—if you want the image of the cardboard to be on the right side of the print, put it on the left side of the stencil paper (the counterproof/template).

When the cardboard shape is in position, pull the proof paper down over the cardboard and stencil paper. Place two damp blotters over the paper and cardboard. (The cardboard is thicker than the aluminum, but not as thick as the intaglio plate—therefore two blotters will be enough to add the needed pressure.) Follow the same process that you did above with the aluminum plate to get the image of the cardboard on both the proof paper and the stencil paper.

You now have two colors on the proof and counterproof (the stencil paper). Place the inked intaglio plate within the colors on the stencil paper. You can place this plate anywhere on the counterproof—you're not limited by the rectangle of colors. Without using blotters this time, follow the same process to get the image on the etched intaglio plate on both the proof paper and the stencil paper.

At this point you have a proof and a counterproof of your assembled plates. You can still make changes or additions, but you should repeat the entire process described above until you're satisfied with the results. The counterproof on the stencil paper is your template—you'll use it to print more collagraphs so that the pieces of the plate will be the same in every print.

After you have a proof and counterproof that please you and you want to print more collagraphs, place the counterproof on the bed of the press. Cover it with a piece of clear mylar—the mylar will act as a shield. The mylar should be longer than the counterproof so it can be caught between the blankets and the bed of the press throughout the entire printing session. This eliminates the need of taping the mylar to the bed of the press—and static electricity will keep the stencil paper in place.

To print with this template, ink all the plates before you print any one of them. Place each plate over its corresponding shape on the mylar over the template and print them one after the other while the template and printing paper remains in place, caught under the roller. Remember to wipe the mylar clean after each piece is printed. See below for one method of printing a collagraph.

CLEANUP

Refer to Chapter 13 for basic cleanup instructions after printing. In addition:

1. Clean your brushes immediately after use—any gesso or Elmer's glue left to dry on them will destroy them.

2. Clean your collagraph plate(s) after printing, and remove all the ink. In addition, a plate made of cardboard, fabrics, gesso, and Krylon needs special attention. Clean it first in the usual manner with a brush and varnolene, and then dry it thoroughly with a clean cloth. Take care that no varnolene has seeped through the gesso into the cardboard—this would tend to loosen the glue, and the plate would fall apart. To avoid this, dust talcum powder over the plate. The talc will absorb any excess moisture which might be left in the plate. Don't put the plate into a plastic bag—rather, leave it in a safe place to air-dry. *Never wash the plate with alcohol*—alcohol would remove the Krylon and soften the gesso. Before printing the plate again, carefully brush the talcum powder off, and spray the plate with another coat of Krylon.

WHAT WENT WRONG AND WHY

Problem	Cause	Solution
Little pieces of gesso stick to the paper of the print.	The gesso wasn't thoroughly dry before you printed.	It's wise to allow the plate to dry for a week or more after you apply the last coat of gesso and before you coat the plate with Krylon. If you're working in a damp or humid environment, this is even more important. When the plate is *thoroughly* dry, it will be sturdy enough to print a large edition.
There are large areas in the print where the paper doesn't pick up the ink.	1. There isn't enough pressure in the press.	1. Look at the back of the print. If the embossing on the back is very shallow, you probably need more pressure. Put a damp blotter or a piece of foam rubber over the paper rather than change the pressure of the press.
	2. There's too great a difference in height between one level of the plate and the next.	2. If the back of the print is deeply embossed, then the areas that aren't printing should be filled with more gesso. Remove the ink and dry the plate thoroughly before applying more gesso. Allow the gesso to dry, and spray on two coats of Krylon before printing again.
There's one flat area of the plate which is lower than the rest—the paper doesn't pick up the ink properly there.	This area isn't receiving the same amount of pressure as the rest of the plate.	Loosen the press slightly on both sides. Put two damp blotters over the paper, and roll the plate through the press. When you lift the blankets, the blotters will be embossed. Without removing the blotters, gently tear out those portions that cover the part of the plate that is printing properly, leaving the blotters only in those areas that were *not* printing well. Put the blankets down on the top of the plate, return the pressure of the press to normal, and print the plate again. If you remove the pieces of the blotter carefully, you can use them again to apply more pressure to the areas which need it. To do this, put the pieces aside carefully. Ink the plate and print as usual. Lift up the blankets, but don't remove the paper. Since the paper will be embossed, you will be able to see exactly where to position the torn blotters. Put them in place, lay the blankets back down, and print again.
After printing, the paper sticks to the plate. It's hard to remove it without tearing it.	1. The Krylon isn't completely dry.	1. Clean and dry the plate. Then spray it again with Krylon and let the Krylon dry *thoroughly*.
	2. The intaglio ink used was too stiff.	2. Add more raw linseed oil to the ink. Intaglio ink used for a collagraph should be a little oilier than the ink used on a metal plate.
It's difficult to wipe the edges of the collagraph before printing, and the plate mark on the print appears dirty.	The edges of your collagraph aren't smooth, and the ink is collecting in the rough edges.	Clean and dry the plate. When the plate is completely dry, sand the edges of the collagraph first with medium and then with very fine sandpaper. Spray with Krylon before printing again.
After the print is dry, the embossing seems to flatten out.	You applied too much weight to the print while it was still wet.	Stack the drying prints with tissues and blotters between them. Allow the prints to dry for a day before putting any weight on them.

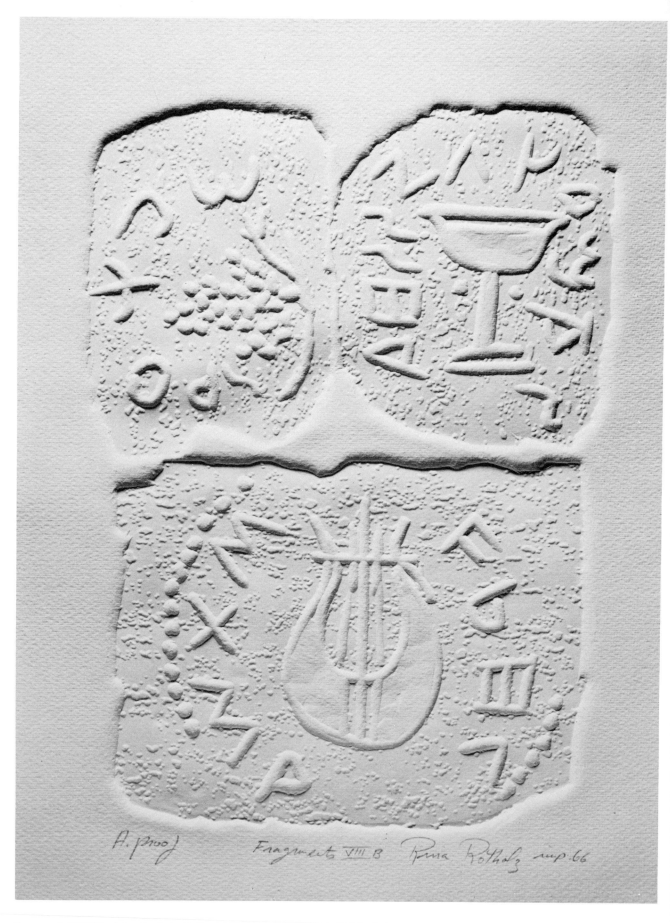

Fragments VIIIB *by Rina Rotholz. Tuilegraph embossment, 20″ x 14″.*

TWENTY-ONE

Tuilegraphs

A tuilegraph is a print made from vinyl asbestos tile, a material only recently available to the printmaker and one which can be treated with great versatility of method. On vinyl asbestos tile you can engrave with a burin, incise with a drypoint needle, or emboss using found objects. The tile can be cut into with woodcutting tools or cut all the way through with scissors to make shaped plates. The shapes can be used alone or in combination with other shapes to make larger images or with other plates to make a collagraph.

By using acetone on the tile, you can create tones which look like aquatint when they're printed. The resulting tile can be printed in intaglio, in relief, or in a combination of the two. Since the vinyl asbestos tile doesn't interact with color, all colors used remain pure. This remarkable material's possible relationship to printmaking was the discovery of Rina Rothholz, an Israeli printmaker who had young children at home and who was reluctant, therefore, to work with techniques that required acids.

WORKING THE TILE

When you have worked the tile, it will have an image that can be printed as an inkless intaglio (an embossment), an intaglio, a relief, or a combination of all three.

Materials and Equipment
vinyl asbestos tile
pencil
Krylon acrylic spray
hot plate
drypoint needle
burin
woodcutting tools
scissors
acetone
bristle brushes
found objects such as flat metal gaskets or thin coins
press set up for printing
blotter larger than the tile
contact paper
razor blade
wax paper larger than the tile

Process. To begin, draw gently on the tile with a pencil. The drawing can be either a simple outline or a complicated design, and you can erase it easily, if necessary, by rubbing with a cloth or with your fingers. Work gently on the surface of the tile with your pencil, as pressure can dent the surface. When you're satisfied with the image, spray the tile with Krylon to fix the drawing. Be sure that the acrylic is dry before you continue to work on the tile.

Warm the tile on the hot plate. A cold tile is brittle, and any attempt to cut into it without warming it first will result in cracked, ragged lines. Take care not to let the tile become too hot to touch—if it does, it will tend to flow like one of Salvador Dali's watches (see Figure 1).

Engrave or draw into the warm tile with a burin or a drypoint needle. Both of these tools will incise fine lines in the tile so that it can be printed in intaglio. Try using woodcutting tools also—you'll find that using them on a vinyl asbestos tile is very much like cutting into linoleum. See Figure 2 for the proper positions of your hands and the tile when cutting. A tile cut with woodcutting tools is usually printed in relief, but it can be printed in intaglio as well.

Figure 1. The tile tends to flow when it's hot.

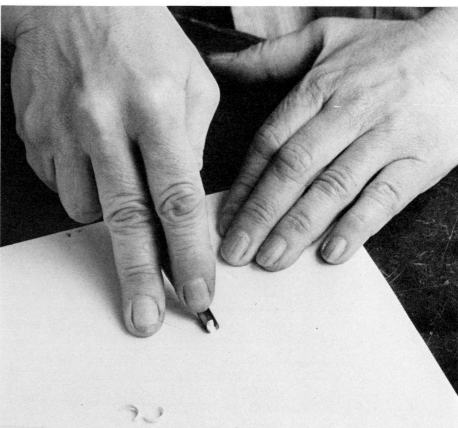

Figure 2. You can cut the tile with woodcutting tools when it's warm. Note the position of the hands.

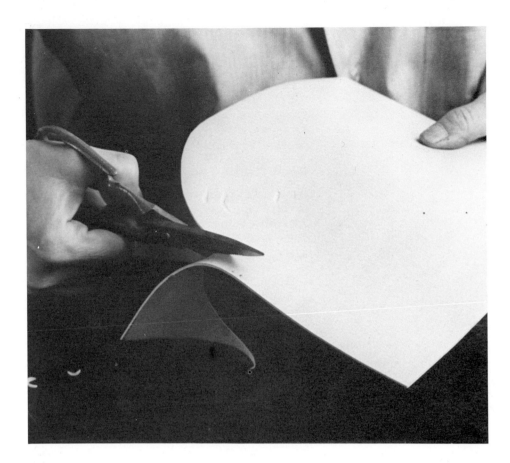

Figure 3. When the tile is warm, you can shape it easily with a pair of scissors.

To impress thin pieces of metal or plastic found objects into a tile, place the tile on the hot plate. Lay the objects on the tile where you want them. Then, when the tile is warm, press the objects into place. Lift the tile up with the objects on it and place it on wax paper on the bed of the press—the wax paper keeps the tile from cooling too quickly when it comes in contact with the cold press bed. Put a blotter over the tile and the objects, pull the blankets down over the blotter, and run the tile through the press. This is the time to use your oldest printing blankets, since the found objects may cut them. When you remove the blankets, the blotter, and the found objects, the tile should have a clear impression of the objects in it. If, however, the tile wasn't warm enough, then the impression of the objects won't show clearly. You'll have to warm the tile again and repeat the process just described.

You can shape the tile by cutting it with a scissors. Just remember to warm the plate before you try to cut it (see Figure 3).

You can also use a brush and acetone to make a tone on the plate which will look like an aquatint or a soft ground tone when the plate is printed. To do this, pour a small amount of acetone into a container—it evaporates very quickly, so keep the larger, original container tightly closed. Brush the acetone on the cold tile in the places where you want a tone. The tone will become darker with each application of the acetone— and be sure to let the plate dry between applications.

Take a proof at any point while working the tile to see how the image is progressing. After printing, you can continue to work on the tile until it's esthetically satisfying.

Since the tile is very brittle when it's cold, you may have to apply contact paper to the back to strengthen it. Then even if the tile cracks, the pieces won't separate, and you will still be able to print (although the cracks will show). Cut the contact paper slightly larger than the tile, and place the tile face down on the table. Remove the protective backing of the contact paper, and place one end of the glued paper on the back of the tile. Smooth it down until it covers the tile. Trim the excess paper from the edges of the tile with a scissors or a razor blade, and then run the tile through the press to remove any bubbles in the contact paper.

PRINTING A TUILEGRAPH

Print vinyl asbestos tiles with intaglio ink in much the same way you would print a metal plate (see Chapter 13). There are a few differences: the ink used for a tuilegraph should be *very* oily—add enough linseed oil so that it runs off the palette knife quickly; use a stencil brush to rub the intaglio ink into the deep crevices of the tile before wiping with tarlatan; and you *must* heat the tile before printing. If you print a warped tile cold, the pressure of the roller will crack it. You can roll surface color as usual over the tile after it has been inked with intaglio ink (see Chapter 15).

REGISTERING THE TILE AND ANOTHER PLATE

A tile may be printed with an additional surface color coming from another plate made of cardboard, aluminum, zinc, or steel, from a second tile, or indeed from any flat surface that will withstand the pressure of the press. The second plate may be any shape or size and can be larger or smaller than the tile. If it's larger than the tile, you'll have to print it first; if it's smaller, then you'll print the tile first; if the tile and the other plate are the same size, then either can be printed first.

Please note that this method of registration is extremely useful when the plates printed together are not the same size *and when exact registration is not crucial to the print*.

Materials and Equipment
tile, inked in intaglio, in relief, or both
second plate of cardboard coated with Krylon, of zinc, aluminum, steel, etc., inked with surface color
press set up for printing with pressure adjusted to accommodate the thickest plate
paper dampened for printing, 12″ larger than the larger of the two plates
2 damp blotters, smaller than the paper but larger than the largest plate

Process. Place the larger of the two plates on the bed of the press and cover it with the dampened paper so that there's a 6″ border of paper at the top and the bottom of the plate.

If the plate is thinner than the tile, place a damp blotter over the paper. Be sure that it covers the plate, pull down the blankets, and roll the bed through the press. Catch the printing paper, but not the blotter, under the roller. Lift up the blankets and drape them over the roller. Remove the blotter—keep it on a flat surface, as you'll use it again. Lay the paper over the blankets, and remove the plate.

Check the bed of the press to be sure it's clean. If necessary, wipe it clean and dry it carefully. Then place the paper down on the bed of the press. Lay two dampened blotters over the paper (use the one you've just removed plus one other). Pull the blankets down over the blotters and paper, and roll the bed through the press. Roll just far enough so that the blotters are free of the roller.

Please note that since there's no plate for you to feel to tell when you've gone far enough, stop at the point that you think is correct, lift up the blankets, and remove the blotters. If you've gone too far, simply put the blankets back down and roll the press back over the 6″ border of paper until it's caught under the roller.

You now have a printed image—a counterproof—of the first plate on the bed of the press. This will allow you to see the plates in relation to one another. Place the second inked plate where you want it on top of the counterproof. If the press is already adjusted to the thickness of this plate, go ahead and print. If, however, you are now printing a cardboard which is thinner than the tile just used, then place a damp blotter over the paper to add enough pressure for the cardboard to print properly. Then pull the blankets down and roll the plate through the press.

CLEANUP

See Chapter 19 for information concerning the care of the tools and for cleanup procedures after printing. In addition, please note that you must store the tiles on a flat surface, as they tend to take the shape of whatever they are resting on.

WHAT WENT WRONG AND WHY

Problem	Cause	Solution
Cracks in the tile appear in the print. Can anything be done to remove them?	The very nature of the tile causes it to crack.	Coat both sides of the crack with Elmer's glue. Hold the tile together, and wipe the excess glue off the surface with your fingers or with a cloth. Put a strip of clear tape across the crack until the glue dries, and then remove it.
The tile is so badly warped that when I put it on the hot plate, only a small part of the tile heats up.	You may have left the tile on an uneven surface.	Place the tile in hot water until it's warm. Then lay it on a flat surface. It will become perfectly flat as it cools.

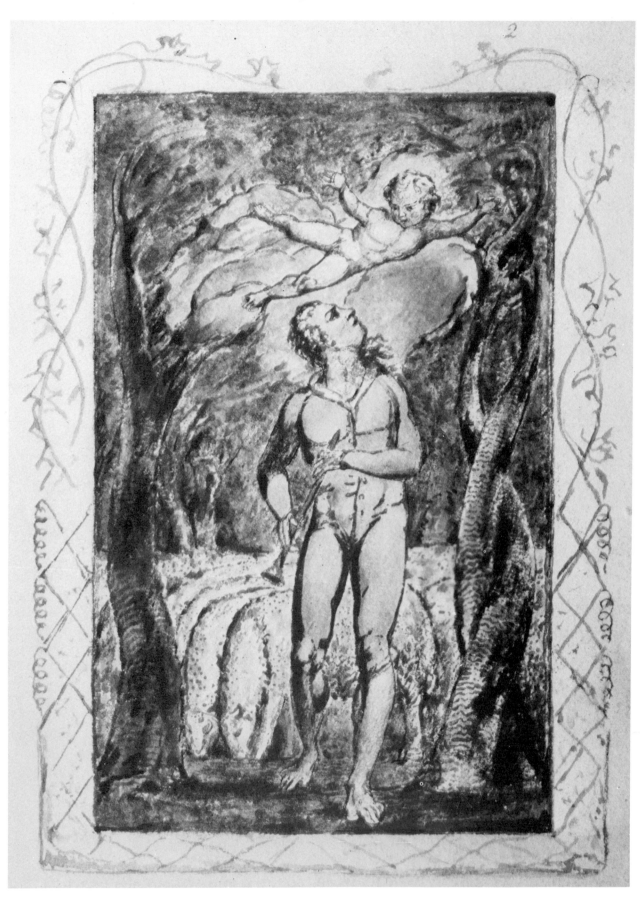

Page from "Songs of Innocence and of Experience" by William Blake (1757-1827). Relief etching, 7" x 5". Courtesy Metropolitan Museum of Art, New York City, Rogers Fund.

TWENTY-TWO

Blake Transfer Method

The poet William Blake was an artist before he was a writer, and throughout all of his life he printed his own books of poems. They were engraved on copper plates, and the prints were later colored by hand by Blake or his wife.

There are difficulties involved in printing or lettering legibly on a plate. The letters must be drawn on the plate in reverse in order to print properly in the finished print—this can be very difficult to do. Harriet Morrel and I have adapted Blake's method of transferring images from the paper to the plate. We draw lettering and other images with special stopout on paper which is prepared with a mixture of gum arabic and tincture of green soap. When the image is transferred to the plate and the plate is placed in an acid bath, the drawn image will protect the plate surface, remaining intact while the rest of the plate is bitten down. Printed in intaglio, the transferred image will be an embossed white. Printed as a relief print, the intaglio will remain uninked.

PREPARING TRANSFER PAPER

You can prepare and dry transfer paper, and then store it until you need it. Whether you plan to store it or not, the paper must be thoroughly dry before it can be used.

Materials and Equipment
2 oz. liquid gum arabic
2 oz. tincture of green soap
vellum or good quality tracing paper
masking tape
piece of cardboard larger than the transfer paper
glass measuring cup
jar with screw top (optional)
2″ flat Bristol brush

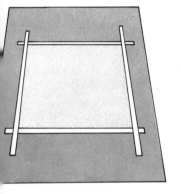

Figure 1. Tape the vellum or tracing paper to a piece of cardboard before preparing it for the transfer method.

Process. Pour 2 oz. of liquid gum arabic into the measuring cup. Add 2 oz. of tincture of green soap, and stir thoroughly to be sure that the two liquids are completely mixed.

Fasten the vellum or tracing paper to the cardboard by taping down the four sides of the paper with masking tape (see Figure 1). Brush the mixture of gum arabic and tincture of green soap over the entire sheet of paper. Then allow the paper to dry completely. The time that it takes to dry will depend on the weather—the transfer paper will dry faster on a cool, dry day than on a warm, humid one. When the paper is dry to the touch, paint another coat of the mixture over the first and allow it to dry for 24 hours. Don't remove the paper from the cardboard—just stand the board with the paper attached in an out-of-the-way corner until you're ready to use it.

If there's any unused gum arabic and tincture of green soap mixture, pour it into a jar with a screw top, and store it for future use.

DRAWING OR WRITING ON TRANSFER PAPER

You should draw or write on the transfer paper just as if you were drawing with India ink on paper.

Materials and Equipment
special stopout (see Chapter 6 for formula)
brush for drawing
dry transfer paper
clean cloth

Process. Draw the image on the transfer paper with the special stopout and a brush. If there are any areas of the drawing that you wish to remove, wipe those areas with a clean cloth before the stopout dries. When you're satisfied with the image or lettering, allow it to dry thoroughly—until you feel that it's dry to the touch.

TRANSFERRING THE DRAWING TO THE PLATE

If you do this step properly, the drawing will be transferred to the plate, and the transfer paper will be almost blank when the process is completed.

Materials and Equipment
transfer paper with drawing on it, completely dry
zinc or copper plate, cleaned and beveled
hot plate, heated
proof paper or newsprint, twice as large as the plate
press set up for printing
garden gloves

Process. To begin, place the zinc or copper plate on the hot plate, and cover it with the transfer paper, image side down. Rub the back of the transfer paper with your fingers until the paper sticks to the plate. Leave the plate and paper on the hot plate.

Fold the proof paper or newsprint in half (when folded, it should be a little larger than the plate) and place it on the bed of the press with the fold nearest the blankets (see Figure 2).

When the plate is *too hot to touch*, put on the garden gloves and remove it from the hot plate, with the transfer paper on top. Place the plate between the folds of proof paper or newsprint on the press bed. Working very quickly, pull the blankets down over the paper, transfer paper, and plate, and roll them through the press.

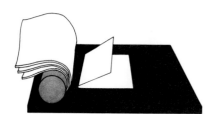

Figure 2. The fold in the proof paper (or newsprint) should face the blankets.

Lift up the blankets, drape them over the roller, and pick up the folded paper. *Don't remove the transfer paper!* Hold the transfer paper down on one side of the plate and raise one corner so that you can see if the transfer was successful. There should be a clear image of the drawing on the plate. If the drawing is spotty and some of the stopout remains on the paper, put the plate with the transfer paper on top of it back onto the hot plate. When the plate is hot, roll it and the transfer paper through the press again the same way you did before.

When the transfer is completed, the plate is ready to be etched. You may add additional special stopout with your brush to reinforce the image if you feel that some of the drawing isn't sturdy enough. Also stop out those areas of the plate which you want to work on in intaglio later on.

Place the plate in a medium nitric acid bath (see Chapter 12 for information on biting plates in acid). Bite the plate until you can see a level between the stopped-out areas and the open plate.

PRINTING A TRANSFER PLATE

A plate prepared by the Blake transfer method is usually rolled with surface ink and a hard roller—the deeply bitten areas with no ink on them appear embossed in the print. These prints are sometimes referred to as relief intaglios. You can also bite these plates for viscosity printing (see Chapter 16).

CLEANUP

See Chapter 7 for general cleanup procedures. In addition:

1. Clean the brush used with special stopout first with varnolene and then with soap and water.

2. Store the mixture of gum arabic and tincture of green soap in a jar with a screw top for use another time.

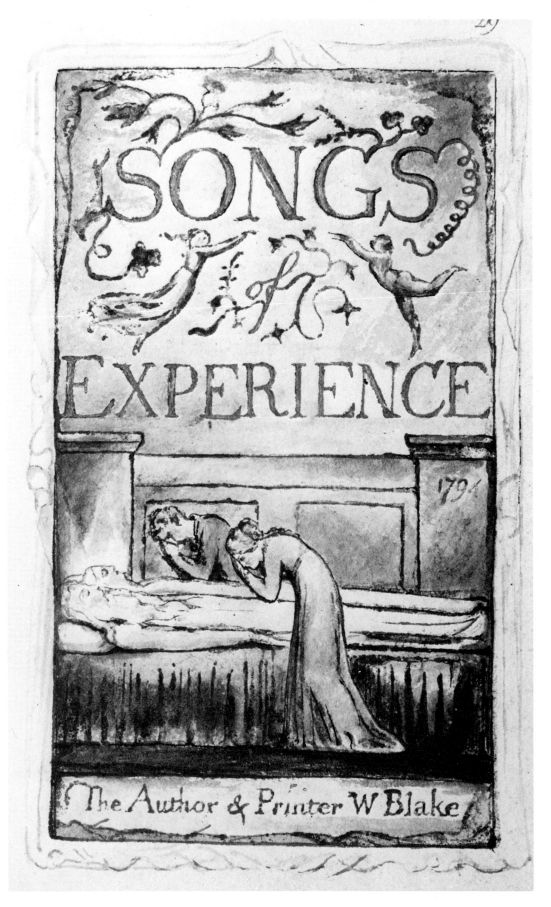

Page from "Songs of Innocence and of Experience" by William Blake (1757-1827). Relief etching, 7" x 5". Courtesy Metropolitan Museum of Art, New York City, Rogers Fund.

WHAT WENT WRONG AND WHY

Problem	Cause	Solution
I heated the plate and ran it through the press several times, but the drawing didn't transfer enough.	Because the folded proof paper or newsprint between the plate and the bed is thin, the bed cooled the plate.	Place a piece of cardboard, larger than the folded paper, underneath it on the bed of the press. Adjust the pressure of the press so it's a little looser (to accommodate the cardboard), and try again.
The image transferred, but it was blurred.	The stopout wasn't completely dry.	Let the stopout dry enough so when you touch it, it doesn't come off on your fingers.
After the plate was bitten, a texture appeared where the mixture of gum arabic and tincture of green soap had been.	That mixture will act as a stopout only for a certain amount of time—then it will break down in the acid and a texture will result from the uneven biting. You'll notice that this happens only in large areas of the plate where no image has been transferred.	Stop out these areas of the plate—they can be bitten another time.

PART FIVE
Appendix

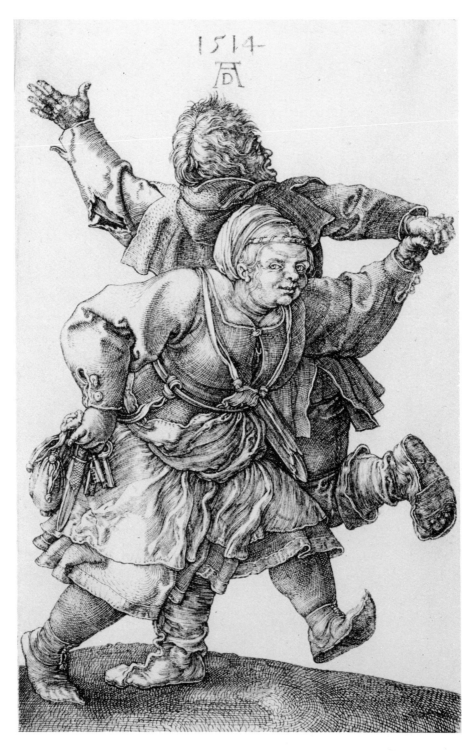

The Peasant Couple Dancing *by Albrecht Dürer (1471-1528). Engraving. Courtesy Metropolitan Museum of Art, New York City, Fletcher Fund.*

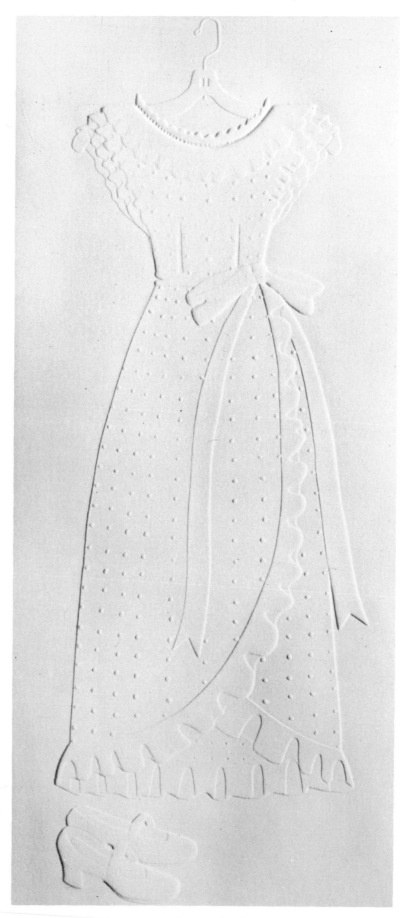

Special Day *by Sondra Mayer. Embossing, 17¼″ x 7⅜″ .*

Things Every Printmaker Should Know and Doesn't Know Whom to Ask

When you decide to print an edition—once your plate is finished—it isn't necessary to print the entire edition immediately. However, you must number the prints, store them as they're made, and protect the plate in order to avoid corrosion. This chapter will deal with the methods of numbering the edition, keeping records, matting, framing, and storing prints and plates. In addition, I will suggest an approach to selling prints.

SIZE OF THE EDITION

There are several factors that determine how large an edition should be; the most important are the durability of the plates and the type of bite. A zinc plate bitten with lift ground, hard ground, or soft ground, could yield an edition of 100 prints, while the same zinc plate bitten with aquatint or white ground could wear out after only 25 prints. Copper, a harder metal, will yield more prints than zinc. A copper plate can, in addition, be steel-faced, an electrolytic process that deposits a thin film of steel over the copper. The advantage of facing a copper plate with steel is that it allows fragile intaglio methods, such as drypoint, mezzotint, and aquatint, to be printed in very large editions. A drypoint edition on plain copper, for instance, might normally be only 10 prints; on a steel-faced plate that edition could be 100 or more. Steel plates will print very large editions with no difficulty.

Another factor to be considered when you're deciding how large an edition should be is how many prints you think you might sell, send to shows, and so forth. Storing many prints for long periods of time can be a problem, and there's little point to pulling 100 prints when you can't realistically expect to sell or use more than 5.

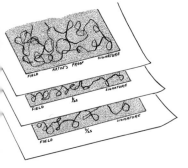

NUMBERING THE EDITION

Figure 1. Prints are signed in pencil. The title is on the left; the numbers indicating the number of the particular print and the edition number, or the words "Artist's Proof" are in the center; and the artist's signature is on the right.

An edition consists of the numbered prints plus the artist's proofs. If a printer is employed to print the edition, he receives another print, labeled "Bon à tirer." This is the first print he pulls, and it's exactly like the proof which the artist brings to him with the plate. This means that a printmaker who has his printing done by someone else must have a perfect print to present to his printer—the pick of the litter, more or less.

Prints should always be numbered and signed in pencil. The name of the print is put in the left-hand corner or in the center, the edition number is in the left-hand corner or the center with the name, and the artist's signature is always in the right-hand corner (see Figure 1). The edition number is stated as a fraction with the total number of prints in the edition as the bottom number and the number of the specific print as the top number. If the edition is 25, the numbers would read 1/25, 2/25, 3/25, 4/25, and so forth.

In the nineteenth century, when entire editions were sold to dealers or publishers, the artist was allowed to keep several prints labeled "Artist's Proof" to sell or to show. Artist's proofs are now a part of every edition, whether the edition is sold or not. Usually, the artist makes 10 artist's proofs, although if the edition is as large as 250, he could make 25. Artist's proofs aren't counted in the size of the edition, but it isn't considered ethical for the number of artist's proofs to exceed the size of the edition.

KEEPING RECORDS

When you finish a plate and begin the edition, you must keep a careful record of the last number printed so there's no duplication of numbers in case you finish printing the edition years later. This would happen if you wanted 50 prints in the edition, but expected to sell only 5. So you might print 10 out of 50. Three years later, when you want to finish the edition, you won't remember what number you're up to unless you keep a record. Also, if the print is in color, keep accurate color notes. You may think that you'll remember the colors, but I can assure you, both through observation of others and from my own sad experiences, that you *won't* remember. If possible, even keep a color swatch of each color used.

Right now, begin to keep a book or a set of file cards to record the following information for each print:

1. Name of print

2. Date the plate was finished

3. Kind of paper used

4. Accurate account of color plus a color swatch

5. Numbers used in the edition

6. Price of the print

7. Number of prints sold

8. Number of prints on consignment and to whom

9. Purchases by collectors or museums, prizes won, etc.

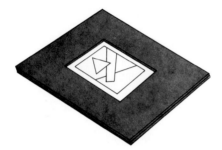

Figure 2. When the book mat is closed, the margins left between the print and the mat allow the plate mark to be seen. There is also room on the bottom for the edition numbers and signature.

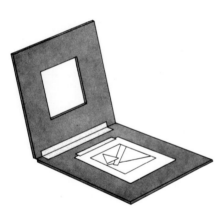

Figure 3. The book mat open. The print is taped to the back-board at the top only. The faceboard, with a window cut out, is taped to the backboard on the top.

MATTING PRINTS

In national shows, prints are often shown matted but not framed. Mats consist of a backboard and a faceboard. They should be the same size; the faceboard should have an opening through which the print shows; and the two should be connected with linen tape.

To mat a print, you should fasten it to a backboard *at the top only* with linen tape or Elmer's glue. As paper tends to absorb the moisture in the air, which causes it to stretch, a print attached to the backboard on all four edges would eventually buckle. The opening in the faceboard should be ¼″ larger than the platemark on the top and sides of the print. The bottom margin should be ½″ larger than the platemark to allow room for the name of the print, the number of the edition, and your signature (see Figure 2).

Mats for shows should be white book mats (see Figure 3). If you expect a print to be in a mat for a long period of time, either in or out of a frame, you should place it in a mat and backboard made of acid-free museumboard or ragboard. Wood-pulp card-board will stain or burn the paper in a few years.

You may be asked often to wrap your matted print in acetate to protect both mat and print. A good weight of acetate for this purpose is .003—when you purchase it, be sure that it's clear and that it doesn't superimpose a color on the print. Tape the ace-tate securely to the back of the print (see Figure 4).

FRAMING PRINTS

The framing of prints has presented a new problem, unique in art work, because of the effect of glass on the paper. Styles in framing change with the times, but you must always use glass to protect the print. However, there's a danger of destroying the print if the glass touches its surface, especially if you want to float the print on a background mat within the frame. The moisture which is always present will collect at the point of contact and will either cause a mold to develop or will turn the sizing in the paper into a glue, causing the print to adhere to the glass. If you want to float the print, then make sure the framer puts a spacer—a strip of matboard—under the rabbet between the backboard and the glass. This strip will take up the space normally occupied by the mat, leaving enough space to allow the print to expand and contract without touching the glass.

Plexiglas can be used in place of glass. It has both advantages and disadvantages. On the one hand, it is not as fragile as glass; it doesn't condense moisture as readily; and it's lighter in weight. On the other hand, plexiglas scratches very easily, and it collects dust because of the static electricity inherent in plastics.

Never use glare-free glass on a print which you consider valuable—to work as a non-reflective material, it must be in direct contact with the print. If it were held away from the paper with a spacer, glare-free glass would distort the image on the print. Finally, glare-free glass gives a living print the dead look of a reproduction.

Remember that the best mat and frame should simply add to the visibility of the print. If someone should compliment you on your lovely frame, then you can be assured that it isn't right for the print.

STORING PRINTS

Moisture and air pollution can cause a great deal of damage to stored prints. Moisture will cause papers to become moldy, and pollution in the air will discolor them. Prints are best stored in a warm, dry room where the humidity is never more than 50% in drawers, blueprint cabinets, or in boxes made of acid-free cardboard. (See *Supplies and Suppliers* for the names of companies where these can be purchased).

Intaglio ink doesn't dry completely for as long as a year. Therefore, you should stack prints with sheets of cellulose acetate or silk paper between them to avoid ink offsetting from one print onto the back of the print above. Newsprint and tissue paper absorb moisture, but they would discolor the rag paper—never put them between stored prints.

STORING PLATES

Plates can be stored for long periods of time without any danger of corrosion if you smear a coat of Vaseline cut with turpentine or brush a hard ground on the *dry* printing surface. To make sure the plate is free of any moisture before applying this protective coating, wipe the surface down with alcohol and a clean cloth after cleaning the plate thoroughly. Since alcohol evaporates very quickly, the plate will be left perfectly clean and dry. Then coat the plate with ground or Vaseline, wrap it in plastic, and tape the plastic securely.

Steel plates must be protected immediately after they are printed as described above, since steel rusts when it's exposed to the moisture in the air.

Plates may be stored upright if they're tied together so they can't bend. You can also pile them on top of one another. This, however, presents problems of weight, since a shelf would have to be very sturdy to withstand the weight of more than a few plates without warping.

CANCELING PLATES

When you complete an edition, you should cancel the plate so that additional prints can't be pulled. Some artists engrave their names in the plate without reversing the letters. Then, if the plate is printed, the reverse signature shows that the artist has canceled the print. Sometimes, however, plates are destroyed by engraving lines across their surfaces.

Plates are very beautiful and can be framed by themselves. To do this, engrave your signature in the plate and ink the plate as though you were going to print it. Allow the ink to dry for several weeks, spray the plate with Krylon—the ink and Krylon will protect the surface of the plate—and your plate is ready to be framed.

PRICING PRINTS

One of the exciting aspects of printmaking is the fact that you can have an original work of art that is produced in multiples so that you can sell it and still have one for yourself. Unlike the manufacturer of a utilitarian product, the artist produces an object of undetermined value. You should price your print at a lower level than if it were a single, original work of art. To determine the price, take into consideration the cost of materials, the time taken to produce and print the plate, and, most important of all, what the public is willing to pay for it. It's better to have prints on people's walls than to store them in print cabinets.

Once you've established the selling price of a print, don't lower it! You have a responsibility to the people who buy your prints—they would be unhappy (to say the least) if they saw them offered at a price that is lower than the price they paid.

AGENTS

Agents, or dealers, differ from gallery owners in that they usually handle the entire graphic output of an artist and deal with the galleries for him. The percentage of the

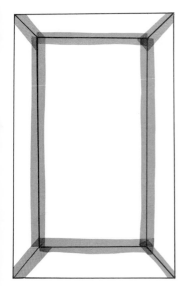

Figure 4. The tape here covers the acetate on the back of the mat wherever there's a possibility of the acetate tearing.

selling price of the print that you, as the artist, receive from an agent is less than you would receive if you dealt directly with a gallery. The advantage of having an agent is that you no longer have to spend time and money on matting prints and emotional energy seeing gallery owners. The agent may show your prints to galleries to which you yourself might not have access; the work is then exposed to a much larger audience, and the chance of being seen and of selling is much greater. A word of warning: whether you deal with a gallery or with an agent, mutual respect and trust must exist, or else the arrangement can't work.

WHERE TO SELL AND SHOW

Every artist has the need to show and possibly sell the work that he does. No matter how much you love the work you're doing, the artistic process won't be complete until it has been seen by others: printmaking, just as much as music or literature, is a form of communication.

There are several ways to show art work. One is to make the rounds of the galleries to find one that is willing to show your work. This is, for most artists, a difficult experience. Galleries and dealers are, for the most part, interested in work that they can sell, which most often means work by artists of established reputation. If you do find a gallery to show your work, most likely they will suggest that it be left on consignment. Works that are left on consignment are paid for only when the print is sold, and therefore, it's wiser for the artist to sell the print to the gallery outright if possible. When you sell a print to the gallery, the gallery owner usually pays you half the selling price of the print.

Another way to show work is to send prints to the many local and national print competitions listed in the current art magazines. If you're accepted in these shows, there's a possibility that a gallery or an agent will seek you out.

There are galleries that contact artists with an offer of a show on the condition that the artist pay a fairly large fee. Before paying for such a show, it would be advisable to investigate the gallery to find out if it would be worth while.

There will be times when you'll be tempted to swerve from your own vision in order to please those who seem to know more about what is acceptable to the public. In my opinion, it's unwise to change your personal development in order to fall into step with what is the current fashion. Trends change so fast that, if you persist on your own course long enough, the pendulum of art fashion is likely to swing back in your direction. If you chase the rainbow, you may never catch it. At any rate, it's a gamble *any* way—you might as well gamble on yourself and at least enjoy it.

Glossary

A la poupée. The use of dollies or daubers, a different color ink for each, in a small area of a plate.

Aquatint. Porous ground made by applying and heating rosin particles on a plate in order to create a tone or varied tones.

Artist's proof. The first prints pulled from a plate. When a publisher purchases an entire edition, the first ten prints remain the property of the artist.

Asphaltum. An ingredient used in making grounds and stopout; also called bitumen.

Bath. Mixture of acid and water used for biting plates.

Beveled edge. The edges of a plate filed to an acute angle to avoid cutting the paper on blankets. A finely beveled edge enhances the print with a clean plate mark.

Bite. Corrosive action of acid on a plate.

Bitumen. See *Asphaltum.*

Blankets. Pressed or woven wool felts used in printing which serve to push the dampened paper into the crevices and lines on the plate.

Bleeding. An error in printing where, on a deeply bitten plate, excess intaglio ink is pushed out from the lines and crevices and runs (bleeds) over the print and plate under pressure.

Bon à tirer. The print pulled by the printer which is most like the proof pulled by the artist and which the artist will accept. It's signed either *bon à tirer* or *printer's proof,* and it belongs traditionally to the printer.

Bridge. A wooden construction used as a handrest to avoid touching the plate with the hand when drawing on a soft ground.

Burin. Tool used to engrave lines in copper, zinc, or steel plates.

Burnisher. Polishing tool used on plates which have been scraped.

Burr. (1) Ridge made by the drypoint needle when it's used to draw on a plate. (2) Excess metal pushed out by the burin in engraving. (3) The rough edge left on a tool after it has been sharpened.

Cancellation proof. The last print pulled after the edition has been printed and after the surface of the plate has been deliberately marred—this print shows that the plate was destroyed.

Charging. The process of covering a roller or plate with surface ink.

Collagraph. A combination of materials and objects glued together or separately which are inked in intaglio or in relief and printed.

Counterproof. An image printed from a wet proof rather than from a plate. The image on the counterproof is identical with the image on the plate.

Crevé. An open space on the plate which will not hold ink well—it's created when lines on a hard ground or a texture on a soft ground remain in the acid too long and the lines and textures widen.

Dauber. A tool made of tarlatan or felt which is used to push ink into an intaglio print. Daubers made of materials such as silk or taffeta with lamb's wool stuffing can be used to apply grounds.

Deckle-edge. The rough edge of handmade or mold-made paper.

Diamond point. A drypoint needle with a diamond chip at the tip, used in making drypoints.

Double intaglio. One plate printed twice in two or more colors superimposed in accurate register, or two or more plates printed in intaglio in accurate register on the same sheet of paper.

Drypoint. A graphic technique in which the plate is drawn into directly with a tool which has a sharp diamond point or hard-tempered steel tip. This tip creates a burr on either side of the drawn line which holds a lot of ink when the plate is inked—this gives the drypoint print its characteristic appearance.

Durometer. A unit of measuring the degree of softness or hardness of the rollers used for surface printing.

Dutch mordant. The acid bath used for copper, consisting of a mixture of hydrochloric acid, potassium chlorate crystals, and water.

Edition. All of the numbered prints pulled from a plate, plus the artist's proofs.

Embossing. (1) A raised image on the print caused by a deeply bitten plate. (2) The print of a deeply bitten plate printed without any ink (inkless intaglio).

Engraving. A graphic technique in which the image is cut into the plate with a burin.

Etching. A graphic technique in which the plate is covered with a ground, the ground is partially removed, and the exposed areas are bitten in acid.

Etching tool. Any pointed tool that will draw through a ground without scratching the plate.

Extender. A colorless lithographic ink that can be added to an intaglio or surface ink to make it more transparent; also called transparent base.

False biting. An error in etching by which areas of the plate bite where no biting was intended due to faulty grounds or carelessly applied stopout; also called foul biting.

Feathering. Using a feather from any waterfowl to brush hydrogen gas bubbles gently off the surface of a plate in a nitric acid bath—this technique can be used with any ground *except* white ground and soft ground.

Foul biting. See *False biting*.

Found objects. Metal, plastic, or paper shapes, packaging materials, small gaskets, materials such as laces, and so on, which can be either inked and printed as they are found, or integrated into other plates and then printed.

Ground. A material which protects a plate from the acid. There are a variety of grounds, each one applied to the plate to produce a different effect. See *Aquatint, Hard ground, Soft ground, Sugar lift ground,* and *White ground.*

Gum arabic. Tree gum used in powdered form as an ingredient in lift ground.

Hard ground. An acid-resistant ground which must be drawn into to expose the plate to acid.

Impression. The printed image of plate; also called a print.

India oil stone. The round stone used to sharpen burins and scrapers; also called polishing stone.

Inkless intaglio. See *Embossing* (2).

Intaglio. Overall term for all the techniques in which a printed image is obtained by applying ink to a plate and then wiping the plate with a tarlatan and possibly paper. Engraving, drypoint, aquatint, white ground, lift ground, hard and soft grounds are all intaglio techniques.

Intaglio relief. A graphic technique in which the surface of a deeply bitten plate is rolled with a surface ink and printed on an etching press. The pressure embosses the paper so the inked surface is lower than the level of the surface of the print.

Lift ground. A ground made mostly of sugar which dissolves in hot water used to draw directly on the plate.

Maculature. See *Rétirage.*

Mordant. Usually a combination of chemicals and acids which makes a bath for biting plates, as in Dutch mordant.

Open biting. Biting that occurs when large areas of the plate are exposed and bitten in acid.

Plate mark. The embossed impression made by the beveled edges of the plate on the paper when the plate is printed under the pressure of the press and blankets.

Plate tone. A faint tone produced by the oil in the ink which remains on the clear surface of the plate when a plate is inked and wiped.

Polishing stone. See *India oil stone.*

Press set up for printing. The press with blankets installed and adjusted to the proper pressure for printing.

Print. See *Impression.*

Printer's proof. See *Bon à tirer.*

Proof. A print taken during the course of working on a plate; also called a working proof. A working proof differs from an artist's proof in that the artist's proof is a print taken after the plate is finished and before the edition is begun.

Pulling a proof. Printing a proof.

Rainbow roll. A roller charged with three colors placed next to each other at the same time and rolled onto a plate.

Register marks. Tape or pieces of cardboard placed on the press to register the paper and/or the plate during the printing process.

Registration. The process by which we make sure that the paper and plate are in the proper relationship to each other when we print one color over another or one plate over another so that the resulting images are aligned. A print that is out of register will appear to be blurred.

Relief printing. The graphic technique in which ink is applied to the surface of the plate with a roller.

Retirage. A second printing of a plate which originally had a heavily inked surface without removing the ink from the plate and without reinking; also called maculature.

Rosin. A distillate of turpentine used for making an aquatint ground or rosin stopout.

Repoussage. Leveling the front of a scraped or bitten plate by the application of tape to the back of the plate.

Retroussage. Passing a soft cloth over the intaglio lines after the plate has been inked and wiped to pull the ink onto the surface.

Roller. A cylindrical tool made of rubber, gelatin, or neoprene used to roll ink onto the surface of a plate.

Roulette. A tool with lines or dots on a wheel which can be used directly on the surface of a plate or on a plate with a hard ground applied.

Scraper. A tool with three sharp cutting edges used to remove unwanted textures, lines, or burrs from an etched plate.

Slip sheet. Tissue paper or newsprint placed between the print and blotter to keep the wet ink on the print from offsetting onto the blotter. It is removed when the print is dry.

Soft ground. An acid-resistant ground which must be either drawn on or pressed into to expose areas of the plate to acid.

Steel facing. An electrolytic process that applies a minute quantity of steel to the surface of a copper plate. A steel-faced plate will print a much larger edition than one that is not faced.

Stencil. A nonabsorbent paper with shapes cut out, used to roll surface color on specific areas of an intaglio plate.

Stopout. An acid-resistant liquid that prevents the acid from biting a plate in the areas where it's applied.

Stopping out. Painting certain areas on a plate to prevent them from biting when the plate is placed in the acid.

Struck off. The amount of an edition that has already been printed.

Sugar lift ground. See *Lift ground*.

Surface-rolled. A plate which has had a hard roller rolled over its surface.

Tarlatan. A material that looks like starched cheesecloth and is used for wiping the ink off the surface of an intaglio plate.

Template. A piece of paper or plastic used as a register in printing.

Transparent base. See *Extender*.

Tuilegraphs. Prints made from vinyl asbestos tiles.

Underbiting. A plate not bitten deeply enough in the acid.

Undercutting. An error in etching which occurs when a plate with a large amount of exposed metal is placed in strong acid, and the acid becomes hot and bites the plate under the ground or stopout.

Water marks. Designs put on printing paper when it's molded in order to identify the maker.

White ground. A ground that is not completely acid-resistant which is painted on the plate in varying thicknesses—the acid will bite through the ground faster where the ground is thin and more slowly where the ground is thick.

Wiping the plate. The process of removing the ink from the surface of an intaglio plate with a tarlatan and sometimes paper.

Working proof. See *Proof*.

Supplies and Suppliers

When trying to find out where to buy something, look both under the specific category and *also* under general supplies. Supplies such as files, flexible shaft tools, jigsaws, hot plates, raw linseed oil, varnolene or paint thinner, kerosene, and denatured alcohol can be found in well-stocked hardware stores. And you will find items such as brushes, palette knives, matboards, oaktag, gesso, modeling paste, acrylic gel, and Elmer's glue in art supply stores. Harder-to-find supplies are listed below.

GENERAL SUPPLIES

Fine Art Materials, Inc.
530 LaGuardia Place
New York, New York 10010
Tools, papers, and inks, including Graphic Chemical inks

Sam Flax
25 East 28th Street
New York, New York 10016
Tools, papers, inks, including Graphic Chemical inks, and more

Graphic Chemical and Ink Co.
Post Office Box 27
728 North Yale Avenue
Villa Park, Illinois 60181
Chemicals, tools, papers, blankets, inks, presses, tarlatan, rollers, and Easy Wipe. Catalog available

Joy J. Industries
Box 36 Northport
Long Island, New York 11768
Asphaltum, rosin, beeswax, tools, rollers, proof and edition papers, grounds, inks, including Lorilleux-LeFranc, oils, blotters, plates, presses, and tarlatan. Catalog available

Rembrandt Graphic Arts Co., Inc.
Crane Farm
Stockton, New Jersey 08559
Presses, papers, tools, trays, plates, chemicals, and more. Catalog available

PRESSES

Glen Alps
6523 40th Avenue
North East Seattle, Washington 98115
Good all-around press

American French Tool Co.
Route 117
Coventry, Rhode Island 02816
Very heavy presses

Charles Brand
84 East 19 Street
New York, New York 10003

Martin Machine Co.
P. O. Box 504
Bayside, New York 11361
Very good presses in a variety of sizes and prices. Also have hot plates. Catalog available

Graphic Chemical and Ink Co.
P. O. Box 27
728 North Yale Avenue
Villa Park, Illinois 60181
Sturges presses

Rembrandt Graphic Arts Co. Inc.
Crane Farm
Stockton, New Jersey 08559
Dickerson Combination presses

PRINTING BLANKETS

Continental Felt Co.
22 West 15th Street
New York, New York 10011
Woven and pressed wool-felt blankets

PRINTING TOOLS

T. N. Lawrence and Son
2-4 Bleeding Heart Yard
Grevelle Street, Hatton Garden
London, England
Tools, small rollers, and general graphic supplies

Edward C. Lyons
16 West 22nd Street
New York, New York 10011
Sharpening stones, burnishers, scrapers, burins, roulettes, and other engraving tools

PAPERS AND PAPER PRODUCTS

Andrew Nelson Whitehead
7 Laight Strret
New York, New York 10013
Imported and domestic printing papers

Jerry's Artarama
117 South 2nd Street
New Hyde Park, New York 11040

Crestwood Paper Corp., Inc.
263 Ninth Avenue
New York, New York 10001
Proof and printing papers, museum board and blotters

Hollinger Corporation
3810 South Four Mile Run Drive
Arlington, Virginia 22206
Acid-free containers for print storage. Also museum board

Technical Paper Corp.
729 Boylston Street
Boston, Massachusetts 02116
Tableau paper in rolls or sheets

ACIDS AND CHEMICALS

Please note: Any large chemical company will supply acids locally.

City Chemical
132 West 22nd Street
New York, New York 10011
Acids, chemicals, and malachite green

TRAYS

May be purchased at any large photo supply company. Purchase the large plastic trays—rubber trays are very heavy and tend to crack.

MAGNESIUM CARBONATE

Handschy Chemical Co.
2525 North Elston Avenue
Chicago, Illinois 60647

PLATE

G. A. Feld Company, Inc.
119 Fulton Lane
Mount Vernon, New York 10550
Cold roll, mild steel, .065 gauge. Also copper and brass

National Steel and Copper Plate Co.
543 West 43rd Street
New York, New York 10036
Plates may be purchased in small amounts

Harold Pitman Co.
515 Secaucus Road
Secaucus, New Jersey 07094

Zinc and copper

TARLATAN

Gross-Kobrick Co.
370 West 35th Street
New York, New York 10001

Must be purchased in amounts over 100 yards. (See General Supplies for where to buy smaller amounts.)

INTAGLIO INKS

Charbonnel
13 Quai Montebello
Paris V, France

Cronite Co.
88th Street & Kennedy Blvd.
North Bergen, New Jersey 07047

Also sell the heavy plate oil used in the making of intaglio ink

Rudolph Faust, Inc.
542 South Avenue East
Cranford, New Jersey 07016

Catalog available

Graphic Chemical and Ink Co.
P. O. Box 27
728 North Yale Avenue
Villa Park, Illinois 60181

PIGMENTS

Tricon Colors, Inc.
16 Leliarts Lane
Elmwood Park, New Jersey 07407

Powdered pigments, beeswax, gum arabic, and Fezan green (which can be used to color rosin stopout). Catalog available

SURFACE INKS

Lorilleux-LeFranc
161 rue de Republique
Puteaux, Seine, France

Excellent for viscosity printing—no dryers added (sold through Joy J. Industries—see General Supplies)

Lewis Roberts
250 West Broadway
New York, New York 10013

Commercial inks including good transparent white

Superior Printing Ink Co.
295 Lafayette Street
New York, New York 10013

Commercial offset inks suitable for viscosity printing

Van Son Holland Inks
92 Union Street
Mineola, New York 11581

Commercial offset inks suitable for viscosity printing

RUBBING INK & LITHOGRAPHIC CRAYONS

William Korn, Inc.
260 West Street
New York, New York 10013

ROLLERS

Apex Printers Roller Co.

1541 North 16th Street
St. Louis, Missouri 63106

Martin Machine Co.
P. O. Box 504
Bayside, New York 11361

Rollers made to order according to specific durometer, size, and weight

Precision Roller Corp.
30 Central Drive
Farmingdale, New York 11735

Rollers made to order according to specific durometer, size, and weight

For small rollers see General Supplies

ACETATE, PLASTIC BAGS, ETC.

S. and W. Framing Supplies, Inc.
120 Broadway
Garden City Park, New York 11040

Catalog available

SAFETY EQUIPMENT

Pulmosan Safety Equipment Corp.
30-48 Linden Place
Flushing, New York 11354

Dust respirators and safety glasses

Willson Products Division
P.O. Box 622
Reading, Pennsylvania 19603

Respirator for filtering acid fumes

Bibliography

ABOUT PRINTS

Adhémar, Jean. *Twentieth-Century Graphics.* New York: Praeger, 1971.

Great Prints and Printmakers. Bentveld, The Netherlands: Wechsler Abrams, N.V.

Hayter, Stanley William. *About Prints.* London: Oxford University Press, 1962.

Hind, Arthur M. *A History of Engraving and Etching.* New York: Dover Publications, 1923, 1963.

How to Care for Works of Art on Paper. Boston: the Museum of Fine Arts, 1971. Pamphlet.

Lindemann, Gottfried. *Prints and Drawings.* New York: Praeger, 1970.

Sachs, Paul J. *Modern Prints and Drawings.* New York: Alfred A. Knopf, 1954.

Sotriffer, Kristian. *Printmaking, History and Technique.* New York & Toronto: McGraw-Hill, 1966.

Zigrosser, Carl, and Gaehde, Christa M. *Guide to the Collecting and Care of Original Prints.* New York: Crown, 1965.

ABOUT PRINTMAKERS

Burke, Joseph, and Caldwell, Colin. *Hogarth, the Complete Engravings.* New York: Harry Abrams.

Goya. *Complete Etchings of Goya.* New York; Crown, 1943.

Kollwitz, Käthe. *Prints and Drawings of Käthe Kollwitz.* Zigrosser, Carl, ed. New York: Dover Publications, 1969.

Peterdi, Gabor. *Gabor Peterdi Graphics 1934–1969.* New York: Touchstone, 1970.

Rembrandt. *Complete Etchings of Rembrandt.* New York: Garden City Publishing, 1937.

Rembrandt. *Rembrandt: Experimental Etcher.* Greenwich, Connecticut: New York Graphic Society, 1969. Catalog.

Rembrandt. *The Unseen Rembrandt.* New York: George Grady Press and the Metropolitan Museum of Art, 1942.

Werner, Alfred, tr. *The Graphic Works of Odilon Redon.* New York: Dover Publications, 1969.

ABOUT PRINTMAKING TECHNIQUES

Brunsdon, John. *The Technique of Etching and Engraving.* London: B.T. Batsford, Ltd., and New York: Reinhold, 1967.

Edmondson, Leonard. *Etching.* New York: Van Nostrand Reinhold, 1973.

Hayter, Stanley William. *New Ways of Gravure.* New York and London: Oxford University Press, 1966.

Heller, Jules. *Printmaking Today.* New York: Holt, Reinhart & Winston, 1972.

Lumsden, E.S. *The Art of Etching.* New York: Dover Publications, 1924, 1962.

Magazines and Annuals 1961–1971. "Artist's Proof." Fritz Eichenberg, ed. New York: Pratt Graphic Art Center.

Peterdi, Gabor. *Printmaking.* New York: Macmillan, 1971.

The Print Review. Andrew Stasik, ed. New York: Pratt Graphic Art Center. Magazine.

Ross, John, and Romano, Clare. *The Complete Printmaker.* New York: The Free Press, 1972.

Wenniger, Mary Ann. *Collagraph Printmaking.* New York: Watson-Guptill, 1975.

Index

Dover Books on Art

VITRUVIUS: TEN BOOKS ON ARCHITECTURE. The most influential book in the history of architecture. 1st century A.D. Roman classic has influenced such men as Bramante, Palladio, Michelangelo, up to present. Classic principles of design, harmony, etc. Fascinating reading. Definitive English translation by Professor H. Morgan, Harvard. 344pp. 5⅜ x 8.
20645-9 Paperbound $5.00

HAWTHORNE ON PAINTING. Vivid re-creation, from students' notes, of instructions by Charles Hawthorne at Cape Cod School of Art. Essays, epigrammatic comments on color, form, seeing, techniques, etc. "Excellent," Time. 100pp. 5⅜ x 8.
20653-X Paperbound $2.25

THE HANDBOOK OF PLANT AND FLORAL ORNAMENT, R. G. Hatton. 1200 line illustrations, from medieval, Renaissance herbals, of flowering or fruiting plants: garden flowers, wild flowers, medicinal plants, poisons, industrial plants, etc. A unique compilation that probably could not be matched in any library in the world. Formerly "The Craftsman's Plant-Book." Also full text on uses, history as ornament, etc. 548pp. 6⅛ x 9¼.
20649-1 Paperbound $7.95

DECORATIVE ALPHABETS AND INITIALS, Alexander Nesbitt. 91 complete alphabets, over 3900 ornamental initials, from Middle Ages, Renaissance printing, baroque, rococo, and modern sources. Individual items copyright free, for use in commercial art, crafts, design, packaging, etc. 123 full-page plates. 3924 initials. 129pp. 7¾ x 10¾.   20544-4 Paperbound $6.00

METHODS AND MATERIALS OF THE GREAT SCHOOLS AND MASTERS, Sir Charles Eastlake. (Formerly titled "Materials for a History of Oil Painting.") Vast, authentic reconstruction of secret techniques of the masters, recreated from ancient manuscripts, contemporary accounts, analysis of paintings, etc. Oils, fresco, tempera, varnishes, encaustics. Both Flemish and Italian schools, also British and French. One of great works for art historians, critics; inexhaustible mine of suggestions, information for practicing artists. Total of 1025pp. 5⅜ x 8.
20718-8, 20719-6 Two volume set, Paperbound $15.00

AMERICAN VICTORIAN ARCHITECTURE, edited by Arnold Lewis and Keith Morgan. Collection of brilliant photographs of 1870's, 1880's, showing finest domestic, public architecture; many buildings now gone. Landmark work, French in origin; first European appreciation of American work. Modern notes, introduction. 120 plates. "Architects and students of architecture will find this book invaluable for its first-hand depiction of the state of the art during a very formative period," ANTIQUE MONTHLY. 152pp. 9 x 12.   23177-1 Paperbound $7.95

THE HUMAN FIGURE, J. H. Vanderpoel. Not just a picture book, but a complete course by a famous figure artist. Extensive text, illustrated by 430 pencil and charcoal drawings of both male and female anatomy. 2nd enlarged edition. Foreword. 430 illus. 143pp. 6⅛ x 9¼.   20432-4 Paperbound $3.50

THE FOUR BOOKS OF ARCHITECTURE, Andrea Palladio. A compendium of the art of Andrea Palladio, one of the most celebrated architects of the Renaissance, including 250 magnificently-engraved plates showing edifices either of Palladio's design or reconstructed (in these drawings) by him from classical ruins and contemporary accounts. 257 plates. xxiv + 119pp. 9½ x 12¾. 21308-0 Paperbound $10.00

150 MASTERPIECES OF DRAWING, A. Toney. Selected by a gifted artist and teacher, these are some of the finest drawings produced by Western artists from the early 15th to the end of the 18th centuries. Excellent reproductions of drawings by Rembrandt, Bruegel, Raphael, Watteau, and other familiar masters, as well as works by lesser known but brilliant artists. 150 plates. xviii + 150pp. 5⅜ x 11¼. 21032-4 Paperbound $6.00

MORE DRAWINGS BY HEINRICH KLEY. Another collection of the graphic, vivid sketches of Heinrich Kley, one of the most diabolically talented cartoonists of our century. The sketches take in every aspect of human life: nothing is too sacred for him to ridicule, no one too eminent for him to satirize. 158 drawings you will not easily forget. iv + 104pp. 7⅜ x 10¾. 20041-8 Paperbound $3.75

STYLES IN PAINTING, Paul Zucker. By comparing paintings of similar subject matter, the author shows the characteristics of various painting styles. You are shown at a glance the differences between reclining nudes by Giorgione, Velasquez, Goya, Modigliani; how a Byzantine portrait is unlike a portrait by Van Eyck, da Vinci, Dürer, or Marc Chagall; how the painting of landscapes has changed gradually from ancient Pompeii to Lyonel Feininger in our own century. 241 beautiful, sharp photographs illustrate the text. xiv + 338 pp. 5⅝ x 8¼. 20760-9 Paperbound $6.50

PAINTING IN ISLAM, Sir Thomas W. Arnold. This scholarly study puts Islamic painting in its social and religious context and examines its relation to Islamic civilization in general. 65 full-page plates illustrate the text and give outstanding examples of Islamic art. 4 appendices. Index of mss. referred to. General Index. xxiv + 159pp. 6⅝ x 9¼. 21310-2 Paperbound $7.00

THE MATERIALS AND TECHNIQUES OF MEDIEVAL PAINTING, D. V. Thompson. An invaluable study of carriers and grounds, binding media, pigments, metals used in painting, al fresco and al secco techniques, burnishing, etc. used by the medieval masters. Preface by Bernard Berenson. 239pp. 5⅜ x 8. 20327-1 Paperbound $4.50

THE HISTORY AND TECHNIQUE OF LETTERING, A. Nesbitt. A thorough history of lettering from the ancient Egyptians to the present, and a 65-page course in lettering for artists. Every major development in lettering history is illustrated by a complete aphabet. Fully analyzes such masters as Caslon, Koch, Garamont, Jenson, and many more. 89 alphabets, 165 other specimens. 317pp. 7½ x 10½. 20427-8 Paperbound $5.50

PRINCIPLES OF ART HISTORY, H. Wölfflin. This remarkably instructive work demonstrates the tremendous change in artistic conception from the 14th to the 18th centuries, by analyzing 164 works by Botticelli, Dürer, Hobbema, Holbein, Hals, Titian, Rembrandt, Vermeer, etc., and pointing out exactly what is meant by "baroque," "classic," "primitive," "picturesque," and other basic terms of art history and criticism. "A remarkable lesson in the art of seeing," SAT. REV. OF LITERATURE. Translated from the 7th German edition. 150 illus. 254pp. 6⅛ x 9¼.   20276-3 Paperbound $4.95

FOUNDATIONS OF MODERN ART, A. Ozenfant. Stimulating discussion of human creativity from paleolithic cave painting to modern painting, architecture, decorative arts. Fully illustrated with works of Gris, Lipchitz, Léger, Picasso, primitive, modern artifacts, architecture, industrial art, much more. 226 illustrations. 368pp. 6⅛ x 9¼.   20215-1 Paperbound $6.95

METALWORK AND ENAMELLING, H. Maryon. Probably the best book ever written on the subject. Tells everything necessary for the home manufacture of jewelry, rings, ear pendants, bowls, etc. Covers materials, tools, soldering, filigree, setting stones, raising patterns, repoussé work, damascening, niello, cloisonné, polishing, assaying, casting, and dozens of other techniques. The best substitute for apprenticeship to a master metalworker. 363 photos and figures. 374pp. 5½ x 8½.

22702-2 Paperbound $5.00

SHAKER FURNITURE, E. D. and F. Andrews. The most illuminating study of Shaker furniture ever written. Covers chronology, craftsmanship, houses, shops, etc. Includes over 200 photographs of chairs, tables, clocks, beds, benches, etc. "Mr. & Mrs. Andrews know all there is to know about Shaker furniture," Mark Van Doren, NATION. 48 full-page plates. 192pp. 7⅞ x 10¾.   20679-3 Paperbound $5.00

LETTERING AND ALPHABETS, J. A. Cavanagh. An unabridged reissue of "Lettering," containing the full discussion, analysis, illustration of 89 basic hand lettering styles based on Caslon, Bodoni, Gothic, many other types. Hundreds of technical hints on construction, strokes, pens, brushes, etc. 89 alphabets, 72 lettered specimens, which may be reproduced permission-free. 121pp. 9¾ x 8.   20053-1 Paperbound $3.50

THE HUMAN FIGURE IN MOTION, Eadweard Muybridge. The largest collection in print of Muybridge's famous high-speed action photos. 4789 photographs in more than 500 action-strip-sequences (at shutter speeds up to 1/6000th of a second) illustrate men, women, children—mostly undraped—performing such actions as walking, running, getting up, lying down, carrying objects, throwing, etc. "An unparalleled dictionary of action for all artists," AMERICAN ARTIST. 390 full-page plates, with 4789 photographs. Heavy glossy stock, reinforced binding with headbands. 7⅞ x 10¾.   20204-6 Clothbound $15.95

GRAPHIC WORLDS OF PETER BRUEGEL THE ELDER, *H. A. Klein.* 64 of the finest etchings and engravings made from the drawings of the Flemish master Peter Bruegel. Every aspect of the artist's diversified style and subject matter is represented, with notes providing biographical and other background information. Excellent reproductions on opaque stock with nothing on reverse side. 63 engravings, 1 woodcut. Bibliography. xviii + 176pp. 9⅜ x 12¼.   21132-0 Paperbound $6.95

THE COMPLETE WOODCUTS OF ALBRECHT DURER, edited by Dr. Willi Kurth. Albrecht Dürer was a master in various media, but it was in woodcut design that his creative genius reached its highest expression. Here are all of his extant woodcuts, a collection of over 300 great works, many of which are not available elsewhere. An indispensable work for the art historian and critic and all art lovers. 346 plates. Index. 285pp. 8½ x 12¼.   21097-9 Paperbound $8.95

CHINESE PAINTING AND CALLIGRAPHY: A PICTORIAL SURVEY, Wan-go Weng. Comprehensive survey of Chinese painting from Northern Sung (960–1127) to early Ch'ing dynasty (1644–1911). 149 reproductions from Crawford Collection, finest private holding in the West. Emphasis on pivotal painters, calligraphers—landscapes from Ming, Sung eras, three classic styles of calligraphy shown. 109 illustrations, including many two-page spreads. Finest reproductions of any Dover book. 192pp. 8⅞ x 11¾.   23707-9 Paperbound $7.95

WILD FOWL DECOYS, Joel Barber. Antique dealers, collectors, craftsmen, hunters, readers of Americana, etc. will find this the only thorough and reliable guide on the market today to this unique folk art. It contains the history, cultural significance, regional design variations; unusual decoy lore; working plans for constructing decoys; and loads of illustrations. 140 full-page plates, 4 in color. 14 additional plates of drawings and plans by the author. xxvii + 156pp. 7⅞ x 10¾. 20011-6 Paperbound $6.95

1800 WOODCUTS BY THOMAS BEWICK AND HIS SCHOOL. This is the largest collection of first-rate pictorial woodcuts in print—an indispensable part of the working library of every commercial artist, art director, production designer, packaging artist, craftsman, manufacturer, librarian, art collector, and artist. And best of all, when you buy your copy of Bewick, you buy the rights to reproduce individual illustrations—no permission needed, no acknowledgments, no clearance fees! Classified index. Bibliography and sources. xiv + 246pp. 9 x 12.
    20766-8 Paperbound $7.95

THE SCRIPT LETTER, Tommy Thompson. Prepared by a noted authority, this is a thorough, straightforward course of instruction with advice on virtually every facet of the art of script lettering. Also a brief history of lettering with examples from early copy books and illustrations from present day advertising and packaging. Copiously illustrated. Bibliography. 128pp. 6½ x 9⅛.   21311-0 Paperbound $3.50